Representing the Unrepresentable

LATIN AMERICA
Interdisciplinary Studies

Gladys M. Varona-Lacey
General Editor

Vol. 3

PETER LANG
New York • Washington, D.C./Baltimore • Bern
Frankfurt am Main • Berlin • Brussels • Vienna • Oxford

Yvonne S. Unnold

Representing the Unrepresentable

Literature of Trauma under Pinochet in Chile

PETER LANG
New York • Washington, D.C./Baltimore • Bern
Frankfurt am Main • Berlin • Brussels • Vienna • Oxford

Library of Congress Cataloging-in-Publication Data

Unnold, Yvonne S. (Yvonne Sabine)
Representing the unrepresentable: literature of trauma
under Pinochet in Chile / Yvonne S. Unnold
p. cm. — (Latin America; vol. 3)
Includes bibliographical references.
1. Chilean prose literature—20th century—History and criticism. 2. Reportage literature,
Chilean—History and criticism. 3. Politics and literature—Chile.
4. Psychic trauma in literature. I. Title. II. Latin America (Series); vol. 3.
PQ7997.U66 868'.640809358—dc21 2001038340
ISBN 0-8204-5677-2
ISSN 1524-7805

Die Deutsche Bibliothek-CIP-Einheitsaufnahme

Unnold, Yvonne S.:
Representing the unrepresentable: literature of trauma
under Pinochet in Chile / Yvonne S. Unnold
–New York; Washington, D.C./Baltimore; Bern;
Frankfurt am Main; Berlin; Brussels; Vienna; Oxford: Lang.
(Latin America; Vol. 3)
ISBN 0-8204-5677-2

Table of Contents

Acknowledgment vii

Introduction 1

History and Literary Representation 25

Testimonio. Genre Delineation and Critique 39

Chilean Autobiography: Between Holocaust Autobiography and Latin American *Testimonio* 85

Chilean *Testimonio* in the Form of Monological Interviews 117

"What is What?" in Historical Fiction 155

Closure? 181

Bibliography 197

ACKNOWLEDGMENT

I would like to express my appreciation to the University of Southern Mississippi, in particular, Dr. Cotton, Vice President for Research and Finance, and Dr. Harper, Dean of the College of Liberal Arts, for their continuous commitment to and support of learning and research.

Essential assistance and advice were also provided by Dr. Anthony Geist, Dr. Cynthia Steele and Dr. Gary Handwerk at the University of Washington.

On a personal note, I would like to thank Javier, Luna, Fauna and Carmela for their love, friendship, and support.

INTRODUCTION

Forty years after Hitler's ascent to power, an ultra right-wing group in Chile strategically prepared for a military coup. In Hernán Valdés' words, fascism was "first hand" introduced to Chile on September 11, 1973, the day on which General Augusto Pinochet, chief of the military operation, overthrew President Salvador Allende's socialist government[1] and named himself head of the new military regime.[2]

Although there is a general agreement that Pinochet entered the planning of the military coup at a rather late stage, he only ascended as head of the military with General Carlos Prat's resignation on August 23, 1973. Upon succeeding with the coup, Pinochet's strategy for remaining in power involved eliminating potential competitors to his position. He has been linked directly to the assassination of Chile's former ambassador Orlando Letelier in Washington, and there is also evidence linking him to the murder of General Prat and his wife in Buenos Aires in September 1974. Investigations into the death of General Oscar Bonilla in a helicopter accident have revealed few details regarding the nature of this accident, yet it has been suggested that Bonilla's death fits into Pinochet's strategy of eliminating competitors to power. Finally, the military junta expelled Gustavo Leigh Guzmán, an air force general under Pinochet because of his public call for a transition from military to civilian rule within a five year time period.[3] Although Pinochet initially announced that the position of chief executive would rotate among the junta members, he manifested his decision to dominate as the single ruling power from the start. He assumed the title of supreme head of the nation and president of the junta by way of decree 527 in June 1974. He named himself president of the republic on December 16, 1974.

With the Junta's reversal of Allende's social reforms, many Chileans were thrown into absolute poverty.[4] The military created concentration camps, tortured victims and clandestinely buried victims dead or alive in the oven of a state owned mine, in mass graves at various other locations; allegedly, prisoners were also flown out and dumped into sea. The Rettig Commission, appointed by President Aylwin (1989–1995) to investigate human rights violations under Pinochet revealed that "a total of 2,279 people had been killed, victims of human rights abuses."[5] Thousands "disappeared" as the result of military actions. The dictatorship invoked a curfew, changed the constitution[6] and censored information. In short: fear, terror, and violence took over and thousands fled into exile. Nearly all families knew of relatives, neighbors or friends taken by force, never to return.

Due to the increasing number of human rights violations, the Pinochet regime provoked extensive concern internationally. The military regime censored the country's access to international media and limited the national news to dictatorship propaganda. After the first few months, and increasingly in the following years, silence grew, in part due to ignorance and denial of the military's human rights violations, and in part because the military[7] met even the smallest sign of resistance with unrestrained violence and persecution.[8] To counter the United Nations vote condemning Chile for continued human right violations, Pinochet called for a national referendum. Held on January 7, 1978, "under a repressive state of siege and with no electoral rolls," the plebiscite indicated a "75 percent approval rate," based on which he asserted that "Chile did not need elections for another ten years."[9]

On October 5, 1988, the Chilean people rejected Pinochet's proposal for continued rule in a public referendum. With 55% in favor of the No vote in the presidential plebiscite, it was constitutionally (Constitution of 1980) legal to schedule competitive presidential and congressional elections in 1989. In the presidential elections that followed, Patricio Aylwin won a majority of the popular votes, becoming thereby "the first civilian president in Chile since 1973."[10] However, despite the change of government from an authoritarian to a democratic system in 1989, the former dictator remained in charge of the Chilean army until 1998. At that time, Pinochet assumed his seat in the Chilean senate as senator for life, in accordance with the 1980 Constitution that he had authored. In spite of increasing vocal opposition, Pinochet continued to receive support from numerous *pinochetistas* who yearned for a return to the years of his dictatorship.

Unlike in Post-Holocaust Germany where the German population was subjected to an immediate intensive denazification program that forced its citizens to face eye to eye the concentration camp horrors, in Chile, public voicing of the human rights atrocities committed under Pinochet began to emerge to the surface slowly and with a long delay, still lacking official authentication. The impunity law,[11] according to Oppenheim, "a sober reminder of the extent of human rights abuses in this early period,"[12] granting military amnesty for any criminal acts committed between September 11, 1973, and March 10, 1978, prevailed as much as the fear originating in the Pinochet dictatorship.[13] Reports and accusations of human rights violations and demands for justice issued by victims, their relatives, as well as by the international community, still lacked judicial attention past the first few democratic elections.

One of the four major components of president Aylwin's plan for achieving democracy was based on the necessity to deal honestly with the human rights violations under Pinochet's rule and to show that the rule of justice has indeed once again returned to Chilean reality. However, in order to restore Chile as a country in which human rights are observed and violations persecuted, the responsible party needed to be identified and accused. This would produce serious consequences for the civil-military relationship under which the post-dictatorship governments have been functioning. The military was clearly the chief violator of human rights under Pinochet, yet any attempt to bring it to justice could provoke a new civil-military confrontation and endanger the newly formed democracy.

Ever since the first accusations have been publicized, the military has been nervous about the possibility of trials of military men for human rights violations. Upon the 1990 discovery in Pisagua in northern Chile of mummified bodies still showing the expressions of horror on the victims' faces, Pinochet, as chief of the military, denounced the discussion of human rights abuses as a campaign to discredit the armed forces. Consequently, he invoked a provocative *dia de enlace*, a day of retreat for the army. This demonstration of the military's disapproval of investigation of human rights violations was repeated in 1993 and was reinforced by

Pinochet as late as 1998.

Cards shifted drastically when Pinochet visited England on a diplomat-visa. In October 1998, Scotland Yard arrested Pinochet on charges of war crimes as an international extradition warrant was extended by the Spanish judge Baltazar Guzón and later joined by several other countries from the European community. With the British High Court rejecting Pinochet's claim of diplomatic immunity and paving the way for the judicial process of a persecution for crimes committed after 1988, it appeared as if the extradition would finally be granted one and a half years after his initial arrest. Then, in what appeared to be a highly controversial and last minute rescue attempt on behalf of the accused, on March 2, 2000, the British Interior Minister Jack Straw declared the ex-commander in chief of Chile unfit to stand trial citing reasons of poor health. Pinochet immediately boarded a plane homeward bound.

For a moment, Pinochet's judicial fate in Chile seemed unclear. In what first appeared to signal a definite shift away from the former "hands-off" approach, the Chilean court decided to reverse the British ruling by declaring Pinochet fit to stand trial in his own country. In the following months, judges moved back and forth from granting charges of authorship versus charges of cover-up; in the end, Pinochet again was declared unfit to stand trial. With this ruling, considered a "serious set-back for the quest for truth and justice pursued for over two decades by the relatives of the thousands of victims of human rights violations committed under Augusto Pinochet's rule,"[14] accusations of crimes against humanity are, once again, piling up on the judicial table where they seem to accumulate more dust than attention. The 1996 call by Families of the Detained and Disappeared regains relevance:

> Our position on the problems of human rights violations is basically legal, ethical and preventative. No healthy, solid, stable democracy can build itself upon a foundation of forgetting the most serious crimes against the right to life, integrity and freedom committed in Chilean history and within a policy of state terrorism that unleashed maximum political violence against society. We reaffirm that there is no ethical nor judicial reason why crimes of human rights violations should remain in impunity. We are asking that crimes against humanity be punished in the same way that common ones are.[15]

In post-dictatorship Chile, it cannot be denied that some progress has been achieved with investigations into the criminal activities committed under the former ruler. However, far from invoking justice, Chile continues to struggle with bringing the principle culprits to stand trial and attempting to heal the wounds resulting from the atrocities. More than two decades after the coup, Pinochet-friendly voices, now faced with opposition, cry out for a halt to the investigations. They argue that Chile has grown tired of looking at the past. Nevertheless, Amnesty International's 1996 report reveals that "large majorities of the population favoured continued investigation into human rights violations (75% and 80%) and a sizeable percentage (62% and 70%) favoured continued prosecutions of those responsible for human rights violations.... [These] results at least call into question assertions that the majority of Chileans wish for investigations into human rights violations under the military period to be closed."[16] Twenty eight years after the military takeover, more than 250 legal complaints are pending in Chile against Pinochet and other former members of the Chilean armed forces; some are also facing human rights accusations in civilian courts.

Prior to the emergence of the fascist regime, Chile enjoyed a level of cultural production that received international attention, in particular in the realm of literary discourse. Under Pinochet, cultural production did not cease, but the military junta censored, "corrected," and destroyed works which they deemed unworthy or not in accord with the fascist sociopolitical agenda.[17] The regime also exercised strict censorship upon international and highly esteemed productions such as *Waiting for Godot*, declaring them "uncultured." Starting with the military coup in 1973, censorship, human rights violations, and persecution were introduced into culturally highly active Chilean communities, and, for the following fifteen years, constituted a constant source of preoccupation for intellectuals and artists. Until the very end of Pinochet's rule, Chilean artists continued to be subjected to military persecution. As late as 1988, more then eighty Chilean artists associated with theater and dance received death threats issued by the military.

Upon the no-confidence vote in 1988, artistic communities and other culturally active sectors of the population called for an immediate return to work. The same year the cultural meeting "Chile crea" was celebrated, followed by a conference of the nation's poets (Encuentro de Poetas) in

1989 in the town of Valdivia. A conference of Chilean writers (Encuentro de Escritores) took place at the same location in 1990, along with a film-festival at Viña de Mar. No such events had been celebrated in Chile for the duration of the military regime.

In literature, the change in government was met by the compilation of the three-volume series, *Chile, la memoria prohibida*, an extensive investigation of human rights violations. Likewise, the film industry responded by broadcasting *Imagen latente* by Pablo Perelman, a film censured by the Pinochet regime because its subject matter deals with the search for a young *desaparecido* or "disappeared" person. Currently, Chilean narrative is undergoing a significant transition. Literary production has changed from an initially "less refined" expression in opposition to, or in support of, the regime to a type of narrative that focuses more on micro-dramas and on the immense Chilean population which identifies neither as victim nor as perpetrator. It is the transition process itself, from the system of dictatorship and censorship to a society that proclaims democratic values and practices, that now preoccupies contemporary cultural, literary, and artistic producers, apparently even more so than recent history.

The present study, *Representing the Unrepresentable: Literature of Trauma under Pinochet in Chile* aims at gaining an understanding of the dimensions, purposes and roles of literary production in reaction to the military coup and the dictatorship headed by General Augusto Pinochet in the years 1973 to 1988. In the literary representation of the sociopolitical environment and experience governed by Pinochet's authoritarian, fascist regime of power, a clear distinction separates official and alternative voices. Official representation presents a discourse sympathetic to dictatorship, issued by the government-controlled media. Alternative representation, in contrast, is produced by victims of the regime that they oppose and seek to change. These representations share an antithetical relationship. They originate out of the particular sociopolitical context whose experience they seek to affect and are intrinsically linked to the sociopolitical and literary agenda of the voices through which they are pronounced.

This discussion entails an analysis of six Chilean literary works here referred to as *literature of trauma* in accordance with the traumatic nature of the experience they relate: Hernán Valdés' *Tejas Verdes* (1974), Sergio Bitar's *Isla 10* (1987), Samuel Chavkin's *The Murder of Chile* (1982), Emma Sepúlveda's *We, Chile* (1996), Patricia Politzer's *Miedo en Chile* (1990), and Isabel Allende's *La casa de los espíritus* (1982). Generically, these works may be distinguished as autobiography (Valdés, Bitar), monological interview (Chavkin, Sepúlveda, Politzer), and historical novel (Allende), but they should also be comprehended as alternative representations of history, and, more specifically, as forms of *testimonio*. In accordance with the generic definition of *testimonio*, this literature of trauma performs the functions of denouncing and challenging an official representation of history, while it serves as a sociopolitical agent in promoting a (trans)formation of a sociopolitical conscience and continues its call for truth and justice.

This literature of trauma in Chile carries the goal of seeking to come to terms with the past. This goal is set by the victim who tries to overcome the trauma endured. It requires a formation of a social conscience that acknowledges human rights infractions, and that shows sympathy to the goal of bringing justice to Chile. Years back, Theodor W. Adorno explained with regard to the highly traumatic German Holocaust that the attempt of coming to terms with the past does not necessarily entail a "serious working through of the past, the breaking of its spell through an act of clear consciousness. It suggests, rather, wishing to turn the page, and, if possible, wiping it from memory."[18] This observation is still valid and pertinent to Chile, even though the Holocaust trauma and the dictatorship trauma do not compare either in nature or in extent. In the Chilean context, Adorno's observation applies not to those who were made victims by the regime but to those who perpetrated the crimes. It reflects the attitude of those who benefited from an authoritarian system of government. Even those who, as a result of fifteen years of dictatorship propaganda, have become depoliticized now demonstrate themselves more eager to learn how to construct a future than to deconstruct an illusory past, and acknowledge crimes that have been denied ever since they were committed.

Patricia Politzer pointed out eleven years into the dictatorship (and with four more to go), "Chile is divided into two clearly defined countries which don't look at each other, don't touch each other and don't know each other; but which recognize each other intuitively and fear one another."[19] This division gradually worked its way to the surface, with Pinochet's victims, like Adorno, calling for an "enlightenment about what happened in the past," and alternative representation, specifically *testimonios*, working above all "against a forgetfulness that too easily goes along with and justifies what is forgotten."[20]

A strong sense of trauma dominates the testimony of victims of Pinochet's regime; however, the relationship between trauma, literary representation, and the overcoming of trauma has not yet been critically addressed in the context of Chilean literary testimony. This study investigates patterns and differences in Chilean testimonial literature of trauma by way of a comparative discourse analysis.[21] It approaches these texts, with the idea in mind that the practitioner of testimonial literary craft may not to be seen as a "bearer of universal values"[22] but as an individual who occupies, and is formed by, a specific position in society, and who, moreover, is guided by a sociopolitical objective.

Alternative representations of dictatorship experiences emphasize specific sociopolitical objectives and situations; as Aman points out, the focus of popular discourse shifted in 1988 from active resistance against the dictatorship to the call for "truth and justice in opposition to the impunity sought by the military."[23] In 2001, on the 28th anniversary of the military coupe, Amnesty International renews its call:

> While important judicial decisions have been passed in Chile, following the arrest of Augusto Pinochet in the United Kingdom in October 1998 and his return to Chile in March 2000, the key bastions of impunity that have obstructed justice and truth in Chile remain in place. "To achieve full justice and truth in Chile, the government must remove the obstacles that have obstructed them during the last 28 years," Amnesty International said. Chief among these is the Amnesty Law (Decree Law No. 2191 of 1978) that must be declared null and void.[24]

Since truth perceived and the formation of perceived truths form an integral part of the sociopolitical and historical sphere, the "truth" about the Pinochet regime must be understood as an element of power in support of, or in opposition to, that which the individual author forms into a narrative. This distinction is of particular importance in the alternative representation that claims truth-value for itself while challenging the legitimacy of the non-fiction status of official historical discourse.

Traditionally, History has been equated with Truth and Reality in the same manner that, in literary representation, a distinction has been made between fictional and non-fictional discourse. A century ago, Nietzsche pronounced that "the origin of historical education...*must* itself in turn be historically understood, history *must* itself dissolve the problem of history, knowledge *must* turn its sting against itself."[25] By extension, this study proposes to analyze alternative literary representations of the sociopolitical crisis in Chile by way of an examination of the interrelationships among the sociopolitical historical environment and the corresponding literary phenomena.

Due to the sociopolitical dimensions of these texts, the theoretical debate on *testimonio* serves well as a starting point for an analytic understanding of the Chilean phenomena. At the same time, the complexity of the Chilean autobiography, monological interview, and historical fiction constitutes a fine basis for a critique of the genre definitions for *testimonio* whose contemporary delineation is, at least partially, problematic.

The Chilean works discussed have not previously been studied as literature of trauma, and the contemporary discussion of the genre of *testimonio* also does not address any element of trauma in the literary practice it seeks to describe. This study is trying to bridge this gap. A significant part of the analysis is guided by observations drawn from post-Holocaust literary criticism relevant to the study of these Chilean texts as a literature of trauma. The discussion of *testimonio* embarks on an understanding of Holocaust literature that recognizes the trauma involved, the link that exists between trauma and literary representation and the processes of coming to terms with trauma.

A main difference between Holocaust literature and *testimonio* is that *testimonio* unfolds as a contestant of official history, one which seeks to challenge the official representation. Here the Chilean context is distinctive, because in this sociopolitical environment the "official history" prevails despite a change in government. The official version of events continues to be nurtured by *pinochetistas*; it is only in recently months that accusations and calls for justice from victims and survivors have received attention.

This present discussion does not entail an actual comparison of autobiographies, monological interview, or historical fiction by dictatorship and Holocaust survivors because the objective is not to establish a comparison between German and Chilean literature of trauma. Instead the aim is to identify a specific sociopolitical environment, cause and purpose in the Chilean texts which that is not paralleled by the post-Holocaust context and its literature. The intent is to facilitate a better understanding of the intricacies of these particular texts.

This selected Chilean literature of trauma manifests a form of *testimonio*; however, rather than redefining *testimonio* as a literature of trauma, the study proposes a modification of the *testimonio* genre delineation to include the particularities of this literature of trauma. Moreover, due to its intrinsic sociopolitical and literary cause and agenda, this Chilean literature also invites a redefinition of the differentiation between fiction and fact which, in turn, ought to be taken under consideration in the delineation of *testimonio*. The "compare and contrast" approach to discourse analysis in this project constitutes a particularly useful tool when applied theoretically, because it allows us to draw observations from Holocaust and *testimonio* critical discourses which will help us comprehend a literature that exceeds the parameters of both discourses.

On the theoretical side, the analysis is informed by three discourses: those on literary genre distinctions, on literary representations of history, and on the significance of literature in relation to trauma. Literary theory, dealing with the Latin American *testimonio* genre, constitutes a point of departure for a delineation of this literary practice and for a discussion of Chilean autobiography and monological interview as testimonial literature. Post-Holocaust theory on literary representation serves as a resource for the understanding of literature as a tool by which to represent sociopolitical trauma. Such theory is useful for a discussion of trauma and its relation to literature, and for a multiple approach to the distinction between fiction and fact in the literary representation of sociopolitical crisis. Discourse theory relevant to the experience, perception, and representation of sociopolitical crisis provides a point of departure for a discussion of a distinction between fictional and non-fictional discourse on the one hand, and fictional and non-fictional representation within the framework of historical fiction, on the other.

The first chapter discusses history as a human construct and literary representation as an extrapolation of such a construct. This chapter outlines the understanding of history, its literary representation, and the possibility of distinguishing between fiction and fact in the representation of history, which forms the basis for the discussion of *testimonio* and the Chilean literature of trauma. It is by way of this (sought out) confrontation, that the truthfulness of official history may be disputed and established as effect rather than fact, and that, vice versa, the same may be seen to apply to alternative history as well. The "dis-authenticity" revelation of official history, of course, depends on a strengthened authenticity on the part of alternative representation.

In what can be seen as a preventative safekeeping against losing the power of representation due to an imperialistically motivated reading, alternative representation of history also establishes itself intra-, extra- and intertextually as composition. The notion of a representation's loss of power is thereby appropriated by the narrative. It emerges as a narrative strategy or tool aimed at re-appropriating the very power it was supposed to have lost: alternative representation of history (re)assigns itself the power to define its own essence at the same time as it also constitutes itself as composition. In identifying itself as composition, however, this literature does not discredit its own ability to represent. More than just a speech act, alternative representation of history establishes itself with a sociopolitical cause (a sociopolitical urgency) and a sociopolitical function (representing traumatic experience, performing an act of solidarity in challenging and denouncing official history and abuse of power, and promoting the [trans]formation of a social conscience). Thereby, this literature also emerges as a sociopolitical tool linked to a sociopolitical agenda.

Due to alternative representation of history's inherent confrontation with official history, even the latter is drawn into the discussion of what it means for a representation to have a sociopolitical cause, function and agenda. Although official history does not necessarily deliberately exhibit its sociopolitical framework, we must acknowledge that it does have one and, by extension, we also come to understand that the genre differentiation of representations constitutes a tool in its own right. One alternative literary representation of history has been theoretically categorized under the rubric *testimonio*. However, whereas official history has been able to thrive by way of its generic constitution, *testimonio*'s genre definitions constitute, above all, a limitation of and to alternative literary representations of history.

Chapter II delineates the literary genre of *testimonio* in accordance with contemporary critical discourse. The discussion of the genre delineation for *testimonio* brings together and juxtaposes theoretic approaches to *testimonio* as they have been formulated diversely within an intellectual discourse maintained by members of US institutions of higher education, but also by literary critics and guerrilla communities and resistance fighters in Latin America. The study presents these heterogeneous approaches, compares and contrasts them against each other and assesses their inherent paradoxes when describing a common concept. Some of these approaches suggest a strict differentiation of *testimonio* and Holocaust literary representations that is problematic. Rather than separating the narratives from each other, observations drawn from Holocaust literature also highlight possibilities in *testimonio* which have not yet been addressed, in particular the significance of trauma to the literary representation of trauma.

The following chapters test the theoretical paradigm of *testimonio* on selected Chilean literary representations of trauma experiences resulting from the Pinochet dictatorship. Chilean trauma literature, specifically, autobiography and the monological interview are discussed as types of *testimonio* literary practice which expose shortcomings of the generic definition. Then attention shifts to historical fiction as a form of the literature of trauma, which is considered incompatible with *testimonio*. The analysis of the polyphony of voices, narrative strategy and the sociopolitical, literary agenda of one particular historical fiction, demonstrates how this literary practice meets the principle characteristics of the *testimonio* previously established and, like the other texts discussed, calls for a redefinition of the genre.

More specifically, Chapter III discusses the autobiographical representation of trauma by comparing Holocaust autobiography to two texts of Chilean autobiographical *testimonio*, specifically Hernán Valdés' *Tejas Verdes* (1974) and Sergio Bitar's *Isla 10* (1987). These two works share *testimonio*'s principle attributes but are narrated without the intervention of an author-editor intermediary, and they expose the fiction-nonfiction paradox in the representation of a sociopolitical crisis. Special attention is paid to the explicit or implicit interplay between fictional and non-fictional elements in self-proclaimed non-fictional representation and the distinction between these texts' "non-fictionality" and their formulation of a sociopolitical agenda. This discussion initiates by observations drawn from Holocaust autobiographies. Holocaust autobiography is here seen as supplementary representation as opposed to Chilean autobiography of trauma, which is defined as an alternative representation that seeks to rectify as much as contradict an existing official representation while serving as a literary tool of resistance.

The discussion of Chilean autobiographical *testimonio* concludes with an understanding of trauma that, in accordance with Bitar and Valdés, identifies trauma as an encompassing effect and prevailing component of victims' experiences that informs the (re)constitution of memory and the construction of narrative. These *testimonios* originate in a sociopolitical situation of urgency, are driven by the commitment to bear witness, and seek to transform a sociopolitical conscience which requires an understanding of the interplay between power, truth, and representation. These works enunciate an attempt to come to terms with the traumatic experiences endured, a challenge to continued sociopolitical oppression, repression and denial, an effort to regain control over the private/public experience and over the power of representation. Above all, Chilean autobiographical literature of trauma distinguishes as an effort to strengthen a sociopolitical agenda of denouncing sociopolitical injustice, human rights violations and misrepresentation, and as an attempt to form a social conscience that is based not on denial but on justice and human rights.

Chapter IV performs an analysis of a type of literary narrative here termed the monological interview. The monological interview constitutes a form of *testimonio*, which is based on oral testimony obtained by way of an interview process. Different from a typescript of an interview, the monological interview entails a process of editorial intervention. By way of this process, the testimony provided in the interview process is extracted by the author, recomposed and represented without reference to or mentioning of the questions, comments, silences and exclamations that intervene, influence and help shape the testimony in its interview setting. The monological interview is discussed as a form of *testimonio* that exposes the power in representation exercised by the author-editor-interviewer in pursuit of a particular sociopolitical and literary objective.

The analysis compares and contrasts the narrative style and strategy of three of the most comprehensive volumes of monological interviews on the Chilean experience published so far: Samuel Chavkin's *The Murder of Chile* (1982), Emma Sepúlveda's *We, Chile* (1996), and Patricia Politzer's *Miedo en Chile* (1990). Thereby the monological interview is treated as a literary discourse that shares *testimonio*'s principle characteristics and that, in turn, provides a tool to test the applicability and sustainability of key components generically attributed to the literary practice of *testimonio*.

This chapter also pays special attention to extra-, intra- and intertextual elements that provide insight into the process of narration, the differentiation between author, narrator and protagonist and the sociopolitical agenda assigned to the text. Sepúlveda and Politzer's editorial intervention at the intratextual level is less apparent than it is in Chavkin's work. Sepúlveda and Politzer construct the coherence of the narrative primarily in their preface or introduction. This should be read as an indication of a difference in narrative strategy that corresponds to the author's sociopolitical and literary agenda and, in particular to the role the author attributes to her/himself. Chavkin, Politzer, and Sepúlveda, reserve the final claim to authenticity in signing the work in the name of author. These authors undermine their influence and role in the representation processes by removing the oral testimony from the original interview setting. They exclude the questions that instigated and directed each testimony and silence their role in the transformation of the oral testimony into literary testimony.

The study of Politzer's monological interview distinguishes her text from the literary practice modeled by Chavkin and Sepúlveda. The individual testimonies that comprise her narrative manifest as harmonious as well as antagonistic representations. Each issues authenticity claims testifying to the validity of the portrayed. In opposition, the separate authenticity claims lose their strength. The dichotomous relationship finds repeated expression, the dichotomy itself gains representation value. This brings to question Sol Serrano Pérez's identification of this text as a testimony based on the removal of the oral testimony from the interview setting and its relocation and transformation into a reconstituted narrative. The editorial process clearly affects a text's testimonial validity. A parallel drawn between the verbal and literary interview experience (based on a transcribed interview) suggests that the latter helps the reader to perform the editorial functions and to apply his/her own judgment and critique in editing out "insignificant noise."

The monological interview carries a different authorship than the original testimony; in the form of an edited, transformed testimony, the monological interview represents the author / editor's experience and perspective, his/her sociopolitical and literary agenda and interpretation of the event. Politzer's editorial performance exposes a narrative strategy aimed at creating the illusion that the individual chapters constitute live testimony. This author defines her agenda and sociopolitical objective as bridging of a gap of communication between adversaries in Chilean contemporary society by extending the predominately one-sided discourse to incorporate multi-perspectivity. Consequently she requires that her readership not perceive her as prejudiced or implicated in the discourse other than as an objective intermediary. However, *testimonio* literary critics have distinguished a sympathetic attitude of the transcriber of oral testimony as characteristic of the *testimonio* literary practice. Since Politzer's narrative entails adversary monological interviews, the question arises as to which side her sympathy is directed toward. Politzer's agenda does not necessarily coincide with the sociopolitical objectives of her individual testifiers, and that moreover, in her own approach to the testimony, the author ignores the possibility that her testifiers may seek to pursue their own agendas.

The issue of trauma enters the discussion as attention shifts to the notion of reader response as suggested by Serrano. The author's own fear is mirrored in and by the book in so far as it exposes Politzer's lack of support to the victims' right and fight for justice. Politzer's overriding sociopolitical agenda, reinforced by perpetrators and the Archbishop, yields a traumatizing effect onto victim testifiers who, in *Miedo en Chile*, explicitly cry out for justice and are unable to accept responsibility for the trauma inflicted upon them. Politzer's overriding sociopolitical agenda exemplifies the author's control over the power of representation. *Miedo en Chile* can be read as an indication that the wrongs of the past prevail and are reinforced in and through the present.

With Chapter V, the discussion returns to the theoretical distinction between fictional and non-fictional discourse in literary representations of history in examining *testimonio*'s defining paradigm against the literary practice employed in Isabel Allende's novel, *La casa de los espíritus* (1982). Several questions prepare the theoretical platform for the analysis that follows: what is truth and what is fiction in literary narrative, and, in particular, in the historical novel? Who can author a judgment in this regard? And what can this judgment be based upon? Historical fiction is here identified as a sub-genre of literary fiction in which a fictional representation of experience is placed into a historical context.

Although individuals differ in their understanding of any given historical point of reference, historical fiction implements the latter as common denominators to identify historical events or to attribute historical validity to an experience without linking it to one identifiable event. The role of author and reader is examined as a distinction is upheld between historical fiction and non-fictional history (Porter, Partner and Foley); the study points to a polemic on whether or not historical fiction enjoys higher popularity and why. The analysis juxtaposes Foley's "qualitative approach to define fictionality" with Goffman's notion of a primary framework that determines a text's cognitive meaning and presents Foley's notion of mimesis as a contract between writer and reader. According to Foley, a mutual contract between these agents defines the conditions under which texts can be composed and comprehended. This approach is significant in particular for an analysis of historical fiction of sociopolitical-literary dimensions.

The analysis of Isabel Allende's *La casa de los espíritus* (1982) approaches the novel by interpolating different frameworks and reading experiences. It examines the role, function, and interplay between author, text, reader and varying sociopolitical, historical environments in the differentiation between fiction and fact in historical fiction. Moreover the study addresses the relationship and role of the processes of writing and reading and the (re)appropriation of the power of representation.

The autobiographical element in the novel consists in the family tradition of writing and sharing life journals, and a familiarity with the sociopolitical environment and with some of the characters depicted. This autobiographical element originates in the author, guides us through the novel, and, consequently, extends toward the role and experience of the reader. The text creates an extended sense of representativity in depicting experiences familiar to all of Latin America and, at the same time, specifically also to Chile as it is informed by the author's personal experience and traumatizing autobiographical witnessing.

In the form of a historical fiction, the text conveys a polyphony of voices, an intricate web and exchange between narrators, informants and protagonists. The text juxtaposes alternative and official history and builds a bridge between the past and present that gears toward a constructive future. The story comprises more than just a family's share of history. In this novel the narrator Alba serves as a rhetorical function as intermediary between sociopolitical differences, times and people. She facilitates a *testimonio* that is representative of a larger experience, and that stands out as an attempt to mediate between ignorance, knowledge, across cultures and across times.

Coddou's identification of this text as a transgressive work provides support for establishing this historical fiction as a literary practice that meets *testimonio*'s sociopolitical agenda. In accordance with *testimonio*'s generic definition, Allende's novel issues sociopolitical criticism "against an official version of history" in order to transform the social conscience. The study discusses in detail a scene from the torture chamber, where the narrator's motivation to perform first mental, but then also literary, *testimonio* originates. This mental testimony denounces official history and exposes the real; in order to be perceived as a precursor for the literary *testimonio*, Allende's narrative strategy relies on the mimetic contract between writer and reader, as specified by Foley. Whereas the narrator's matriarchal family tradition has consistently issued testimony in the privacy of a personal life journal, the narrator Alba enables these testimonies to transgress the public sphere. From the hidden presence of the rhetorical narrator, a polyphony of voices relates the experience and point of view of the victim(s) in this society.

Urgency governs this *testimonio*, and its mission, clearly, consists in a battle against official history and the lack of social conscience. This official history, constituted by the grandfather's autobiographical testimony from a patriarchal point of view, routinely intersects the narrative. The comprehensive narrative thus entails dichotomous representations of a common external referent: the narrator facilitates both without mediating between them. The contradictory representations enhance rather than diminish the testimonial effect, in that the discrepancies are limited to the depiction of the grandfather's criminal activities.

The task of deriving the underlying relationships between these types of alternative and official representations of history is here, like in Politzer's monological interview and in Bitar's autobiographical *testimonio*, reserved for the reader. Indeed, the achievement of the text's sociopolitical literary agenda to transform a social conscience requires that the reader heed the writer's mimetic postulate. The *testimonio* must be understood as a non-fiction work, in which the imaginary world that dominates this text embodies a "metaphorical substitute for reality." In general the text is designed as an informant. In this sense, it is directed to an audience that has chosen to ignore the sociopolitical environment of repression and oppression not uncommon in Latin America. However, this text also aims at issuing a solidarity statement, a statement in favor of the socio-politically oppressed and underrepresented.

The study focuses on the pluralistic representation value of this text and the sociopolitical agenda issued by both author and narrator. In accordance with this agenda, narrator and author promote a continuous process of reading and writing, rereading and rewriting. The text illustrates such a spiral process. It argues that meaning changes from the moment that it is first pronounced to the moment that it is perceived by one and then by another. Above all, however, it advises that by sharing memories of traumatic experiences, we can learn of people's torments and also deduce meaning from them.

Unlike other texts discussed in this study of literature of trauma in Chile, Allende's *La casa de los espíritus* ends with an "epilogue" which serves not as a conclusion or afterword, but as an opening chapter of a new book. This new book is one to which we shall contribute and in which we are asked to participate, a book which can grow out of an understanding of reality that gives voice to that which official history silences; this new book is one in which traditional fact is turned into fiction and fiction emerges as fact, a book which is built not on a concept of charity but on a call for justice.

NOTES

1 As a consequence of the military coup and law 1967, the parties that had made up Allende's coalition were banned. The rest were declared in recess and, 1977, dissolved by the military junta. Although underground political activism continued to a limited extent, not until the last years of the Pinochet regime was the forming of political organizations again constitutionally permitted. See Oppenheim 1993, 20.
2 For a comparison of Chile's authoritarian rule with others in South America, see Remmer 1991, 174–182.
3 See Oppenheim 1993, 129.
4 Pinochet engaged in "shock treatment" to reduce inflation. As a result, unemployment began to increase drastically. See Oppenheim 1993, 128.
5 See Oppenheim 1993, 216–7.
6 Pinochet presented the nation with a new constitution on August 11, 1980. At the same time, Oppenheim explains, "Pinochet publicly announced that a plebiscite would take place in thirty days to ratify the new Constitution. The president's position was clear. He stated that, in the unlikely case the Constitution was voted down, 'this would signify the return to the political and juridical situation existent in Chile on September 10, 1973'" (Oppenheim 1993, 134).
7 Similar to Uruguay and Argentina, the Chilean military "engaged in the widespread and systematic use of torture and persecution against perceived leftist subversives in an effort to 'cleanse' their nation."

See Perelli (1990) for a concise description of the military's mentality.

8 The repression was not limited to Pinochet's earlier years in power but continued throughout his rule. Regarding the heightened repression in 1983 and 1984 incited by a fierce economic crisis Oppenheim writes: "The government adopted a two-pronged plan to end the crisis, a carrot and stick approach. On the one hand, Pinochet named right-wing civilian Sergio Onofre Jarpa as minister of the interior in August 1983 in order to negotiate with the opposition. He also allowed some exiles to return. On the other hand, Pinochet stepped up repression. During the same month in which he named Jarpa, Pinochet also called out 18,000 soldiers to put down that month's protests.... There are other striking incidents demonstrating the regime's willingness to use harsh measures. One horrifying example of Pinochet's use of repression was his response to the national strike by the Civic Assembly for July 2 and 3, 1986. Among the acts of repression with which the strike and associated public acts of defiance were met was the deliberate setting on fire of two young Chileans. One, Rodrigo Rojas, died of his burns, and the other, Carmen Gloria Quintana, was severely burned and disfigured. Pinochet also continued to make selective use of his secret police apparatus. On March 28, 1985, three professionals, who were secret Communist Party members, were taken away by the police and killed. Two, José Manuel Parada and Manuel Guerrero, were dragged away from their place of work, the Colegio Latinoamericano (Latin American School), in broad daylight. The three dead men, their throats slashed, were found two days later. Pinochet also called two states of siege during the 1983–1986 period, during which time mass protests were effectively prevented. The first, which lasted about six months, was called after the October 1984 protest, which had become a kind of general strike. The second was imposed in September 1986 after the attempted assassination of Pinochet" (Oppenheim 1993, 186–7).
Regarding the 1983–84 repression also see Maza (1985).

9 With the new Constitution in place by 1980, Pinochet could "legally" remain president of the nation until 1989, when, according to this Constitution, a plebiscite would permit the vote on a "presidential candidate named by the junta." At the same time, the junta was constitutionally determined to "act as a legislature" until a new Congress was permitted to form in 1990. See Oppenheim 1993, 130–34.

10 Oppenheim 1993, 140–41.

11 See the Amnesty International Report on the Decree-Law 2.191 of April 1978 aimed at designed to prevent "the prosecution of individuals implicated in certain criminal acts committed between 11 September 1973 and 10 March 1978," online posting at http://web.amnesty.org/ai.nsf/Index/.

12 Oppenheim 1993, 127.

13 "There has been much discussion about fear in Chile and how Pinochet was able to utilize this fear to stay in power. For example, at the individual level, there was the fear of speaking out, of participating in some public action, and the fear of being taken captive, tortured or killed. This fear can be paralyzing, preventing people from taking action. The Chilean journalist Patricia Politzer deals with how fear affected people and how some managed to overcome it in her book of interviews, *El miedo en Chile*.... Another is a more collective fear, the fear of a society that has been terrorized. Many believe that this has still not been overcome, that there is still much fear in Chile. The report of the Rettig Commission (named by Aylwin) on human rights violations was an important factor in overcoming it, as was the discovery of long-buried bodies; only by publicly acknowledging what really happened, can Chileans begin to overcome their past" (Oppenheim 1993, 195–6).

14 Amnesty International 2001.

15 From the Statement, on 23rd July 1995, by the Group of Families of the Detained and Disappeared; quoted in Amnesty International's report, "Transition at the Crossroads: Human Rights Violations under Pinochet Remain the Crux," March 1996, here cited from the British "Remember Chile" online posting at http://www.remember-chile.org.uk/.

16 Amnesty International 1996.

17 See Monckeberg 1986, 11, regarding a renewed and reinforced censorship of media and news services under Pinochet in November 1984.

18 Adorno 1986, 115.

19 "Chile está dividido en dos países claramente definidos que no se miran, no se tocan y no se conocen; pero se intuyen y se temen" (Politzer 1990, 11).

20 Adorno 1986, 125.

21 I utilize the term "discourse" in accordance with Hayden White's concept of discourse as formulated in *Tropics of Discourse* (White 1990, 4–5).

22 Rabinov 1984, 73.

23 Aman 1991, 7.

24 Amnesty International 2001

25 Nietzsche 1980, 45.

HISTORY AND LITERARY REPRESENTATION

The experience and the making of history form the basis of history's literary representation.[1] In order to discuss a distinction between fiction and fact in the representation of history in and through literature, we also need to question "what is what" in history, knowledge and language. This first theoretic sketch draws from and modifies some ideas from Foucault's *The Order of Things* (1970) for a theoretical approach to the role the human being in history, in both the experiencing and the making of history.

As human beings, we actively partake in history; we are surrounded by it at the same time, as we constitute ourselves in our own "historicity." Foucault refers to a "historicity of man which is itself its own history but also the radical dispersion that provides a foundation for all other histories."[2] With us as object as well as executing subject, history and knowledge emerge as human constructs lacking universal validity; indeed, we may question the validity of knowledge and even knowledge itself. Foucault identifies knowledge as an "anterior and indivisible mode of being between the knowing subject and the object of knowledge." Consequently, he argues, knowledge cannot account for the "possibility of an analysis sufficiently radical to discover elements of origins," because it would thereby neglect the link between these assertions and what made them possible.[3]

Foucault redefines knowledge as "non-knowledge" whereby fact becomes non-fact and the totality of history may be said to separate into histories. This redefinition ought be modified to identify knowledge not by its antithesis but as composition whereby fact may translate into composed fact and the plural compositions of histories may serve as an approximation to that which perception, experience, composition is thought to reflect. The development from experience and perception to representation and reading ought not be viewed as evoking an incremental increase in the distance between a Real (a totality) and the real (an individualistic or pluralistic composition). Instead, any one of these compositions can be seen as an attempt to approximate what the totality of human experience is thought to embody. A redefinition of knowledge as "non-knowledge" in Foucault's terms implies, at the very least, a "profound breach in the expanse of continuities."[4] However, this "breach" may be bridged by acknowledging that knowledge and reason cannot be genetically defined or decoded like a scientist may attempt to define or decode a human cell. As compositions, knowledge and reason are shaped by the linking—yet not always linked—elements and forces that transgress but also thrive in our inter-textual universe.

In traditional terms, history may be understood as constituted by human experiences of the past. Whereas the momentum of a human experience may be located at any given point on a time line, the exact factors determining when, how and why an experience entered the subject's and other subjects' consciousness are difficult to determine. History is thought to encompass experiences of the past. Nevertheless, we may also understand history as a human perception and construct, which finds manifestation within the present experience: metaphysically, as a mental re-composition of events and thought processes of the past, and semi physically, by way of an interplay between metaphysics and perceivable constructs of representation such as literary work.[5] Historical constructs help us form a historical consciousness, which, in turn, enters, influences, and assists us in interpreting present experience and in establishing theoretical paradigms of knowledge and reason. We may interpret and assign meaning to a present experience under consideration of an internal/external information data bank or reference. First, however, an event must be registered by entering human consciousness.

As intertextuality helps us create and process our understanding of history, our perception of history may also be comprehended as representation or text. A perception, reflection, and representation of an event is subjective and relative by nature. We may complement or challenge a composition by referring to a different array of intertextuality than the one consulted in the composition of the former. There may be as many or more different understandings of history as there are genetic, social, political, generation, temporal, geographical, and personal differences among individuals. What we understand as history is a representation in itself, and that representation is as multifaceted and diverse as our imagination allows it to be. Roland Barthes explains,

> the only feature which distinguishes historical discourse from other kinds is a paradox: the 'fact' can exist linguistically only as a term in a discourse, yet we behave as if it were a simple reproduction of something on another plane of existence altogether, some extrastructural 'reality.' Historical discourse is presumably the only kind which aims at a referent 'outside' itself that can in fact never be reached.[6]

Accordingly, historical discourse strives to undermine its composite nature by identifying external referents as its object of representation. Its purpose and objective is knowledge formation. Yet, knowledge, in turn, is "rooted in a life, a society, and a language that have a history."[7] This, according to Foucault, prevents it from achieving universal validity, even regarding its own history or origin. Historical discourse may also seek to nurture human imagination, conscience and a sociopolitical consciousness, yet these too are acknowledged to have a history.[8] Whereas thought may be seen to encompass the composition of knowledge and imagination, it would seem to be consciousness that enables thought. Reason, an active agent of thought, may perform the task of questioning the foundation of knowledge and, at the same time, turn toward itself and examine its own composition and the realm and agents which allow it to function. Consciousness, conscience and thought help us process input and provide the means and medium that enable us to formulate knowledge and representation.

In accordance with Foucault, neither knowledge nor our understanding of history may be attributed universal validity. However, even though thought helps us process and produce knowledge and representation, it cannot claim universal validity for itself either because it cannot separate from the universe that constitutes it. To deny thought's inherent ties to life, society, language, and history, and, moreover, to a changing sociopolitical historical consciousness, would deny thought its very essence.

Foucault imposes a theoretical distinction between history as the compilation of actual events, and History as a modality of knowledge. Thereby, he is able to identify the latter not "as the compilation of factual successions or sequences as they may have occurred; [but as] the fundamental mode of being of empiricities, upon the basis of which they are affirmed, posited, arranged, and distributed in the space of knowledge for the use of such disciplines or sciences as may arise."[9] The understanding of History as a substantial element of thought forms the basis of the aforementioned argument that the questioning of History may promote an interrogation of thought itself:

> History, as we know, is certainly the most erudite, the most aware, the most conscious, and possibly the most cluttered area of our memory; but it is equally the depths from which all beings emerge into their precarious, glittering existence. Since it is the mode of being of all that is given us in experience, History has become the unavoidable element in our thought...and it will necessarily lead thought back to the question of knowing what it means for thought to have a history.[10]

In turning to the history of any given thought, we may stumble upon an incomprehensible network of cognitive interrelations. We will inevitably fall short in our attempt to approximate an origin or prehistoric composition of thought. As we question the composition of knowledge and seek to understand the workings and interplay of intertextual elements in the composition of experience and perception, we may not succeed in deconstructing the system of reason but only the argument that denies its composite essence.

Language forms the basis of our thought and enables its pronunciation. Yet society evolves and we continue to develop, change, translate and interpret language. Histories mingle within our thought in the form of ever changing perceptions forming an indivisible part of our present experience. Impregnated, manipulated and processed by perception, experience and reason, thought dresses our consciousness in words and imagery. Our use of, as well as our attitude toward, the powers of language is intrinsically related to our "Weltanschauung," our understanding of the universe, humanity, and, of course, our concept of history. Neither reason nor language is devoid of subjectivity; to the contrary, both are truly only exempt from objectivity. Certainly we can question reason, we may even question our entire system of epistemes, however, we cannot surpass thought and we can not arrive at any objective form of representation. Language alone does not enable reason, perception is involved as well. Events, as stated earlier, must be perceived in order to enter a consciousness constituted by images and ideas. A literary representation of an event cannot surpass the composite essence of perception, understanding, imagery, and thought process which, among other elements, influence in the constitution of the event. Literary representation is subjective in essence but may nevertheless intend to express meaning and serve for knowledge formation.

The preceding discussion establishes subjectivity as a natural element in experience, perception, reason, knowledge and representation. Thereby it lays the groundwork for our analysis of the possibility and significance of a distinction between fictional and non-fictional discourses, as well as between fiction and fact within the framework of a representation of history. For it is in the context of literary representation of human experience that a seemingly endless discussion of the possibility to distinguish right and wrong, truth and lie, mimesis and distortion, fiction and fact, and different genres continues to thrive. Indeed, the interplay between fictional and non-fictional discourse, between fiction and fact in discourse, comes to carry ever more significance when literature seeks (or is thought) to represent a history of society's wrong doing at a time, when victims and perpetrators continue to sustain a dichotomous sociopolitical presence, objective or stake in life.

It is in this context, that literary discourse may serve to express more than just a particular "Weltanschauung," a particular manner of understanding and perceiving events, humanity and history. It is in this context that a distinction between fiction and fact can correspond to a denial of experience versus a denunciation of such a denial or silencing of experience. It is in this context also that two literatures—official and alternative representation—may assign equal authenticity and representativity value to contradictory informing truths of a common sociopolitical historical experience. Fact may thereby come to represent fiction and fiction may attempt to represent fact.

Literary and historical criticism that tackles the issue of fiction and fact in literary representation of history is dominated by a set of opposed schools, neither one of which appears willing to accept that their separating line is anything other but shaky. Suzanne Gearhart distinguishes their approaches as either democratic or imperialistic and explains:

> [All theories of literature and all theories of history] have consistently sought to fix the boundary between them and to establish once and for all the specificity of the fields in one of two ways: democratically, in that each accepts a mutually agreed on boundary which grants to each its own identity and integrity; or, just as often, imperialistically, in that each tries to extend its own boundary and to invade, engulf, or encompass the other.... In the second [case, the other genre] is overcome, cannibalized, incorporated into the sameness of the imperializing field.[11]

In the context of the literary representation of history, the imperialistic approach formulated by Gearhart tends to be employed in favor of a pro-fiction agenda determined to overcome its separation from fact by relocating the latter within its own boundaries, i.e. by redefining it as fictional discourse. This approach may be seen as an extension of the foregoing analysis that identifies all perception, experience and representation as composition. Foucault echoes this concept in identifying all explanatory paradigms as fictional, including his own: "I am well aware that I have never written anything but fictions.... One 'fictions' history on the basis of a political reality that makes it true, one 'fictions' a politics not yet in existence on the basis of a historical truth."[12] Despite the logic implied, this imperialistic approach may result in performing a double standard: it may be read as formulating an all-inclusive principle whose formulation is consequently located outside of the premises it formulates. Barthes arrives at a similar conclusion regarding historical discourse and declares it a "fake performative, in which what claims to be the descriptive element is in fact only the expression of the authoritarian nature of that particular speech-act." [13] Yet even this statement can be seen as an "expression of the authoritarian nature of that particular speech-act," which suggests to exclude its own explanatory criterion from the domain of fiction.

According to Foucault, traditional representation (History), based on the model of an organic structure, focuses upon its link to "functions essential to the living being, and upon relations of importance that are no longer merely a matter of description." When "the notion of life" is considered "indispensable to the ordering of natural beings," representation, he says, entails both the "visible and the invisible" and implies a permanent rupture between history and History.[14] Foucault maintains that, as long as the principal means of representation, language, "was defined as discourse, it could have no other history than that of its representations: if ideas, things, knowledge, or feelings happened to change, then and only then did a given language undergo modification, and in exactly the same proportion as the changes in question."[15]

It is at this moment, in which language is denied autonomous characteristics because its tools and applications are placed in relation from one use to another, that the notion of historicity merges "into the density of the spoken word itself."[16] And because of these inherent changes in language, Foucault suggests that the discourse sustained through language, i.e. representation, "has lost the power to provide a foundation—with its own being, its own deployment and its power of doubling over on itself—for the links that can join its various elements together. No composition, no decomposition, no analysis into identities and differences can now justify the connection of representations one to another."[17] In essence, Foucault distinguishes two stages in the development of representation: A primordial stage in which language is attributed autonomous characteristics and considered able to represent History, and a latter stage, throughout which language has been transformed and changed. Given the processes of this later stage, Foucault can then argue that "Representation is in the process of losing its power to define the mode of being common to things and to knowledge," and that the "*very being of that which is represented* is now going to fall outside of representation itself."[18]

These two issues are important here, because they point to an ongoing transformation of representation and they essentially challenge that a representation's authenticity claim is self- sustainable. When, with the passing of time or the changing of a sociopolitical, cultural environment, the "very being of that which is represented" may no longer be defined and is relocated outside of representation, then the authenticity claim of representation may be reformulated and established as effect rather than fact. Likewise, a "dis-authenticity" feature attached to historical fiction may also be reconstructed. Such reformulating would require a reader's acknowledgment of a transformation of representation similar to that described by Foucault. At the same time, the notion of representation's loss of power, also referred to by Foucault, may be appropriated by the narrative and emerge as a narrative strategy or tool aimed at re-appropriating the very power it was supposed to have lost.

In the theoretic differentiating between fictional and non-fictional literary representation, the democratic approach referred to by Gearhart constitutes a more traditional and popular practice. It (re)assigns literature the power to define its own essence. From this point of view, we are told fiction and nonfiction are two very different pots on the stove: A creative work of representation (fiction), seasoned for taste with a sprinkling of "real" spices, may not be confused with a dish of purely wholesome, organic, yet raw historical vegetables. We are to suppose that fiction is issued primarily for entertainment, and non-fiction for the purpose of knowledge formation. In the case of any one particular literary work, however, it would be important to know how the fiction – nonfiction paradigm is established or articulated. Moreover, it would be significant to test if a theoretic differentiation of fictional and non-fictional discourse and fictional and non-fictional elements within a framework of a literary representation may maintain general application even in the context of representations of sociopolitical crisis. By this I mean a context, where alternative representation proclaims non-fictional status while challenging the legitimacy of an official representation as non-fictional discourse, and where, at the same time, the historical novel can constitute a popular means to denounce and challenge official voice and representation by way of an interplay of fictional and non-fictional representation within its own framework.

Both texts, official representations of history and *testimonios*, assign truth value to their content, yet *testimonios* are intended as alternative representations of a history which official representation is said to misrepresent, silence or deny. In essence, *testimonio* challenges the validity of official representation as much as the latter challenges the former. In opposition these forms of representation void each other, perhaps as much as any other opposing poles in our epistemological system of dichotomies. Perception, perspective and interpretation enter our calculations in a judicial function, guiding our reading and, essentially, constituting each text. Neither official history nor *testimonio* may avoid their inherent, yet extratextual, constitution. They may yield influence, yet fall short of determining their own essence. The mere existence of such dichotomous forms of representation of history thus sheds a light on the redefinition of knowledge into non-knowledge. It would seem to leave little ground for argumentation, if official representation of history and *testimonio* were not at the same time joining forces in a different dichotomy, that which distinguishes fiction from non-fiction.

In an unusually harmonious relationship, official representation and *testimonio* coincide in their claim of inherent difference, otherness, from literary representational narratives, identified as fiction.[19] Their claim for otherness, for being distinct from fiction, however, is not an isolated, one-sided event; rather, it is a reciprocal feature: fiction, too, claims to be different from non-fiction. Consequently, both sides, fiction on the one hand, and non-fiction on the other, shape the coin of literary narrative in tradition and in modern-day practice. If, however, at the same time we are asked to understand *testimonio* as alternative discourse to official representation of history, moreover, if it is perceived as a given that *testimonio* as resistance literature maintains a reciprocate, inharmonious relationship with official representations of history by unveiling a reality different from that represented by official versions, then we must concede that at the base of this relationship lies a dispute over the authenticity, truthfulness and honesty of the representation of reality. Both official and *testimonio* representations of history make authenticity claims for their respective content despite the contradictory representation and responses to inquiries like "Are there or are there not 'disappeared'?" "Has a torture taken place or has it not?" Even only partially contradictory statements suggest that the veracity of either official or testimonial representation, or both, needs to be challenged.

Hayden White upholds the conventional[20] differentiation that "*historical events* differ from *fictional events*." He suggests that "[h]istorians are concerned with events that can be assigned to specific time-space locations, events which are (or were) in principle observable or perceivable, whereas imaginative writers—poets, novelists, playwrights—are concerned with both these kinds of events and imagined, hypothetical, or invented ones."[21] The problem in representation of history under authoritarian regimes, however, lies in the *fact* that the claims by which events are assigned to specific time-space locations and are/were said to have been observable and perceivable are disputable in themselves. Consequently, even this conventional differentiation must be challenged. Moreover, in questioning the theoretic distinction between fictional and non-fictional representation, we can only point to the inherent subjectivity implied in representation. Clearly, neither challenge is intended to discredit literary production's ability to represent. For representation it remains indeed. In depicting images, suggesting meaning, reflecting worldview and expressing experience, literary representation achieves its goal. And such literary representation of, for example, "history" can take different forms, forms which traditionally we have distinguished generically as historiography, *testimonio*, autobiography, historical fiction, and so on.

With regard to the "authenticity" value of any of these productions, we lack the authority *either* to assign *or* to discredit the representativity of a particular production, for representation it is. As critics we may advocate that any given representation be taken with a grain of salt. We cannot equate the intra-, inter-, or extratextual claim of authenticity with a guarantee of truth. Nor may a similar claim of "fiction" give us cause to deny the possibility of truth-value. Although, on a personal level, we may take a (possibly political) stand and support or challenge a particular (intra-, inter-, or extratextual) claim for authenticity, our attempt to decipher a text's multifaceted "meaning" ought be complemented by a study of the agenda that a representation may serve. If we learn to understand literary representation of history in any given form as a sociopolitical, literary tool, then we may arrive at an understanding that the genre differentiation of representations constitutes a tool in its own right.

The revisionists' attempts to dispute the existence of the Holocaust through a re-writing of history is a clear attempt of falsification and denial of history; "content truth value" cannot be attributed to those or other representations contrary to internationally upheld historical fact and awareness. Hayden White writes: "Every mimetic text can be shown to have left something out of the description of its object or to have put something in that is inessential to what *some* reader, with more or less authority, will regard as an adequate description. On analysis, every mimesis can be shown to be distorted and can serve, therefore, as an occasion for yet another description of the same phenomenon, one claiming to be more realistic, more 'faithful to the facts.'"[22] This may well apply to representations of history that share a, primarily, homogeneous, complementary relationship, within the margin of which a text's realistically is challenged in degree and not disputed as such. However, the relationship shared by official representation of history, proffered in accordance with an authoritarian, oppressive system of government, and *testimonio*, issued by victims of that government, distinguishes as intensely antagonistic. In this situation it is not a question of who is more faithful to the facts but who speaks the "truth" and who does not. In opposition, the former discourse denies and silences the latter and the latter denounces and challenges the former. Both representations claim truth-value and it is our task to examine how these claims are formulated and maintained through intra-, inter-, or extratextual elements.

A comparative analysis of authenticity effects and related narrative strategies in heterogeneous representations of history will serve as a tool to discuss the (inter)relation and (inter)dependency between these discourses and particular sociopolitical endeavors. It will also be useful in distinguishing between literature by agents who control the power of representations and meaning, and discourses by individuals who seek to regain access to and control over the power of representation. As White reminds us, "every representation of the past" or the 'present,' for that matter, carries "ideological implications."[23] In discussing *testimonio*, this study therefore points to the ideological implications and examines the authenticity effect as a necessary requirement for this literature's transformation into a sociopolitical tool. It pursues the question and implications of the explicit or implicit interplay between fiction and non-fiction elements in self-proclaimed non-fictional representation further in the discussion of Chilean trauma literature, specifically autobiography and the monological interview, as types of *testimonio* literary practice. The last chapter extends the discussion of this interplay to historical fiction and discusses in particular, Isabel Allende's novel, *La casa de los espíritus*, challenging its supposed incompatibility as *testimonio*, here seen as based on inadequate notions of history and its representation under, and in the aftermath of, authoritarian regimes of government.

NOTES

1 At the same time, we may consider the perception and experience of history as a representation that is shaped by an indeterminable interplay of cognitive elements.
2 Foucault 1970, 369–70.
3 Foucault 1970, 252, 303.
4 Foucault 1970, 217.
5 Literary representation constitutes only one such form of manifestation, other forms include (but are not limited to) acoustic and visual compositions.
6 Barthes 1970, 153. Also see Foley 1986, 33.
7 Foucault 1970, 373.
8 Indeed, imagination and human consciousness are said to have undergone a significant change most recently due to the Holocaust. According to Lawrence Langer, "The existence of Dachau and Auschwitz as historical phenomena has altered not only our conception of reality, but its very nature" Langer 1975. And Edward Alexander explains: "The nature and magnitude of the Holocaust were such as to mark almost certainly the end of one era of consciousness and the beginning of another. … The human imagination after Auschwitz is simply not the same as it was before" (Alexander 1979, 1–2). See also Foley 1986, 12.
9 Foucault 1970, 219.
10 Foucault 1970, 219–20.
11 Gearhart 1984, 4. Also see Foley 1986, 34.
12 Foucault 1980, 193. Also see Foley 1986, 13.

13 Barthes 1970, 154, see Foley 1986, 34.
14 Foucault 1970, 226–30.
15 Foucault 1970, 236.
16 Foucault 1970, 236.
17 Foucault 1970, 238–9.
18 Foucault 1970, 240. My emphasis.
19 Hayden White suggests that historians' refusal to acknowledge "the fictive element in their narratives" may be linked to their fear of a "degradation of historiography to the status of ideology or propaganda" (White 1990, 99). Indeed, in the context of representation of history in accordance with the official voice of an authoritarian system of government, I suggest, we may well liken these representations to propaganda. That this equation is not limited to this type of socio-politically-motivated narrative is clear, but this should not keep us from applying it here. White argues further that "we are always able to see the fictive element in those historians with whose interpretations of a given set of events we disagree; we seldom perceive that element in our own prose" (White 1990, 99). This points to a different connotation of "fictive element." It is the composite nature of representation that we cannot deny or avoid. The fictive element in pro-dictatorship representations that deny or silence the victims' traumatic experiences is that they deliberately construct a reality that contradicts that of the victims.
20 According to White, one that goes back as far as Aristotle. See White 1990.
21 White 1990, 121.
22 White 1990, 3.
23 White 1990, 69.

TESTIMONIO. *GENRE DELINEATION AND CRITIQUE*

Nietzsche speaks of
"a time when one will wisely refrain from all constructions of the world process
or of the history of mankind, a time when one no longer considers the masses at all
but once again the individuals who constitute a kind of bridge
across the wild stream of becoming.
These do not, as it were, continue a process but live in timeless simultaneity,
thanks to history, which permits such co-operation....
The task of history is to be the mediator between [the present and the past]
and so again and again
to provide the occasion for and lend strength to the production of greatness."
Nietzsche 1980, 53

Latin American testimonial practices "derive from a long oral history of witnessing"[1] and have developed into a tradition still practiced today, in an environment where the need to communicate and promote awareness of historical sociopolitical events becomes ever more urgent. The oral "recalling of history" and the "call to awareness" of past and present suffering form an essential component of the daily practices of individual activists; at the same time, they correspond to an integral and long standing tradition in communal ceremonies.[2] In Latin American literary production, traditionally a distinction has been drawn between "fictional" and "non-fictional" narratives. With both forms coexisting side by side, Latin American testimonial writings are said to have emerged out of a diverse tradition of the latter: non-fictional works,[3] such as the chronicles of the colonial period, the literature of manners, political writings by Simón Bolívar and José Martí, and romantic biographies. It is only in recent years that testimonial writings have entered the realm of mainstream literary discussion and found recognition as a separate literary genre.[4] Official recognition of the *testimonio* did not materialize until the 1970s. Then, the renowned Cuban publishing house, Casa de las Américas, established a prize category for testimonial writings in its literary contests[5]; an "institutional legitimization" identified as "arguably, one of the most important events of the past two decades in Spanish American literary history."[6]

As *testimonio* was officially determined to form part of twentieth-century "Latin American literary evolution," literary scholars did not hesitate to point out its inherently transitional literary form. Beverley explains:

> Like its ancestor, the picaresque novel, *testimonio* is a transitional literary form appropriate to the dynamics of a period of global social and historical transition, but also destined to give way to new forms of cultural representation as that transition moves to new stages and the human collectivities that are its agents come into possession of new forms of power and knowledge.[7]

Testimonio has turned into more than a mere literary complement to oral testimony. Retrospectively defined as a genre, it is distinguished as a literary discourse of ever-higher significance, set apart from other testimonial and documentary literature.[8] Critics have evoked a distinction between testimony and testimonial literature on the one hand, and *testimonio* and testimonial discourse on the other. Unlike the concept "testimonial literature," "testimony" is not limited to literary production but encompasses other testimonial forms of expression, including oral testimony, generally considered the precursor of literary *testimonio*. In distinguishing between *testimonio* and testimonial discourse the emphasis is shifted from a Latin American testimonial practice to a more intellectual discipline carried out to a great extent in US institutions of higher education. This distinction may serve to set a terminological basis for a discussion of the development, intertextuality and literary locus of *testimonio*. It also serves to illustrate a tendency toward establishing *testimonio* as a singular, exceptional genre.

Since the emergence of *testimonio* as a separate genre, numerous Latin American texts have been identified retrospectively as *testimonio*, while new publications today enter the market pre-classified.[9] In delineating *testimonio* as a genre of its own, critics have had to draw fine lines differentiating this genre from other testimonial discourses. Autobiographies, biographies, diaries, letters, documentaries, poetry and novels were placed under scrutiny and, for one reason or another, were disqualified as *testimonio* by not meeting all requirements established for this genre alone. *Testimonio*, on the other hand, became known as a pluralistic genre that could contain or appropriate elements of other forms of discourse while preserving its singularity.

By considering oral testimony a precursor for literary *testimonio*, the emergence and/or development of *testimonio* can with difficulty be traced to a specific point of time in history. Nevertheless, its establishment as a genre is said to entail a "challenge to the category of literature itself." Understanding literature as an ideological form of expression in providing "imaginary representations of real social relations," Rice Sayre locates *testimonio* "between 'literature' in its more traditional forms and real social relations."[10] Defined by Jara as "a trace of the real,"[11] *testimonio* is attributed literary and extra literary qualities. By way of an "explicit interplay between the factual and fictional, between aesthetic aspirations to literariness and scientific claims to objectivity," Sklodowska explains, "testimonio has consistently defied the critics by departing from a traditional system of assumptions about truth and falsity, history and fiction, science and literature."[12]

Literary critics have located *testimonio* at the crossroads of the literary and the real, in that it shares characteristics of both spheres, while evading a strict classification into either realm. "Testimonio is testimonio," writes Moreiras, "because it suspends the literary at the very same time that it constitutes itself as a literary act: as literature, it is a liminal event opening onto a nonrepresentational, drastically indexical order of experience."[13] As a sociopolitical agent with particular ramifications and objectives, *testimonio* must overcome its literary constraints and assert itself as a sociopolitical tool. According to Moreiras, it may be conceived as an act of solidarity and resistance in quest of support and action:

> Testimonio provides its reader with the possibility of entering what we might call a subdued sublime: the twilight region where the literary breaks off into something else, which is not so much the real as it is its unguarded possibility. This unguarded possibility of the real, which is arguably the very core of the

testimonial experience, is also its preeminent political claim. The significance of testimonio, [...] is more political than it is literary.[14]

Oral and literary exercises, which constitute, in traditional terms, both fictional and non-fictional representations of experiences in history, are considered precursors for the literary genre of *testimonio*. Whereas *testimonio* may be distantly rooted in "memoirs and historical analyses emanating from military, laboral, and political circles,"[15] in and of itself the tree which it resembles is considered singular and different from these (distant, or not so distant) predecessors. In establishing itself as alternative representation of history, *testimonio* challenges the truthfulness and completeness of official representations of history. In order for this tree to engender any fruit, it must thrive, blossom via publication, attract (and be accessible to) a positively inclined readership, and finally be deemed worthy of life by receiving a pollination of approval and support. Only a successful fertilization will enable this tree to produce fruit and enter the market under the classification of *testimonio*. The contemporary definition of *testimonio* entails specific attributes, and it is their number that, in essence, constitutes this genre's attributes.

"Despite all the critical attention it has received, *testimonio* remains undefined," writes Elzbieta Sklodowska.[16] Undefined, perhaps, yet closely delineated. For *testimonio* is no empty term. Rather it is filled to capacity with expectations and connotations and, as such, is said to be set apart from the literary arena as a special kind of cultural production entailing both the literary and the real. John Beverley authors one of the more explicit delineation for *testimonio* and touches on the majority of characteristics generally attributed to the literary practice. Beverley states,

By *testimonio* I mean a novel or novella-length narrative in book or pamphlet (that is, printed as opposed to acoustic) form, told in the first person by a narrator who is also a real protagonist or witness of the events he or she recounts, and whose unit of narration is usually a "life" or a significant life experience. *Testimonio* may include, but is not subsumed under, any of the following categories, some of which are conventionally considered literature, others not: autobiography, autobiographical novel, oral history, memoir, confession, diary, interview, eyewitness report, life history, *novela-testimonio*, nonfiction novel, or "factographic literature."...The situation of narration in *testimonio* has

> involved an urgency to communicate, a problem of repression, poverty, subalternity, imprisonment, struggle for survival, and so on.[17]

Beverley addresses several emblematic characteristics of *testimonio*. First, the identification of author or narrator as protagonist or witness of the represented significant event; second, the integration of other literary or nonliterary practices within *testimonio*; and third, the inherent and underlying urgency to represent out of socioeconomic, political necessity. The first attribute may be linked to the authenticity and reality considered central to *testimonio*, since they facilitate it to emerge as an alternative representation of an external referent. In juxtaposition to official representation, *testimonio* challenges the validity of the former in presenting survivor accounts and claiming validity for itself. This identification of author / narrator as protagonist or witness also aids to establish the link between literary representation and socioeconomic and political urgency. In assuming the role of a spokesperson, the author / narrator may transform the personal experience into a public experience and reconstruct the author / narrator's personal call for awareness and action into a public outcry.

The first and third characteristics named by Beverley do not emerge in isolation or complementary relationship to each other but form an inherently interdependent alliance. As for Beverley's second characteristic, the integration of multiple literary or nonliterary forms of expression and representation into *testimonio* assumes the role of facilitator in this interdependent relationship. The multiplicity of voices and integration of sub-genres facilitates the chain of transformations from author/narrator to spokesperson, from the personal to the generally valid experience, and from the individual to the public outcry. Furthermore, this multiplicity enables the emergence of the *testimonio* as a literary representation of history and, at the same time, as a sociopolitical tool.

The truth and reality effect forms a central element in *testimonio*, given that this literary genre is aimed at representing real events and at serving as a sociopolitical tool. In the 1970s and 1980s many studies supported these objectives as a distinguishing trait of *testimonio*. Today, however, more critics are suggesting that *testimonio*'s authenticity claim be questioned based on central notions of subjectivity. Coinciding with a growing tendency to challenge the traditional separator between objectivity and subjectivity in literary representation, George Yúdice suggests reviewing the implications of an author or narrator's political orientation and situation in the context of truth formulation:

> Following the studies of Barnet (1969, 1981), Fornet (1977), González Echevarría (1980), and Casas (1981), testimonial writing may be defined as an authentic narrative, told by a witness who is moved to narrate by the urgency of a situation (e.g., war, oppression, revolution, etc.). Emphasizing the popular, oral discourse, the witness portrays his or her experience as an agent (rather than a representative) of a collective memory and identity. Truth is summoned in the cause of denouncing a present situation of exploitation and oppression or in exorcising and setting aright official history.... My argument regarding testimonio and its challenge to master discourse relies on those texts that are written as collaborative dialogues between activists engaged in a struggle and politically committed or empathetic transcribers/editors. The reason for this is that many texts do not really abandon the forms of subjectivity inscribed in certain master discourses.[18]

Yúdice problematizes the truth claim of *testimonio* in highlighting that the text's subjectivity is linked to a sociopolitical objective. Considering that no literary discourse may circumvent the interference of subjectivity in representing "reality", Yúdice's argument seems to imply that a discourse which does not summon truth in the cause of a sociopolitical objective may be more successful in overriding its own subjectivity. And, indeed, traditional historical discourse, i.e. official representation, is generally not challenged due to subjectivity. However, such representation also does not tend to engage voluntarily in dialogic discourse.

Official representation of history does not identify a sociopolitical objective as cause for its representation, and does not "summon truth" because it pretends to represent the truth. In contrast, *testimonio* is brought forth as alternative representation. It is conceived as a discourse which must "summon truth" because official discourse presents as truth what the *testimonio* author or narrator perceives as a misrepresentation, a distortion, a denial, a silencing of reality. Unlike official history, *testimonio* succeeds in exposing subjectivity, at the very least, the subjectivity entailed in the discourse it challenges. Empathy and popular political commitment help shape the socioeconomic and political cause and objective ascribed to *testimonio* as much as pro-government commitment helps shape official history. The relationship between official and alternative representations of traumatic experiences in history under military rule corresponds to the antagonistic relationship shared by perpetrator and victim. Their representations clash, manifesting the abyss that divides the "truth" of one from that of another.

Both official history and *testimonio* attach authenticity value to their representations of history. As a nation's official history tends to concord with the contemporary political agenda in order to serve that agenda, this alliance in point of view tends to be less explicitly formulated on an intra-textual level in these representations than in *testimonio*. By way of the juxtaposition of official and alternative representation, the question of an implicit point of view in representation moves into the foreground and culminates in a challenge of the other's self-identification as non-fictional discourse. In a discussion of such dichotomous representations of history, implications of subjectivity are often linked to the point of view of representation but do not necessary result in a challenge or discrediting of a narrative's representation value. In response to Yúdice's and Beverley's definition of *testimonio*, Sklodowska points out:

> To any poststructuralist, post-boom, or postmodern reader the give-away in Yúdice's definition is the notion of "authentic narrative". The critic succumbs to what Foucault calls "the will of truth" and finds testimonio's authenticity in an unquestioned origin of the word.... In [Yúdice's and John Beverley's] definitions testimonial writing is politically principled and strongly action oriented, which detracts from exploring its discursive armature. In strictly formal terms, it is simply perceived as a curious brand of life document, autobiography, and forensic patterns of confession, which takes the form of a novel.[19]

Testimonio issues an authenticity claim regarding the truthfulness and validity of its representation. It does not question the underlying concept of authenticity; nor do certain critics. According to Sklodowska, the overemphasis of the extra literary cause and purpose of *testimonio* distracts from its identity as a literary construct, in the form of a novel. These issues are of interest here, in particular because they pertain not only to *testimonio* but to official history as well.

Both *testimonio* and official history are designed as representations of external referents. They are also conceived as representations whose value ought not to be disputed. *Testimonio* issues authenticity vouchers ensuring that the representation does not distort the external referent in its representation to the extent of changing its content substantially. *Testimonio* assures that a crime is not attributed to an innocent person who has not committed the crime and that the nature of the crime committed (i.e. murder, rape, beating, etc.) is not misrepresented as something else. Official history, in contrast, does not issue but implies authenticity guarantees. In a sociopolitical environment of crisis, as constituted by the Pinochet dictatorship in Chile, official history constitutes the voice of the ruling power.

The official voice constitutes a paradigm of truth, the only truth permitted in the sociopolitical environment which it rules. Truth here equates to life. The mere insinuation of the possibility of an accusation or an opposing view that might challenge the legitimacy of official representation is met with censorship, persecution, torture and death. The official voice establishes external referents in accordance with its sociopolitical agenda, it provides justifications and explanations which help further the sociopolitical objective of the ruling power. Its highest concern is to prevent the rising of an opposing voice which could challenge the official representation of truth / history and thereby the legitimacy of the ruler.

Under Pinochet, a new constitution is installed, impunity laws are brought into effect, and the judicial system is newly aligned to meet the Junta's sociopolitical agenda. Official representation of Chile under military siege does not issue authenticity claims; instead it eliminates the mere possibility of questioning its legitimacy together with the possibility of expressing of opposing views. The military junta controls all information stations, the radio, the television, and the news media. International telecommunication and media services are either banned or submitted to strict censorship.

As Sklodowska points out, *testimonio* authorizes a claim of authenticity that is observed by critics, questioning neither its legitimacy nor the origin or implications of the concept of truth upon which it is based. If this claim were scrutinized critically, Sklodowska suggests, *testimonio* would need to be recognized as what it is, a text. But *testimonio* is more than just a text. Like official representation of history, it is a tool, a sociopolitical tool that originates out of a sociopolitical urgency and aims at furthering a sociopolitical goal. *Testimonio* challenges official history by appropriating that representation's own weapon: the claim to truth. *Testimonio* enunciates and reinforces its veracity claim extratextually as well as intratextually: the author / narrator identifies as protagonist / witness in addition to spokesperson and issues an authenticity claim that identifies the narrative as representing an experience in accordance with that experience. The text is said to document the experience. At the same time, it also documents trauma and the possibility that trauma continues to impact the narrator's contemporary experience, process of recollection and narration.

Whereas official history is created to rule alone, alternative history originates out of a need to resist the overruling power. It is history created in defiance of the authoritarian regime. It is created as a challenge and out of a challenge. In Chile, those who were made victims of and by the ruling power write *testimonio*. It is written by survivors whose voice and experiences are silenced, denied, and outlawed. *Testimonio* identifies its external referent as autobiographical experience; the ruling power identifies the external referent of official history as truth. Official history does not elaborate on the composite nature of representation; it completely undermines its literary constitution. *Testimonio*, on the other hand, identifies as a literary work: it addresses the act of its composition, the nature of its content, the cause and purpose of its existence. It asks to be acknowledged as a sociopolitical tool in literary form.

In *testimonio*, the authenticity claim is manifested and reinforced from within the narrative; official history manifests a truth that is enforced by the ruling power. Both narratives constitute literary constructs and, at the same time, sociopolitical tools. Both represent "truth", yet in opposition. One truth challenges the other as non-truth. In consideration of this antagonistic relationship and the literary and sociopolitical constituency, *testimonio* may be seen as a literary weapon devised to re-appropriate the power of representation lost as a result of authoritarian imposition of military rule. Nonetheless, as much as *testimonio* resists the sociopolitical regime of the ruling power, according to Sklodowska, it also defies the rules of literary standards, avoiding the imposition a strict genre definition.

> By establishing an explicit interplay between factual and fictional, between aesthetic aspirations to literariness and scientific claims to objectivity, testimo-

> nio has consistently defied the critics by departing from a traditional system of assumptions about truth and falsity, history and fiction, science and literature. While it is clear that an unambiguous definition of testimonio keeps eluding us, amid the debates still resonating in the field of Latin American testimonio criticism there must be, one should assume, a fairly general agreement as to what testimonio represents. After all, if testimonio was given an identity in our recent (re)readings of Spanish American letters, this rereading must have been informed by a common understanding of what counts as testimonio.[20]

Sklodowska's call for a reformulation of our concept of *testimonio* may at the same time be extended to a reformulation of our concept of historiography and representation of history in general. For just as *testimonio* "suspends the literary at the very same time that it constitutes itself as a literary act,"[21] historiography, too, needs to be reexamined as a sociopolitical literary activity. *Testimonio* and historiography are in temporal or local, sympathetic or antagonistic fashion linked to the sociopolitical panorama of the moment in history that is object of representation. Whereas we may conclude that the "significance of testimonio,...is more political than it is literary,"[22] we should also confirm that the significance of historiography or official representation of history is not only literary but also political and may certainly serve a sociopolitical function.

Marc Zimmerman distinguishes *testimonio* as a source for historical and cultural data based on which prognosis for future developments and understandings of present / recent events may be derived. Consequently, he speaks of Guatemalan *testimonio*[23] as a cadre literature[24] which in its communication of structural transformations among populations and its role in the identification of causes and limitations of particular resistance movements has developed into a dominant literary tool central to the Guatemalan experience it represents.[25] According to Zimmerman and Beverley, *testimonio* ought not be understood as a mere "reenactment of the function of the colonial or neocolonial 'native informant', nor a form of liberal guilt."[26] Instead, they argue, *testimonio* aims at increasing solidarity on the local, national, and international arena.[27]

In focusing on particular struggles, *testimonio* has gained recognition for "linking rural and urban contexts of struggle within a given country, and...maintaining and developing the practices of international human rights and solidarity movements in relation to particular struggles,"

Moreiras explains.[28] *Testimonio* serves as a source of information for studies of political, economic and historical development in particular regions. On the basis that "literary and social considerations are necessarily intertwined in *testimonio*," *testimonio* has been legitimized as a reliable informant for outsiders. It is said to reveal "hidden secrets of popular tradition in relation to questions of resistance"[29] and give "access to situations and modes of thought unknown or poorly understood by officially sanctioned culture."[30]

Testimonio may carry a dual role in modern day civilizations. On the one hand, it may serve to reveal information and insight into popular practices, modes of thought and traditions in situations of resistance to uninvolved populations; on the other hand, it may serve as a tool of action for the involved parties.[31] *Testimonio* is given historical significance precisely because it may represent experience that is silenced or denied in official representation. In reference to the social and political interpretation of military and social developments in Guatemala between 1981 and 1985, Zimmerman explains accordingly:

> Although many explanations have been given for this crisis, there is no doubt that the quintessential written expressions of the crisis are the countless testimonials to various events and processes in the period, by Indian and often women representatives. And there is also no doubt that, of all the testimonios, none is richer and more complete than that of Rigoberta Menchú.[32]

Yet *testimonio*'s sociopolitical function is not limited to its role as a source for information in representing the otherwise underrepresented or unknown. *Testimonio* is an actual participant and activist in the struggle it represents.[33] More than merely a means to enunciate "popular ideologies and cultural modes," Zimmerman commends *testimonio* as "a means of popular-democratic cultural practices closely bound with the same forces that produce political and military insurgency."[34] In identifying *testimonio* as an essential tool for invoking changes of national implications, Zimmerman reinforces the notion that the underrepresented must form part of any democratic process or true social progress and that, therefore, they must find representation. This is a task which *testimonio* is thought to fulfill.

In literary *testimonio*, literary representation and social political relevance cannot be separated. Indeed, we may consider the interplay of these factors a key feature of *testimonio*.[35] In Burgos-Debray's work, the Guatemalan Indian, Rigoberta Menchú, emphasizes that the past is intrinsically connected to the present situation and that the future can only be different if a change is provoked in the here and now. It is this change in which she and her interlocutor want the *testimonio* to assume an active role. "Rigoberta has chosen words as her weapon and I have tried to give her words the permanency of print," explains Elisabeth Burgos-Debray, underlining the political message entailed in this *testimonio*.[36] As Duchesne points out, by way of its actual and political relevance, *testimonio* is able to "resist a formal autopsy which pretends to isolate the literary from the non-literary.... Rigoberta Menchú's struggle," she writes, "is a struggle to modify and break the bonds that link her and her people to the Ladinos, and that inevitably implies changing the world.... She is fighting for the recognition of her culture, for acceptance of the fact that it is different and for her people's rightful share of power."[37] In this struggle her *testimonio* is transformed into a sociopolitical tool.

As an alternative representation of history, *testimonio* may function as a sociopolitical tool in a struggle against officially sanctioned misrepresentations of moments of terror, which in their own existence serve as strategic implementations or stepping stools directly linked to a larger reign of terror. Cavallari manifests such attributes in Fernando Alegría's novel, *El paso de los gansos* (1980). This novel, he explains, "is oriented toward a deconstruction of the fascist 'version' of the historical events which articulate and define the military coup of 1973." Accordingly, it may be seen as a text which "like Salvador Allende's final statements and action" proposes "simultaneously a 'message' and a 'model' of resistance against fascist violence."[38]

Testimonio "signifies the need for a general social change," a need which, according to Beverley, places the reader's own "stability and complacency" into question.[39] Authors of *testimonios* expose their own vulnerability at the same time as they call for help and justice. Just as the readership learns about local injustice, local government enforcement agents can uncover the whistleblower's identity and cause further harm. In order to prevent the risk of provoking negative backfire, these authors have generally needed to disguise or change data referring to their identity or location or they moved into exile. This comes as a consequence of this literature's identity as a sociopolitical, alternative (non-sanctioned) representation and its role as a tool in resistance movements.[40] Indeed, it is in this that we may find literary *testimonio*'s closest tie to its oral predecessor.

Rice-Sayre supports the notion that oral testimony forms part of a cultural tradition. Moreover, she argues that a change in our attitude toward literature may be called for: "Perhaps a key feature of the testimonio is not that Indians are suddenly speaking for themselves but rather those of us outside the network are finally hearing them for the first time. The reason we are hearing these testimonios as more than mere recordings of historical fact and are beginning to pursue their study as literature may have less to do with any newly discovered literary qualities in the testimony than with a challenge to the category of literature itself."[41] Due to the joint literary and sociopolitical constituency of *testimonio*, the separation between literature and its external referent is challenged. Whereas, literature has primarily been studied for its literary qualities in the interpretation of fictional or non-fictional aspects attributed to external referents, *testimonio* pretends to form part of an external referent at the same time as it constitutes it through composition. *Testimonio* says it is relevant to a sociopolitical prevailing experience. It requires itself to be seen within the context of this experience and implores the reader to utilize it as a sociopolitical disclaimer against official history and the ruling power that it serves. Many see oral testimony as a precursor of literary *testimonio*, but, at the same time, literary *testimonio* is not perceived as a mere extension of oral testimony.

According to Rice-Sayre, autobiographies and biographies, as well as giving homage, may be considered testimonial works in so far as they provide evidence and bear witness.[42] She states that in the form of a novel, poem, or essay, *testimonio* gives expression to suffering through an often-simple form of linguistic representation.[43] Rhythms and diction of popular speech are captured, adding an even further realistic touch to the representation. The incorporation of popular speech tends to reinforce the local setting and the author's participation in the event not as an onlooker, but as a participant and member of the local society. However, rhyme can also highlight the traditional contradiction between the demand for literary aesthetics in the face of content-horror. As Prada Oropeza suggests, it is in the lack of aesthetic intentionality in the face of the sociopolitical goal that *testimonio* distinguishes itself from fictional novels and stories, as well as from the documentary chronicle and anthropological and ethnological writings.[44] Accordingly, *testimonio* is seen as a representation of a sociohistorical external referent from the point of view of a narrator/protagonist, who assigns *testimonio* a sociopolitical rather than a literary aesthetic function and intentionality.

Some critics and authors[45] explicitly undermine the significance of *testimonio*'s literary-aesthetic attributes so as not to distract from the sociopolitical significance of the work. *Testimonio*, they argue, is not aimed at causing a literary aesthetic and aesthetically pleasing reading experience but at representing an experience truthfully to raise awareness and promote change.[46] The sociopolitical intentionality and purpose in literary *testimonio* is paramount, they affirm, and that is what distinguishes literary *testimonio* from otherwise transmitted oral testimony. Beverley explains:

> In oral history it is the intentionality of the recorder—usually a social scientist—that is dominant, and the resulting text is in some sense "data." In testimonio, by contrast, it is the intentionality of the narrator that is paramount. The situation of narration in testimonio has to involve an urgency to communicate, a problem of repression, poverty, subalternity, imprisonment, struggle for survival, and so on, implicated in the act of narration itself. The position of the reader of testimonio is akin to that of a jury member of a courtroom. Unlike the novel, testimonio promises by definition to be primarily concerned with sincerity rather than literariness.[47]

Beverley maintains that literally transmitted oral history is not intrinsically linked to a context of sociopolitical urgency because a recorder may pursue a social scientific rather than a sociopolitical agenda. Decisive in Beverley's observation is that oral testimony is transmitted by a mediator and that the text's intentionality is determined by the agent who controls the text. In oral history the speaker accounts as principal agent of the representation. When an intermediary or recorder is involved in the act of representing oral history, the power of representation is transferred to that agent. According to Beverley, a social scientist obtains oral history with a social scientific agenda in mind, which, in turn, determines the intentionality of the text. However, we must account for the possibility that a recorder's agenda may not always be apparent to a speaker just as the speaker's agenda may not always be apparent (transparent) to a recorder.

The imposition of a social scientific agenda onto oral history may be seen as a strategic interference or manipulation of "data" in which an intermediary deliberately overrides a speaker's intentionality to serve his or her own agenda. The recorder of oral history controls the power of representation, the power to override the intentionality of the speaker and to erase any trace of it. Given this scenario, the distinction between social scientific and sociopolitical agenda will be difficult to draw because the speaker's intentionality may have been deliberately erased from the text. Whereas Beverley constitutes a recorded oral history based on the intentionality of the recorder alone, he suggests that literary *testimonio*, preceded by an exchange of oral testimony, is determined by the intentionality of the speaker. Nevertheless, the role of the intermediary in constructing *testimonio* also needs to be accounted for. In order for literary *testimonio* to be determined by the intentionality of the speaker it must override the intermediary's own agenda. Although the latter controls the power of representation, this agent would need to subordinate his own agenda to that of the speaker, appropriate the speaker's sociopolitical urgency and present it as a cause "implicated in the act of narration itself," all of this in order to fabricate a *testimonio*.

The majority of indigenous, guerrillas, and other economically and politically oppressed groups have such low literacy standards that many, indeed, the most renowned *testimonios* consist of transcriptions of oral accounts. Such transcriptions[48] of oral testimony by people, like Rigoberta Menchú (Guatemalan Indian), Domitilia (Bolivian mine laborer) and Huillca (Peruvian farm worker), is proffered by journalists or social activists with different ethnic/social/cultural backgrounds than the narrators. Nonetheless, the interlocutors tend to inform the reader that their own input and/or manipulation of the original material are minimal. Naturally, interlocutors try to emphasize that it is their aim to provide a voice to people who otherwise find no active representation. In accordance, Beverley writes,

> Testimonio gives voice in literature to a previously voiceless and anonymous collective popular subject, the *pueblo*, but in such a way that the intellectual or professional, usually of bourgeois or petite bourgeois origin, is interpellated as being a part of, and dependent on, this collective subject without at the same time losing his or her identity as an intellectual.[49]

Although we tend to refer to *Me llamo Rigoberta Menchú y así me nació la conciencia* as Rigoberta Menchú's *testimonio*, anthropologist Elisabeth Burgos-Debray authored this text. Menchú issued oral history, Burgos-Debray configured the literary representation, and the final version received their joint approval. It is in this final version that it is difficult to distinguish between the different agents involved. In keeping with the literary genre of *testimonio*, the narrative constitutes an intricate narrative web that interpolates witnessing with biography and autobiography. The claim for pluralistic validity is formulated on intra- and extratextual levels, the voice(s) are legitimized as representative of an entire community. Rice-Sayre explains: "It is not Menchú's uniqueness that makes her life story worth telling; rather, her life story is important because it repeats the experience of so many others.... This type of testimony holds the tenuous position of document: it is neither literature nor reality but a verbal recording of the real."[50]

In this form of a "verbal recording," Menchú emerges as the spokesperson for a larger population. It is her voice, "[t]he voice that speaks in testimonio,...the testimonial voice, and not [...] the paratextual voice of the author or mediator," which Moreiras identifies as "metonymically representative of the group it speaks for."[51] Despite her decisive contributions to the *testimonio*, Menchú is attributed neither authorship nor co-authorship of the text. The authorship still rests with Burgos-Debray, on the other hand, her role and function as author of the text fades in the very process of its creation. Beverley points out, "[t]estimonio involves a sort of erasure of the function, and thus also of the textual presence, of the 'author.'"[52] In applying Miguel Barnet's terminology, Beverley explains "the author has been replaced in testimonio by the function of a 'compiler' (*compilador*) or 'activator' (*gestante*).... The erasure of authorial presence in the testimonio, together with its non-fictional character, makes possible a different kind of complicity—might we call it fraternal?—between narrator and reader...."[53] It remains to be determined, however, if this complicity is also representative of the relationship between transcriber and narrator.

Of interest is Menchú's retrospective disagreement and critique regarding this lack of authorial credit by which she adds extratextual support to the intratextual claim of authenticity—it is, after all, (also?) her story—, as well as to a suggested intratextual self-authorization as narrator. For, as Doris Sommer has pointed out quite eloquently, amid its data based on oral history, this particular text cites silence or refusal to comment on the grounds that there are aspects of the indigenous experience which the narrator Menchú believes "no-one should know."[54] It is remarkable that

> Rigoberta's refusals remain on the page after the editing is done.... Either the informant, the scribe, or both were determined to keep a series of admonitions in the published text. Uncooperative gestures may be typical of ethnographic interrogations, but they are generally deleted from the scientific reports as insignificant "noise." Here, however, scientific curiosity turns out to be impertinent, a conclusion we draw from the refusal to respond. Are we being warned that the curiosity may be an impulse to warm our cold bodies with the fuel of passionate and violated lives? Ironically, in the backhanded logic of metaleptic effects, our curiosity—the cause of Rigoberta's resistance—is a product of her performance.[55]

Scientific impertinence or honesty in representation on the part of the interlocutor, calculated rejection, a "potentially humiliating scene of interrogation" or "an opportunity for self-authorization"[56] on the part of the informant—intentionality may certainly be located in the foreground of this representation. At the same time, this intentionality remains difficult to define. Moreover, it may place in jeopardy the complicity between narrator and reader Beverley referred to. Participating readers might be moved to reconsider the extent of complicity permitted when their freshly aroused, growing curiosity is fiercely halted and, unlike the narrator's own struggle, restrained:

> Therefore, my commitment to our struggle knows no boundaries nor limits. This is why I've traveled to many places where I've had the opportunity to talk about my people. Of course, I'd need a lot of time to tell you all about my people, because it's not easy to understand just like that. And I think I've given some idea of that in my account. Nevertheless, I'm still keeping my Indian identity a secret. I'm keeping secret what I think no-one should know. Not even

> anthropologists or intellectuals, no matter how many books they have, can find out all our secrets.[57]

Clearly, no author or voluntary narrator needs to include information considered irrelevant or obtrusive to a sociopolitical, literary agenda. Secrets form part of our life; we all have them, some we share and others we don't. *Testimonio* already provides many insights into the private/public experience; it follows the victims into the torture chambers, re-witnesses their experiences of rape, torture and humiliation representing violence enacted against the most private part of the human being, the body, the mind, one's sensations and emotions. And these representations are far from sketchy; they are detailed, visual, near real. *Testimonio* depends on an authenticity in order to carry out the sociopolitical function it has been assigned. And that authenticity, in turn, must imply a pluralistic validity, for the sociopolitical agenda is significant only in that the urgency which underlines it is shared by so many.

Identity formation in *testimonio* may take the form of a reverse anonymity. A first person narrative thereby signifies not "the loss of personal identity, of the proper name, but the multiplication of those things; not the faceless sociological average or sample or least common denominator, but corresponds to the association of one individual with a host of other names and other concrete individuals."[58] This reverse anonymity resembles a narrative strategy that leads to the formation of identity as much as of otherness.[59] It establishes an identity consisting of a common social class, ethnic group, political affiliation, or sociopolitical experience, which enables the represented to enter into a dichotic, antagonistic relationship with a dominant group that has placed them in need of national, and often also international, solidarity.

In testimonial writings, then, the reader is urged to acknowledge both the narrator and the represented experiences as real and representative of a larger social class. Although the narrator speaks in a singular voice, this voice is simultaneously real and pluralistic. According to Beverley, "testimonio involves an erasure or attenuation of the role and thus also of the textual presence of the author.... Even where there is not an interlocutor and the narrator speaks or writes for him- or herself, the intention is not to achieve the magisterial or omniscient point of view of the author."[60] It is this identification of *testimonio*'s narrator as spokesperson that is then said to facilitate *testimonio*'s definition "as a non-fictional, popular-democratic form of epic narrative."[61]

Clearly the speaking voice in *testimonio* is illusory because the reverse anonymity also entails "the multiplication of proper names" in the narrator-author relationship in that, according to Jameson, "these second appended names [such as Elisabeth Burgos-Debray] are not merely those of editors or collators" whose work may be seen "in analogy to the creativity of the translator."[62] Nonetheless, Beverley and others argue that it is pertinent to acknowledge that *testimonio* discourse is created by an actual participant or witness of the event "who is not a fictional construct" but "speaks directly to us, as an actual person might."[63] It is in this special identification of narrator as a non-fictional construct that *testimonio* stands out:

> The dominant formal aspect of the testimonio is the voice that speaks to the reader in the form of an "I" that demands to be recognized, that wants or needs to stake a claim on our attention. This presence of the voice, which we are meant to experience as the voice of a real rather than a fictional person, is the mark of a desire not to be silent or defeated, to impose oneself on an institution of power like literature from the position of the excluded or the marginal...testimonio constitutes an affirmation of the individual self in a collective mode.[64]

In *testimonio*, the narrator may emerge as "real" and, simultaneously, assume a three dimensional role as witness, actor, and, at the same time, judge.[65] Moreover, it is the "erasure of authorial presence" which consequently facilitates a "complicity between narrator and reader" and thereby adds another distinguishing characteristic to *testimonio*. For the relationship between reader and narrator in *testimonio* is suggested to be "different from what is possible in the novel or story, whose fictional character and degree of aesthetic elaboration require a distancing on the part of both novelist and reader from the fate of the protagonist."[66] In *testimonio*, the complicity between reader and narrator is requisite because it facilitates the cause. Even when *testimonios* such as that of Rigoberta Menchú / Burgos-Debray stand out by explicitly limiting the information presented to contain only data which narrator or author perceive necessary for the purpose or sociopolitical function of the *testimonio*, the attainment of this cause depends on a sympathetic readership.

According to Doris Sommer, in *testimonio* author or narrator may isolate vital information from cultural insights that are not explicitly linked or pertinent to the cause and assume that the reader respectfully acknowledges such censorship as justified.[67]

Although the implied complicity between reader and narrator in some ways serves to bridge the distance[68] that separates them, this does not set the basis for identification between reader and narrator or protagonist. Instead, the reader in *testimonio* is merely invited to accompany and provide support to the latter without ever identifying with him or her. Sommer explains: "The testimonial 'I' in these books neither presumes nor even invites us to identify with it. We are too foreign, and there is no pretense here of universal or essential human experience."[69] In Menchú, however, the narrator identifies herself as singular yet representative, which "helps to explain why, like autobiographers, she uses a singular pronoun, 'I', not 'we'" while trying to avoid substituting "her community in a totalizing gesture." At the same time, however, this narrator "refuses intimacy with the reader;" Menchú's "singularity represents the plural, not because it replaces or subsumes the group, but because the speaking is a distinguishable part of the whole. This is where we can come in as readers, invited to be (*estar*) with the speaker rather than to be (*ser*) her."[70] Indeed, this is where the dividing line between the narrator's relationship with the implied reader versus the relationship with the mediator may be less defined and share common traits.

The implied readership finds enunciation in a number of instances in Menchú, as well as in other *testimonios*, such as Omar Cabezas' *La montaña es algo más que una inmensa estepa verde*. Yet on this intratextual level, the readership never exceeds the status of mere implication. Although in Cabezas' work, the narrator repeatedly addresses a second-person singular by way of a "tú" or a "vos,"[71] the identity of this subject is not revealed. The choice of pronoun establishes an informal relationship between spokesperson and the addressed which, due to this utilization of the direct subject pronouns, may be assumed to be present and a witness to the narration (by speech or letter) in process. As Duchesne points out, in this text, "the second person, which the repetitive 'you' of the monologue refers to, which never speaks and is not spoken of, only exists as a discourse polarity, a sole mold of a mediator in which the perspective of the reader may as well reside."[72] Whether or not the pronoun responds to a mediator, a reader, or both, may be of less significance here than the connotation that *testimonio* does indeed imply its readership or audience on an intratextual level.

Critics maintain that *testimonio* share with testimonial literature the reality effect, the auto- or biographical narrative structure, an inherent link to an experience in history, and, possibly even its literary form. Nevertheless, *testimonio* stands out by being more future oriented, by serving a distinct sociopolitical purpose, indeed, by standing with one foot in reality and the other in the world of representations, and, finally, by implying its own audience. This last attribute is now applied to aid Latin American *testimonio*'s theoretical juxtaposition to testimonial representations of the Holocaust as part of the ongoing trend to uphold *testimonio*'s singularity. Gugelberger argues accordingly: "Most certainly we do not wish to identify Holocaust testimonies, which are basically documentary, with the testimonio that wants to effect change and is quite different from documentary writing.[73] The one has no audience, or perceives its audience as having vanished apocalyptically, while the other definitely lives from the hope and will to effect change or at least raise consciousness."[74]

Gugelberger differentiates Latin American *testimonio* from Holocaust testimonies based on the notion that the sociopolitical environment of urgency prevails throughout much of Latin America and Holocaust ceased to exist at the moment of liberation. However, as Chilean *testimonios* on dictatorship experiences will easily reveal that the trauma persists past the gates of the concentration camp experience and past the historical date of liberation. Clearly, Latin American *testimonio* and Holocaust testimonies have an audience and are written specifically with an audience in mind.[75] Neither Holocaust nor Latin American *testimonios* may effect a change of experience retrospectively. Yet both may succeed in their efforts to raise consciousness. Chilean *testimonios* make a point in stressing that their sociopolitical agenda aims at denouncing injustice, at returning the voice to the voiceless so that justice may be served, and, above all so that history will not be repeated.[76] Of course, many Latin American *testimonios* are written at a time in which there is still hope for the other victims, yet even these works cannot take for granted that they will gain publication and circumvent censorship restrictions within that critical period. In many other instances the only hope that remains is that of retrospectively raising awareness and consciousness, which, of course, also applies to Holocaust representations.

As discussed above, *testimonio* may entail the intervention of an intermediary who transcribes oral history in an effort to provide a voice to the voiceless. Whereas hardcore *testimonio* definitions tend to highlight an autobiographical presence in this literary practice, some critics have shied from such strict genre delimitation and suggested reading poems such as *Our Father* by Alfonso Quijada Urías[77] as literary *testimonio* with sociopolitical intentionality.[78] This third person homage to a priest slaughtered by the military expresses no expectation of the priest's survival, nor does this poem entail a contrasting analysis of the past. On the other hand, the poem entails the hope that the voice is returned to the voiceless. The highly accusatory tone of this work mirrors the priest's own identification as "voice of the voiceless," whereby the poem takes up the role of voice provider for which the former had been known and, eventually, killed. In this voice and hope generating narrative, a specific possibility for the future is enunciated: the possibility that resistance through the act of reclaiming and revitalizing voice and representation may eventually lead to overcoming the traumatic experience in history.

Despite the third person narrator, the priest may be compared to Menchú in her self-elected role as spokesperson. Although it is exile that facilitates Menchú's survival, it may be of interest to note that she locates the moment of liberation in the moment of giving testimony. As mediator and recipient of Menchú's oral testimony, Burgos-Debray recalls: "One day she told me that until then [until telling her story to Burgos-Debray] she had never been able to sleep all night without waking up in panic because she had dreamed that the army was coming to arrest her."[79] Giving testimony for Menchú consequently translates into a sense of survival and relief, as if her *testimonio* could indeed prevent a fatal retaliation by the military and insure her survival. However, as the poem *Our Father* illustrates, oral testimony may rather be directly linked to the violent death of the spokesperson that even literary *testimonio* could not prevent. Nevertheless, the poem also demonstrates that literary *testimonio* may contribute a life-generating function in assuming the role of oral testimony: by giving homage to the importance of testimony it can carry on the role of providing a voice to the voiceless.

The priest's mission survives in and through the poem: at this stage, neither the voiceless nor the priest have been able to retain their speech in life. It is the poem that has become the "spokesperson." Like the priest, Menchú assumes the role of a spokesperson to enhance the awareness of the communal suffering and to present her own experience as representative. She does this also because her community is voiceless without her: "my experience had been very painful...and it's not my grief alone, it's the grief of a whole people. It's the grief of a whole people, and all of us orphans who've been left must bear it."[80] As Beverley points out, *testimonio* is, without doubt, "a fundamentally democratic and egalitarian form of narrative in the sense that it implies that *any* life so narrated can have a kind of representativity."[81]

Generally it is the protagonist/author who emphasizes the pluralistic validity of the testimony because of the general validity ascribed to it. Domitilia, a Bolivian mineworker exemplifies this, as she clarifies her role in *testimonio* representation:[82]

> The story I am going to tell, I don't want it at any moment to be interpreted only like a personal problem. Because I think that my life is related with my people. What happened to me could have happened to hundreds of people in my country. I want to make that clear because I recognize that there are some who have done much more for the people than I, but they have died or haven't had the opportunity to be known. That's why I say that I don't want to do only a personal story. I want to speak of my people. I want to give testimony of all the experience which we have acquired through so many years of struggle in Bolivia, and to contribute a little grain of sand to the hope that our experience will somehow serve the new generation, the new people.[83]

Domitilia, like Menchú, constitutes an I-narrator who "never loses conscience of her social constitution" despite individuality, suggests Prada Oropeza. Her *testimonio* pronounces the "powerful textual affirmation of the speaking subject itself."[84] In underlining the author / narrator's identity as individual as well as pluralistic, the author / narrator / protagonist reinforces the realness of the event and demonstrates the "desire not to be silenced or defeated" despite political, social or ethnic marginality. These *testimonios* succeed in pronouncing a strong political call to action and awareness, yet we should not conclude that the absence of the "speaking subject itself" in *Our Father* prevents that text from issuing an equally strong decree.

One of the most prominent calls for literary action comes from Ernesto Che Guevara, whose example of testimonial guerrilla writing is cited by many as the most motivating. In his work *Pasajes de la guerra revolucionaria* (1969), Che Guevara writes: "Many survivors remain of this action and every one of them is invited also to leave record of their memories to incorporate them and to complement history better. We only ask that the narrator be strictly truthful; that it never be to clarify a personal position or to amplify it or to simulate having been at a location or never to say something incorrect…."[85] In this call for political involvement through literary activity, Che Guevara unequivocally pronounces *testimonio*'s inherent function as an active connection between the literary and the real, the literary and political initiative and change.

Regarding guerrilla *testimonio*, Duchesne explains "guerrilla experiences not only play the passive role of providing themes for the narrations…. they form part in the revolutionary process which they describe, because, in essence, they belong to the cultural and ideological dimensions of the revolution wars as important instruments of communication."[86] Accordingly we may identify this genre as a literature that is written a) by the people, b) from within the experience, c) for the people, and d) to challenge and change the preexisting sociopolitical event through partisan collaboration.

Indisputably, Che Guevara's call for action has been heard and repeated by many. On the other hand, Latin Americans nevertheless need to overcome illiteracy, financial hardship, oppression, censorship and other barriers in order to carry out this call for literary action. Even the motivated Menchú first needed to acquire a second language, escape the sociopolitical environment, and travel to Paris in order to deliver oral testimony to an intermediary of a different culture in hope of publication and support in and from the international arena. And Chilean intellectuals Sergio Bitar Hernán Valdés and Rolando Carrasco Moya[87] who were inspired to write *testimonio* on the spur of the moment when memory was still fresh, first had to wait patiently in order for this moment to be located in liberty or exile rather than imprisonment and torture.

Unfortunately, we may say, neither of these *testimonios* reached their concentration camp comrades at the time of imprisonment and Menchú's indigenous contemporaries still lack basic reading skills in Spanish as well as the economic means necessary to gain access to this *testimonio* as readers. Hence, in contrast to the guerrilla model outlined above, such non-guerrilla *testimonio* would need to be reconsidered as a literature written a) *not necessarily directly* by the people *but rather indirectly through the intervention of a mediator,* b) out *of the memory* of the experience *recollected in exile*, c) for the people *not as readers but beneficiaries of a different readership's solidarity*, and, d) to raise *international* awareness through alternative representation of the preexisting or concurrent sociopolitical event.

Given that this delineation differs in each of the four criteria previously outlined regarding guerrilla *testimonio*, the shared genre identification is brought into question. The first two criteria pertain to the process of creating *testimonio*, and significant discrepancies or differences in this process of writing may suggest that inherent differences could also be found in the final product. Such differences may be reflected in the perspective, agents and voices represented, and the content contained. The third and fourth criteria pertain to the consequences of *testimonio* and include specific implications regarding the sociopolitical purpose, readership and reader response assigned to *testimonio*.

In guerrilla and the non-guerrilla *testimonio* here referred to, we may need to concede that the "real," sociopolitical function ascribed to *testimonio* instigates change either from the local (partisan) or the international field and, moreover, that the attainment of this trajectory is more implied than guaranteed. Consequently, we ought to address the question of what happens to *testimonio* the moment the sociopolitical purpose of provoking change is obliterated either by complete devastation or resolved by an event in history possibly not directly linked. Does *testimonio* shed its generic label the moment the experience is overcome? Or is the sociopolitical purpose of *testimonio* then redirected to provide an alternative representation and raise consciousness like Holocaust narratives?

It is along these lines that we may want to compare the sociopolitical objective of *testimonio* to that of Holocaust representations and question if the notion of witness and transmitter indeed differs in these representations. Could we apply Rosenberg's affirmation—"[e]ven to say we are still living in the generation of witness is important, and further: We've become transmitters, whatever we say"[88]—to both Latin American *testimonio* and Holocaust representation? We can affirm that, across the ages, cultures and nations, representation entails the transmission of ideas and perspectives, and that this holds true as well for the discourse of a testifying witness in either *testimonio* or Holocaust representation. On the other hand, unlike Holocaust literature, Latin American *testimonio* traditionally has emphasized the immediacy and temporal proximity that links it to the sociopolitical event.

Testimonio authors, narrators and protagonists tend to foreground the urgency of representation and, indeed, to use it as a disclaimer for the underachievement of aesthetic literary standards. Moreover *testimonio* seems to be based on the notion that the greater the temporal proximity to the event, the greater the possibility of achieving the desired sociopolitical objective. Yet that does not imply that survivors of, for example, the torture chambers in Chile do not share with many Holocaust survivors the sensation that a distancing in time, as well as in location, comes to be a necessary prerequisite in order to attempt trauma representation. This certainly does not underscore the urgency with which Holocaust victims wrote and continue to write, or the urgency, with which delayed Latin American *testimonios* were and are conceived. Rather it can be seen as an indication of the extent of horror that victims suffered, witnessed and continue to experience. As is true for traumatic experiences in Latin American society as well, the suffering in the Holocaust was not overcome by the end of the Holocaust, but continues to prevail, even though to a different extent, throughout post-Holocaust history and into the present day.

Germany officially commemorated the liberation of Auschwitz on January 27, 1998. This serves, at the very least, to illustrate that the process of raising consciousness and coming to terms with this horrific past has not even yet reached its fullest potential, and, in my opinion, a strong analogy can here be made to the Latin American arena. For even as dictatorships, and the savagery, torture and immediate trauma they inflict, may be of temporal nature, the pain and sorrow caused surpasses all temporal and spatial barriers and prevails, even when acknowledged only by the victim. Indeed, according to Osvaldo Bayer, we could use this controversial occasion of the Auschwitz commemoration day to question the process of coming to terms with the past and acknowledging guilt in Latin American post dictatorship societies and suggest a Day of Civil Courage in Argentina in commemoration of the Madres de la Plaza de Mayo, or else ask: "How long will our deputies and senators, our governors and intendents delay; how long will our people delay, how long will we delay, in reflecting upon the horror?"[89] In light of these observations, a delineation of the genre of *testimonio* may expand the attributed socio-political agenda to include a post-event contribution to the process of coming to terms with the past and to the continued task of raising consciousness.

Whether or not *testimonio* representation covers a life story or limits itself to a specific event in history, *testimonio* essentially implies an act of remembering and an act of representing the remembered. When oral testimony constitutes the act of remembering, the act of representing oral testimony through literary *testimonio* corresponds to a mediator. The formulation of literary *testimonio* thereby implies an extensive interaction between the mediator as interviewer and the interviewee who provides oral testimony. Literary *testimonio* consequently also implies the act of editing as direct quotations are removed, an order of representation is determined, and language and content is edited to aid comprehension and *testimonio*'s agenda—all of which may also be considered part of the literary strategy.

When, in contrast to Burgos-Debray and others, the mediator does not limit him/herself to one source (Menchú), but represents a multiplicity of voices in order to provide a panoramic vision of the experience, then we arrive at a work like *The Murder of Chile: Eyewitness Accounts of the Coup, the Terror, and the Resistance Today* (1982) by Samuel Chavkin. This is a narrative, which falls if not outside than at least at the margins of the concept of *testimonio* discussed thus far.

Menchú's and Domitilia's testimonies maintain their representativity based on the narrators' identification as spokespersons. Chavkin's narrative is also built on a notion of representativity, in that each individual interviewee identifies as spokesperson for the larger population of victims under Chile's recent dictatorship. At the same time, however, Chavkin's text also illustrates that, despite its representative value, a *testimonio* may nevertheless be distinguished as singular, because individuals experience trauma differently and undergo different traumas. Indeed, the explicit multiplicity of voices in Chavkin's text (in contrast to the implicit multiplicity of voices in other *testimonios*) may be linked to a desire to enhance the authenticity effect through an augmented representativity. This, in turn, stands in direct correlation to the legitimization of *The Murder of Chile* as an alternative representation that aims at raising consciousness and provoking change. The author explains the process of remembering and the purpose of his narrative in these terms:

> Recalling their suffering, and the brutality their relatives and friends underwent at the hands of the Junta, took courage; indeed, it was a searing experience. Nevertheless, they [the interviewed] took part in this project in the belief that the epic story of Allende and the Popular Unity government, as well as that of the Fascist orgy of sadism that followed, should be told again and again. This book is a collection of personal accounts by the victims and resisters of the putsch, which when pieced together gives perspective to the drama of the Chilean tragedy. Though many of the survivors of this group have been hurt psychologically and maimed physically after years of terror in concentration camps, they remain astonishingly optimistic, confident that the Chilean Junta will not continue to rule for long.[90]

Chavkin's eyewitness accounts are inserted into the narrators' review of Allende's politics, the Allende years and other post-coup experiences. Although the accounts are only seldom interrupted, no indication as to their completeness or omission is provided. The coherence of this narrative is upheld by the narrator's own text, whereas the eyewitness statements serve as data and information to illustrate particular suffering and consequences of the coup. When comparing Chavkin's narrative to that of Menchú / Burgos-Debray, one could argue that the former contains more documentary value and principle than the latter. Nevertheless, the eyewitness accounts add a personal touch[91] to the narrative, and, perhaps, the truly remarkable differences are that Menchú's narrative approaches that of a life story and that Menchú, as narrator, has taken the liberty to speak for others rather than let them speak.[92]

It has been maintained that literary Latin American *testimonio* generally appears in the format of a novel or narrative, told (in most cases) by a first-person narrator who, in addition to his/her function as narrator, identifies as protagonist, participant or witness in the depicted events. The identification, in general terms, of *testimonio*'s narrative time span and content as corresponding to that of a life story, does not aid the argument for *testimonio*'s singularity. Even though, in Sklodowska's words, "testimonio's creative use of the 'life story' formula—as we know it from the studies of Oscar Lewis—places it within the tradition of the Chicago school of sociology with its concern for retrieving voices of people who had seldom been heard," this ought not imply a clear demarcation between *testimonio* and life story: "L. Langness' definition of life story as 'an *extensive* record of a person's life told to and recorded by another, who then edits and writes the life as though it were autobiography' (1965, 4–5) applies to testimonio as well."[93]

On the other hand, the choice of narrative time span is significant in *testimonio* because it aids the sociopolitical purpose and reinforces the reality effect. First, we can observe that the time span of narratives like those of Burgos-Debray and Viezzer (1977) mirrors a life story because the sociopolitical problem illustrated emerges not as a sudden change in reality, but as a long standing tradition. In the experience of the Guatemalan Indian and the Bolivian mineworkers, sociopolitical inequity, oppression, torture and killings are commonplace, not an exception to the rule. Moreover, the life-story presentation serves as identity construction of an "other." Consequently, it may be vital to the sociopolitical agenda of representation because it helps clarify Western civilization's relative unfamiliarity with the culture and living conditions of these oppressed populations.

The majority of *testimonios* that are object of the main stream critical discourse on *testimonio* entail such larger time spans—from childhood to the present—(see Burgos-Debray 1984 and Viezzer 1977). Nonetheless, there are, of course, other *testimonios* whose narrative time span is restricted to a significant period of life or temporal events, such as concentration camp terms experiences (see Valdés 1974, Bitar 1987, Carrasco Moya 1991). In these latter works, the reduction in time span is often substituted by a more detailed zeroing in on events. Here the narrators often identify themselves as spokespersons for having shared an experience with others, yet, having been fortunate to survive and escape the experience prematurely while others continue to be subjected to it. Another variation consists of the narration of a particular perspective and personal experience which, when complemented by other related narratives, aims at shaping a more representative picture.

It is necessary to recognize that any attempt to define *testimonio* will have to recognize considerable diversity and plurality in the experience, the process of remembering, representation, narrative style and strategy, and, finally, sociopolitical implication. Undefined, "historically derived"[94] rather than "logically prescribed"[95] the term *testimonio* has become a signifier for a developing rather than a fixed literary practice. *Testimonio* may be understood as a "shorthand for a whole spectrum of narrative conventions" sharing similarity with "the picaresque narrative and the bildungsroman," while depending "on specifically forensic patterns of argumentation as well as on the narrative conventions of autobiography and the traditional realist novel."[96] Yet, *testimonio* has, perhaps, most successfully been distinguished in its singularity and otherness derived from its sociopolitical implications.

With the implied sociopolitical purpose in mind, *testimonio* is identified as a political tool that emerges principally out of the political necessity to include literature in the sociopolitical struggle of modern day. According to Yúdice, *testimonio* hence consists of "an authentic narrative, told by a witness who is moved to narrate by the urgency of a situation (e.g., war, oppression, revolution, etc.). Emphasizing popular, oral discourse, the witness portrays his or her own experience as an agent (rather than a representative) of a collective memory and identity. Truth is summoned in the cause of denouncing a present situation of exploitation and oppression or in exorcising and setting aright official history."[97] Like a courtroom witness "at once engaged in an appeal and bound by an oath," the *testimonio* narrator thus lays bare the memory of past and concurrent experiences in the name of truth, as Felman says, in order to "*address* another, to impress upon a listener, to appeal to a community."[98]

Yet, *testimonio* is not a lone fighter against oppression, torture and misrepresentation in the literary arena. Ellis explains:

> with the impetus towards political change has come a steady tide of literature, produced by people who unreservedly dedicate their talents to the revolutionary

> struggle and want their poems, novels, short stories, and testimonies to serve as tools in the building of a radically different society. This dedication hardly seems to come out of a self-conscious decision to write socially committed literature. It reflects, rather, the absorbing, preoccupying, inescapable impact of a brutal, oligarchic repression clashing with a people's aspiration to social, economic, and political justice.[99]

In the face of imminent censorship and imprisonment, torture or fatal retaliation by the military regime on home turf, *testimonio* narrators like Chavkin, Bitar, and Valdés, as well as Menchú, turn to the international arena and foreign publishing houses for support. Their inability to mobilize activism through *testimonio* in home territory speaks for the implications of the authenticity value attributed to these representations in terms of censorship. Nevertheless, Ellis maintains that "[l]iterature is crucially involved in this [national or local] movement for political change" and that the emergence and function of testimonial resistance literature in El Salvador is, in essence, analogous to "the historical relationship between literature and society in other parts of Spanish America."[100] *Testimonio,* by definition, aims at presenting an alternative discourse that denounces and corrects a pre-established official representation of the event/situation. Moreover, it helps "recast the distortions, presenting a rectifying view of an embattled society from the other side of the front-line." Consequently, in Jara's words, "testimonial writings seem indeed to be inseparable from the war itself: one of its primary functions consists of inscribing its insistent presence into the bosom of a society that wants to escape to misery, privation, disaster and death. The testimonio is a blow against the conscience."[101]

According to Beverley, *testimonio* achieves such a far reaching political purpose in calling a critical reality to the attention of people who otherwise would not necessarily be aware of the alternative perspective neglected in official representation:

> Generally speaking, the audience for testimonio, either in the immediate national or regional context or in metropolitan cultural centers, is that reading public which is still a partially class-limited social formation. The complicity a testimonio establishes with this public involves the possibility of its identification with a popular cause normally distant, not to say alien, from its immediate experience.[102]

Interestingly, not much work has been done regarding reader response to *testimonios* within the concurrently affected or surrounding population and evidence of a "blow against the conscience" on the national level is still lacking. Clandestine limited circulation of particular *testimonios* have certainly reached out to a selected few; this circulation however, is generally restricted to those who can see the work in its solidarity function rather than as a blow against the conscience. The possession, even temporarily, of a censored product always presents a danger to the holder and to the person from whom it was received. Those who volunteer to participate in this exchange are generally aware of the sad reality which surrounds them and which the text denounces. Menchú, Valdés, Carrasco Moya, and others have chosen to participate actively in history and have tried to turn literature into a sociopolitical tool and response to an actual, ongoing conflict.

There is little evidence that the sociopolitical implication of *testimonio* in particular significantly surpasses its status as mere "implication" in the national arena, indeed, we can safely maintain that the vast majority of *testimonio*'s readership resides outside the area of sociopolitical conflict and urgency. On the other hand, although their clandestine circulation may be minute, we should not discredit its possibilities and impact either. Carrasco Moya's *testimonio PRIGUÉ* obtained two clandestine editions in Chile, in 1977 and 1978. Maybe these did not serve to enlighten those who preferred ignorance to knowledge and chose not to lay their hands and eyes on nonofficial history. Yet to their readers they provided an eyewitness/survivor insight into a sad reality which the majority of Chileans may have suspected but not seen or experienced first hand. With each disappearance of a family member friend or neighbor under Pinochet, "newcomers" joined others in the seemingly endless, hostile, and agonizing journey of trying to learn about the disappeared's fate. *PRIGUÉ* provides insight into the experience of one survivor, the horrors, torture and humiliation he suffered together with the rest of inmates. What is significant, however, is that the validity and sociopolitical urgency ascribed to the text on the national level does not decline with the closure of the concentration camp experience. The publication of non-clandestine editions continues to enhance its sociopolitical agenda and function. In the 1991 preface to *PRIGUÉ*, Jorge Insunza affirms:

> Rolland Carrasco's book will be, today as it was yesterday, a contribution to bringing value to the powers of truth. Many Chileans who did not have access to the earlier, heroic but necessarily limited, editorial efforts, will look in on the world of the concentration camps under dictatorship, to the torture centers, the evil of those in uniform who did not hesitate to stain their honor to protect the interests of a minority. They will also learn of the decency and humanity, the confidence in their ideals and the optimism of the assaulted, whom the humiliations and the pain inflicted did not degrade. The one or the others are listed by their names when these were known. There will be those who will be exalted by what is revealed about their martyrdom and their strength to endure. There will be others who, when their crimes are known, their own children will not be able to respect them from now on.[103]

Justice has not been served in Chile; the sociopolitical urgency, the call for truth, justice and a "Never Again" prevail as long as perpetrators remain unpunished, victims not recognized and the threat for a repeat military coup prevails. *Testimonio* forms part of that struggle, yet we should note, it is not alone and maybe, it is also not all too different from other literary works and genres.

Isabel Allende's first novel, *La casa de los espíritus*, does not meet the strict definition of *testimonio* as established by Beverley and others. Yet it was met by a similar reception as *PRIGUÉ*. Allende explains the novel's success in infiltrating censored Chile and obtaining legitimacy status:

> Due to the strict censorship prevalent in Chile in 1982, I supposed that *La casa de los espíritus* could not circulate in my homeland. I was resigned to the idea that my co-nationalists would not read that story which speaks of the injustice, the fear and the pain, but also of the solidarity, the courage and love of a people like my own.
>
> I never imagined what happened.
>
> The book entered Chile as a pirate copy, hidden in the baggage of audacious travelers or sent by mail without cover and separated into two or three pieces, so that they could not identify it. The few copies that thereby entered the country then multiplied as if by magic. Those who owned one, made photocopies which were passed from hand to hand, there were lists of people interested in reading it and I heard about some who offered it for rent. Months later, the government considered it necessary to suppress the censorship of books to better its public image, although their grip continues to suffocate all mass media.

> Together with other books which had been banned for ten years, *La casa de los espíritus* entered Chile legally and leads the bestseller lists from August until today [March of 1984].[104]

As this study will show, the genre delineation of *testimonio* may require modification in order to account for testimonial works like *La casa de los espíritus* which meets many of the sociopolitical objectives *testimonio* desires but does not necessarily accomplish. The actual (rather than the desired) sociopolitical effect or consequence of *testimonio* may yet need to be defined. On the other hand, the cause for the sociopolitical purpose attributed to *testimonio* is far less debated. At the root of the testimonial discourse lies the "(pre) existence of a socio-historical fact"[105] (for example, the persecution and death of the priest in Quijada Urías' poem *Our Father*), a fact for which *testimonio* may intend to provide proof via alternative representation, raise awareness and instigate change. As Prada Oropeza explains, "all testimonial discourse is referential and pretends a validity of truth; furthermore, it is always intertextual because, explicitly or implicitly, it supposes another version or interpretation (other text) of the object (reference)."[106] These issues will first be addressed in the discussion of the autobiographical *testimonios*, *Tejas Verdes* (1974) by Hernán Valdés and *Isla 10* (1987) by Sergio Bitar, and then also in the analysis of three monological interviews, Samuel Chavkin's *The Murder of Chile* (1982), Emma Sepúlveda's *We, Chile* (1996), and Patricia Politzer's *Miedo en Chile* (1990). Finally, attention is turned toward Isabel Allende's *La casa de los espíritus* (1982) to assess the applicability of the genre of *testimonio* to this historical novel.

NOTES

1 Rice-Sayre 1986, 49.
2 See Burgos-Debray 1984, 67.
3 The differentiation between literary works of fiction and nonfiction represents a dichotomy of exclusion; it does not allow for a middle ground. This critique of genre definitions such as *testimonio* proposes to challenge the logic and validity attributed to this practice. The differentiation between works of fiction and nonfiction has now developed into a polemic among contemporary literary critics: it continues to be upheld and perpetuated by some, while at the same time it is challenged by others. I will make reference to the designations 'fiction' and 'nonfiction' throughout my analysis to demonstrate the extent in which this differentiation has shaped and, indeed, constitutes the very foundation upon which contemporary genre definitions have been developed and are maintained.
4 Gugelberger describes a three-stage development in *testimonio*: "At first glance the genre of the testimonio was a Latin American 'thing,' originating in Cuba in the immediate years of the revolution, then manifesting again in Bolivia before it became nearly a Central American genre. The second stage was the critical response to the testimonio by 'progressive' intellectuals in the United States, a majority of whom were women, just as the majority of the producers of the testimonio were women. The third stage in the development of testimonio was the response of critics in the United States, many of whom were of Latin American origin, who struggled with the issues of 'lo real' and started to refute the presumed

'left' 'poetics of solidarity, going 'beyond' the unconditional affirmation of the genre as represented in [*The Real Thing*] by Barbara Harlow and in the Latin American Perspectives collection by the majority of the contributors" Gugelberger 1996, 5.

5 See Beverley 1990, 173.

6 Sklodowska 1996, 84.

7 Beverley 1990, 207.

8 In Prada Oropeza's words, "the Latinamerican literary evolution, at least as far as the narrative is concerned, in time presents—next to a testimonial literature (novels, stories and chronicles) and documentary literature—a discursive manifestation ever more tenacious and significant: testimonio or, as we prefer to call it, testimonio discourse" ["...la evolución literaria latinoamericana, al menos en lo que a la narrativa se refiere, presenta en nuestros días—al lado de una literatura testimonial (novelas, cuentos, crónicas) y documental—una manifestación discursiva cada vez más tenaz y significativa: el testimonio o, como preferimos llamarlo, el discurso-testimonio"] Prada Oropeza 1986, 10.

9 Duchesene identifies the emergence of the guerrilla *testimonio* with the beginning of the Cuban revolution and writes: "The contemporary guerrilla testimonio is an expression of the revolutionary process which develops in Latin America since the 1970s, of whose initiation the Cuban Revolution has come to constitute a common point of reference" ["El testimonio guerrillero contemporáneo es una expresión del proceso revolucionario que se desarrolla en América Latina a partir de los años sesenta, de cuyo inicio la Revolución Cubana constituye ya un común punto de referencia"] Duchesne 1986, 85.

10 Rice-Sayre 1986, 52.

11 "una huella de lo real" Jara 1986, 2. Jara clarifies: "history is recognized through its traces, through the value of the present it contains. In this manner, testimonio places us, the historian of the past and the present, in the threshold of the real, in the jambs of death, pain and hope." ["la historia se reconoce por sus huellas, por el valor de presente que contiene. De este modo, al historiador pasado y pre-

sente, el testimonio nos pone en los umbrales de lo real, en los dinteles de la muerte, el dolor y la esperanza"] Jara 1986, 3.

12 Sklodowska 1996, 86.

13 Moreiras 1996, 195.

14 Moreiras 1996, 195.

15 Zimmerman 1996, 103.

16 Sklodowska 1996, 84.

17 Beverley 1989, 12–13, in Gugelberger 1996, 9.

18 Yúdice 1996, 44.

19 Sklodowska 1996, 86.

20 Sklodowska 1996, 85.

21 Moreiras 1996, 195.

22 Moreiras 1996, 195.

23 Zimmerman esteems Guatemala as the most appropriate location for the search and "testing of testimonio's origins and functionality," because "Guatemala is one of the places where, even long before the institutionalization of the form in Cuba, testimonio as such had developed and served as a prime mode for expressing the critical problems and situations of various marginalized and subaltern sectors whose active presence would be central to any serious national transformations" Zimmerman 1996, 102.

24 Also see Beverley who observed: "Testimonios centered on participation in guerrilla activity proliferated all over Latin America, in part as a form of propaganda for armed struggle directed toward a progressive general public, in part as a kind of cadre literature internal to the revolutionary organizations themselves" Beverley 1990, 174.

25 Also see Zimmerman 1996, 128.

26 Zimmerman 1996, 128.

27 Like other authors of alternative representation of autobiographical traumatic events, Sergio Bitar manifests this objective in his preface and writes: "This testimonio is also an expression of solidarity with whom I shared my prison at Dawson, as well as a modest contribution and recognition for the thousands of Chilean women and men who have suffered most in these years" ["Este testimonio es tam-

bién una expresión de solidaridad con quienes compartí mi prisión de Dawson, así como una modesta contribución y reconocimiento a los miles de chilenas y chilenos que más han sufrido en estos años"] (Bitar 1987, 14).

28 Moreiras 1996, 196.

29 Rodriguez 1982, 85–6, in Zimmerman 1996, 101.

30 Zimmerman 1996, 101.

31 Likewise, official history may serve to reveal information pro-government agents esteem most beneficial to their sociopolitical agenda. Official history answering to a society's inquiry regarding the persecution, detainment and disappearance of family, friends and neighbors, may provide little truth about the course and nature of events but much truth about the ruling power's agenda to calm a society's anxiety and unrest.

32 Zimmerman 1996, 101.

33 In concordance, Beverley affirms: "Testimonios continue to be produced and to be of great importance in understanding the nature of social struggles in Central America and in projecting their future patterns and possibilities. As we have argued, they serve not only to reflect the praxis of emerging subaltern social and ethnic sectors in the region, but also to generate it, addressing various publics that are both internal and external to the popular movements themselves as records of human experiences that might otherwise remain anonymous, vehicles for local and international solidarity, models of new forms of personal and collective subjectivity places to test and evaluate experience and strategy. In this sense, testimonio remains one of the most important ideological weapons of the Central America revolutions" Beverley 1990, 207.

34 Zimmerman 1996, 101.

35 This interplay generally manifests itself in one sole narrative account. However, Ernesto Che Guevara's texts, *Pasajes de la guerra revolucionaria* (1969) and *La guerra de guerrillas* exemplify one interesting exception to this norm. Here the representation of an ongoing historical event and its future relevance is spread over two separate discourses, with *Pasajes*...providing a depiction of

guerrilla action (i.e. praxis) and *La guerra...*providing a guide for such action (i.e. theory).

36 Burgos-Debray 1984, xviii.

37 "se resiste a una autopsia formal que pretende aislar lo literario de lo no literario" Duchesne 1986, 86.

38 "se orienta hacia la deconstrucción de la 'versión' fascista de los hechos históricos que articulan y definen el golpe militar de 1973..." "...la conducta y las últimas palabras públicas de Salvador Allende...." "...a la vez un 'mensaje' y un 'modelo' de resistencia a la violencia fascista" Cavallari 1986, 162.

39 Beverley 1990, 178.

40 See Hernán Valdés (1974), Sergio Bitar (1987), and Rolando Carrasco Moya (*PRIGUE: Prisionero de guerra en* Chile, 1991; first clandestine edition in Chile 1977).

41 Rice-Sayre 1986, 49.

42 See Rice-Sayre 1986, 5.

43 In some cases this may be due to the narrator's lack of linguistic / literary education. However, there are also skilled writers of *testimonios* who deliberately emphasize the lack of linguistic / literary finery to underline that priority is placed on the urgency of publication. See Valdés (1974) as an example.

44 See Prada Oropeza 1986, 19, 20.

45 See John Beverley 1990, 1996.

46 Also see Yúdice 1996, 46.

47 Beverley 1996, 26.

48 See Beverley's explanation and interpretation of this phenomena: "Because in many cases the narrator is someone who is either functionally illiterate or, if literate, not a professional writer, the production of a testimonio generally involves tape-recording and then transcription and editing of an oral account by an interlocutor who is an intellectual, often a journalist or writer. (To use the Russian formalist term, testimonio is a sort of *skaz*, a literary simulacrum of oral narrative).... What needs to be noted here is that the assumed lack of writing ability or skill on the part of the narrator of the testimonio, even in those cases where it is written instead

of narrated orally, also contributes to the 'truth-effect' the form generates" (Beverley 1996, 26–7).

49 Beverley 1990, 176.

50 Rice-Sayre 1986, 52.

51 Moreiras 1996, 197.

52 Beverley 1996, 29.

53 Beverley 1996, 29.

54 Burgos-Debray 1984, 247; 1983, 377. See Sommer 1996, 135.

55 Sommer 1996, 135.

56 Sommer 1996, 136. Sommer later continues this thought and observes: "Rigoberta's secrets are doubly strategic. They stop avid readers in their appropriate tracks that threaten to overstep the narrator's authority by assuming that the textual terrain is unobstructed and accessible to their mastery. Also, and more subtly, the secrets serve to whet anemic appetites by producing intrigue that can turn into productive, collaborative, political desire. If her secrets are so important, they must be interesting, no?" Sommer 1996, 141

57 Burgos-Debray 1984, 247.

58 Jameson 1996, 185.

59 Frederic Jameson elaborates further in identifying the notion of reverse anonymity as "a concept, then, that is both literary (having to do with the nature of a certain kind of narrative discourse and its basic category of the character, or more particularly the protagonist—the hero or heroine) and also a social concept insofar as it offers what I think is a new conception of collectivity and collective life—very different from the threatening mobs and faceless masses of First World fantasy—and specific to the culture and experience of the Third World itself" Jameson 1996, 186.

60 Beverley 1990, 175–6.

61 Beverley 1996, 27.

62 Jameson 1996, 185.

63 Beverley 1990, 177. See also Rosenberg who, in the context Holocaust testimony Rosenberg argues that "To make personal is a form of testimony..." (Rosenberg 1989, xiii)—in Latin American *testi-*

monio, making personal is a form of pluralistic representation / validity.

64 Beverley 1996, 28–9.

65 Jara writes: "The presence of the 'I'—which can remain more or less isolated, multiply in a *we*, or dilute itself with a rhetorical impersonality—ought be assumed in its triple connotation of witness, actor and judge" ["La presencia del yo—que puede hallarse más o menos delimitado, colectivizarse en un *nosotros*, o diluirse con impersonalidad retórica—ha de asumirse ... en su triple conotación de testigo, actor y juez"] (Jara 1986, 1).

66 Beverley 1990, 176.

67 See Sommer 1996, 146.

68 A distance based on cultural and ethnic differences, among others.

69 Sommer 1996, 146.

70 Sommer 1996, 146.

71 In her *testimonio*, Menchú also addresses a "you" which can be seen to correspond to the intermediary receiving the oral testimony, or to the reader caught in the process of reading. *La montaña es algo más que una inmensa estepa verde* is authored by the Nicaraguan Omar Cabezas without the mediation of a third party, like Elisabeth Burgos-Debray. As Duchesne points out, Cabezas' text "embraces the development of the author-narrator-protagonist's political military activity and, in his story, the guerrilla experience.... In addition, Cabezas does not pretend to narrate the history of a particular guerrilla detachment, but his personal experience in the guerrilla and the impact it has on his life—already dedicated to the sandinist revolution" ["[a]barca el desarrollo de la militancia política del autor-narrador-protagonista, y en su cuento, la experiencia guerrillera.... Además, Cabezas no pretende narrar la historia de un destacamento guerrillero particular, sino su experiencia personal en la guerrilla y el impacto que tiene en su vida—entregada ya a la revolución sandinista"] Duchesne 1986, 117.

72 "La segunda persona a quien parece dirigirse el repetido 'tú' (o 'vos') del monólogo, la cual nunca habla y de la que nunca se habla, sólo existe como polaridad del discurso, puro molde de un inter-

locutor donde también puede alojarse la perspectiva del lector" Duchesne 1986, 117.

73 We may juxtapose this notion of documentary writing to Ellis' argument that the choice of first-person narrator may aid a literature regardless of its genre identification to gain a documentary character. See Ellis in the introduction to *Mirrors*, 6: "Another important factor in the creation of simple authenticity is the prominence of the first-person narrator. This device not only connects the reader to a certain existing consciousness but also gives a documentary character to the writings, whether they be lyric poems, short stories, novels, or literally, testimonies" Yanes 1985.

74 Gugelberger 1996, 4.

75 Indeed, Holocaust narratives frequently address their audience on an intra- as well as an extratextual level in a similar fashion as *testimonio*.

76 A central motive in Holocaust representations certainly consists of raising awareness and denouncing the protagonist's horrific suffering and the victims' demise. Holocaust survivors, their offspring, friends and supporters, continuously insist on raising consciousness so that "Never again" may history repeat such gruesome slaughter.

77 Yanes 1985, 67–8.

78 It is difficult to distinguish, at times, whether or not critics intend to invoke or are conscious of a distinction between *testimonio* and literary testimony because when the Spanish translation of these terms is identical.

79 Burgos-Debray 1984, xv.

80 Burgos-Debray 1984, 236.

81 Beverley 1990, 175.

82 Also see Menchú's self-identification: "My name is Rigoberta Menchú. I am twenty-three years old. This is my testimony. I didn't learn it from a book and I didn't learn it alone. I'd like to stress that it's not only *my* life, it's also the testimony of my people. It's hard for me to remember everything that's happened to me in my life since there have been many very bad times but, yes, moments of joy as well. The important thing is that what has happened to me has

happened to many other people too: My story is the story of all poor Guatemalans. My personal experience is the reality of a whole people" (Burgos-Debray 1984, 1).

83 Viezzer 1977, 13.

84 Prada Oropeza 1986, 12.

85 "Muchos sobrevivientes quedan de esta acción y cada uno de ellos está invitado a dejar también constancia de sus recuerdos para incorporarlos y completar mejor la historia. Sólo pedimos que sea estrictamente veraz el narrador; que nunca para aclarar una posición personal o magnificarla o para simular haber estado en algún lugar, diga algo incorrecto…" (Guevara 1969, 113).

86 "Los acontecimientos guerrilleros no sólo cumplen el rol pasivo de proporcionarle temas a las narraciones...forman parte del proceso revolucionario que describen, pues pertinecen, a fin de cuentas, a la dimensión cultural e ideológica de la guerra revolucionaria, como importantes instrumentos de comunicación" Duchesne 1986, 85.

87 See: Bitar 1987, Valdés 1974 and Carrasco Moya 1991.

88 Rosenberg 1989, xiv.

89 "¿Cuánto tardarán nuestros diputados y senadores, nuestros gobernadores e intendentes; cuánto tardará nuestro pueblo, cuánto tardaremos nosotros, en meditar sobre el espanto?" Bayer 1997.

90 Chavkin 1982, 7.

91 See Yúdice who emphasizes the importance of the personal experience in testimonial writing: "Testimonial writing, as the word indicates, promotes expression of personal experience. That personal experience, of course, is the *collective* struggle against oppression from oligarchy, military, and transnational capital" Yúdice 1996, 54.

92 Regarding Menchú, Yúdice writes: "Throughout her life in Guatemala, however, she learned who she was by participating in a collective struggle for material and cultural survival. She identifies herself as one of the 'people,' meaning by this all who are exploited," and hence formulates an analogy which applies to the eyewitness narrators as well. Like Chavkin's eyewitnesses, Menchú also "gives a personal specificity to those marginalized and op-

pressed elements of which she herself is one" without becoming an "elite speaking for or representing the 'people.'" Moreover we may consider Chavkin's account as much "a practice, a part of the struggle for hegemony" as Yúdice does with regard to Menchú's narrative (Yúdice 1996, 55–57).

93 Sklodowska 1996, 85.

94 Regarding the origin of testimonial writings, Marc Zimmerman observes: "If fictional and nonfictional portrayals of dictatorship are starting points for the importance of testimonial tendencies in modern canonic Guatemalan prose, certainly many documentaries and portrayals of Guatemalan history appeared throughout the century, especially in the 1940s and on to the present. However far removed they may finally be from that specific combination of attributes that correspond to any normative definition of testimonio, many of these treatments do contain at least some of the elements that are essential to the constitution of the genre; they stand as the immediate discursive context for the reception, if not always the production, of specifically testimonial texts. This is especially so with respect to memoirs and historical analyses emanating from military, laboral, and political circles.... Perhaps the most fully testimonial text of the Intervention and the years that follow is *Guardias infernales* by Rubén Barreda Avila (1960).... Barreda published his book depicting the 1,096 days he spent in his 'prison purgatory.' Standing as an indictment of the regime, the volume was a clandestine text used throughout the 1960s as a kind of primer for new cadres; it is a bridge work, then, between the literature of the Reform period and the documentary and testimonial-oriented literature that would characterize subsequent phases of Guatemalan history" Zimmerman 1996, 103.

95 Lohafer, 11 in Sklodowska 1996, 84.

96 Sklodowska 1996, 84.

97 Yúdice 1996, 84.

98 Felman 1992, 204.

99 Ellis "Introduction" in Yanes 1985, 5.

100 Ellis "Introduction" in Yanes 1985, 5.

101 "...el testimonio, al parecer, es inseparable de la guerra: una de sus funciones primarias consiste en inscribir su presencia impostergable en el seno de una sociedad que se quiere ajena a la miseria, las privaciones, el desastre y la muerte. El testimonio es un golpe a las conciencias..." Jara 1986, 3–4.

102 Beverley 1990, 177.

103 El libro de Rolando Carrasco será, hoy como ayer, una contribución para hacer valer los fueros de la verdad. Muchos chilenos que no tuvieron acceso a los esfuerzos editoriales anteriores, heroicos pero obligatoriamente limitados, se asomarán al mundo de los campos de concentración de la dictadura, de los centros de tortura, de la maldad de uniformados que no vacilaron en manchar su honor para proteger intereses de una minoría. Conocerán también de la decencia y el humanismo, de la confianza en sus ideales y del optimismo de los agredidos, a quienes las humillaciones y el dolor inferidos no degradaron. Unos y otros están con sus nombres, cuando fueron conocidos. Habrá quienes serán enaltecidos por lo que conozcan de su martirio y de su decoro para hacerle frente. Habrá otros a quienes, al conocer de sus hechos, ni sus hijos podrán respetarlos de aquí en adelante" Jorge Insunza (Carrasco Moya 1991, 8).

104 "Debido a la estricta censura que había en Chile en 1982, supuse que la *Casa de los espíritus* no podría circular en mi patria. Me resigné a la idea de que mis compatriotas no leerían esa historia que habla de la injusticia, el miedo y el dolor, pero también de la solidaridad, el coraje y el amor de un pueblo como el mío.

Nunca imaginé lo que ocurrió.

El libro entró a Chile como un pirata, oculto en las maletas de viajeros audaces o enviados por correos sin tapas y partido en dos o tres pedazos, para que no pudieran identificarlo. Los escasos ejemplares que así ingresaron al país, se multiplicaron por arte margia. Quienes poseían uno le sacaban fotocopias que iban de mano en mano, había listas de interesados en leerlo y supe de algunas personas que lo ofrecían en alquiler.

Meses después el Gobierno consideró necesario suprimir la censura de libros para mejorar su imagen, aunque la mordaza se mantiene asfixiante en todos los medios masivos de comunicación.
Junto con otros libro que habían sido proscritos durante 10 años, entró *La casa de los espíritus* legalmente a Chile, donde encabeza las listas de venta desde agosto hasta ahora" (Allende 1986, 20).

105 "la pre-existencia de un hecho socio-histórico" Prada Oropeza 1986, 9.

106 "todo discurso testimonial es siempre referencial y pretende un valor de verdad; además es siempre inter-textual pues, explícita o implícitamente supone una otra versión o interpretación (otro texto) sobre su objeto (referente)" Prada Oropeza 1986, 9.

Chilean Autobiography: Between Holocaust Autobiography and Latin American Testimonio

This chapter discusses Chilean autobiography as a means of representing experiences resulting from oppression, persecution, torture and genocide by way of two novels, *Tejas Verdes* (1974) by Hernán Valdés and *Isla 10* (1987) by Sergio Bitar. The analysis is aided by observations drawn from the extensive, continuous stream of investigative reports on the Holocaust thematic which serve to bridge the near vacuum of studies on Chilean autobiography as a traumatic experience in history, and provide insight into areas not before studied in the Chilean context. At the same time, a comparison and contrastive analysis with the Latin American genre of *testimonio* will establish a literary theoretic point of reference in discussion of these autobiographical representations of Chilean concentration camp trauma.

Susan Rubin Suleiman turns around the autobiographical imperative "Everyone has at least one book in them—their autobiography" in order to apply "not only to writing about one's life but to reading about it; reading *for* it; reading, perhaps, *in order to* write about it."[1] This reversed imperative applies to Suleiman and she also sees it reflected in the renowned Holocaust scholar Elie Wiesel. As an immediate reaction to the Holocaust experience, Wiesel imposed upon himself a "ten-year vow of silence,"[2] limiting his initial post trauma reflection to an inner, private exchange nurtured through continuous input from the public, literary sphere. During this ten-year period from 1945 to 1955, Wiesel says, "I never spoke about it; I never made notes; I only read. I read every single book that appeared on the Holocaust. I still do. I'm a voracious reader of Holocaust Literature and World War II Literature. I still want to understand what happened."[3] Once Wiesel did enter the literary ambience with his own production on various Holocaust themes, he began to participate incrementally in the associated public literary, sociopolitical, historian and cultural discourse. His first novel *Night* is, according to Wiesel, his only autobiographical work, at the same time, however, he also maintains that "[a]ll the stories are one story."[4] For the post-*Night* author Wiesel, who "must continue to read and to write over and over,"[5] *Night* appears to assume the role of a second well of infinite memories from which to draw in his urge to represent the "unrepresentable."

This drive to communicate the Holocaust experience shared by many survivors, is said to originate out of the experience itself. "So acute was the fear that their experiences would remain, in Himmler's horrifying words, 'a never-to-be-written page in history,' that 'literary testimony' became for many victims the sole reason to survive," suggests James Young. He adds that "[w]hen survival and the need to bear witness become one and the same longing, this desperate urge to testify in narrative cannot be underestimated."[6] Nonetheless, as the struggle for surviving the Holocaust is replaced with the struggle for survival in a post-Holocaust, victim antagonistic environment, the survivor's imperative to testify "may be accompanied by the equally strong feeling that any attempt to communicate their experience will ultimately fail."[7] Given that no single representation suffices in the attempt to depict the "unrepresentable," the plurality of representations may be seen to translate into one story; notwithstanding that, in Elie Wiesel's case, only the first is considered "autobiography."

In the context of representations of traumatic events in history, the generic title "autobiography" translates into "personal history," enunciating the interdependence between the personal and the historical. Autobiographies of traumatic events in history comprise histories of clearly personal, subjective character, due to a strict author-protagonist relationship and identification. Barbara Kosta explains:

> First, the term "personal histories" encompasses the transition of personal experience into language from a subjective viewpoint, which creates a narrative of

> the self.... Second, joining the terms personal and history calls attention to the dissolution of the traditional boundary between the private and the public. It illustrates the interdependence between these mistakenly separated spheres and also the artificiality of dichotomizing them. At the same time, the combination of personal and history highlights the subjectivity of history and the construction of knowledge.[8]

In autobiographical representations of experiences during the Holocaust or the Chilean dictatorship, personal history is combined with a larger, social history. Moreover, in contrast to autobiographical works, in which the personal-private surpasses the public, sociopolitical historical context, in Holocaust / dictatorship representations, historically recognizable events move into the foreground; they overshadow and determine a particular personal experience. As these personal-public histories implicate the public as antagonistic agent in the historical event, the representations fall subject to higher scrutiny and censorship.[9] They have been known to provoke even excessive antagonistic reader reception. Political disagreement with the form and content of the portrayed has in several cases prompted "the greatest indignity human beings can inflict on one another: telling people who have suffered excruciating pain and loss that their pain and loss were illusions."[10]

Like autobiographical representations of the Holocaust, autobiographical writings on Chile's dictatorship obtain historical relevance in representing personal/communal experiences that the narrator witnessed or participated in. Victims of the Pinochet dictatorship were persecuted under a 25–year military agenda designed, in Hernán Valdés' words, "to exterminate the Marxist roots in Chile" and "to de-politicize the country."[11] They were subjected to excessive violence[12] and turned to literary representation out of an urge or necessity similar to Holocaust survivors. However, Holocaust and dictatorship representations by victims differ in that the former assumes the role of a *supplementary* and the latter[13] assumes the role of an *alternative* discourse on a social historically acknowledged fact.

The sociopolitical purpose of Holocaust representations is to supplement an existing representation of the Holocaust, which is considered valid yet incomplete because of the multiplicity of experiences entailed. By way of literary representation of personal experiences, Holocaust survivor autobiographies hence aim at facilitating an approximation to the actual dimensions of the event. In contrast, survivors of the Chilean dictatorship assign their autobiographical writings the sociopolitical function of serving as alternative mediums of communication to rectify as much as contradict an existing official representation. Although both forms of writings share the goal to represent a non-represented experience (Holocaust autobiography in the sense of supplementation, dictatorship autobiography in the sense of contradiction), Chilean autobiography moreover assumes the function of a literary tool of resistance.

Unlike Elie Wiesel, Hernán Valdés did not hesitate to take up the pen upon his liberation. He wrote *Tejas Verdes* "with great hurry, 'in the heat of the moment'"[14], approximately a month and a half after completing his sentence. Rather than wanting to know what happened, the situation of this narrative involves, in conformity with Beverley's observation on *testimonio*, an urgency to make known a problem, repression, imprisonment and struggle for survival.[15] Specifically, Valdés aims at representing and simultaneously denouncing the persecution, imprisonment and torture he and other Tejas Verdes prisoners endured under Pinochet's military junta. As if he were responding to Erika Hoerning's question "who, for whom, why and at what time?,"[16] Valdés embraces the role of bearing witness in identifying himself as protagonist and witness. In this respect, too, the work concords with Beverley's characterization of *testimonio*, "told in the first person by a narrator who is also a protagonist or witness of the events he or she recounts, and whose unit of narration is usually a 'life' or a significant life experience.'"[17] Nonetheless, Valdés shies away from calling his work a *testimonio*. He defines it as a retrospectively written diary created for a specific audience:

> The reader has before him the diary of one of the prisoners in one of the sectors of the military concentration camp of Tejas Verdes.... The writing of these memories has provoked profound repulsion in me, however, if I have assumed this task, it was not with the objective to exhibit or communicate a disgracing personal experience, but, rather, to illustrate through this experience the *current* experience of the Chilean people.... This book...is principally addressed to those who, in Chile, want to conserve the innocence among their complicity and promiscuity with fascism..., and to those abroad who think that the military coup that finished up with the government of the Unidad Popular, is already a

> fact of the past. This book shall remind them that the coup continues taking place, in other forms, on a daily basis.[18]

Valdés explicitly addresses a plural national readership that he identifies as antagonistically implicated in the traumatic experience, as well as an international population that he charges with ignorance. Valdés demands this anticipated large readership to approach the text as a representation of a historically accurate and concurrent Chilean experience. By way of this introduction, he invokes a highly visual authorial command aimed at encompassing both narrative and reading experience. This emphasized authorial command seem disproportionate considering that it is integrated into a literary work and not an oral testimony, in which the "author" and "narrator" are unmistakably identified as one. In this literary context, it challenges the contemporary understanding of the role and function of the author's signature in autobiography. According to Kosta,

> The author's signature, as we have known it, is no longer privileged and paternal, belonging to someone who 'owns' the text, whose intention is primary and who controls and assigns meaning as the unifying agent outside the text. Rather, the author appears only as a 'guest' in the text.... With the author no longer identified as originator, the text lives in relation to a larger network of intertexts. The dispossession of the author as the sole creator of meaning transfers the production of meaning to the reader. Through this displacement, the text remains open to a number of possible interpretations.[19]

Valdés reverses this practice in appropriating the role as primary creator of meaning and transferring the production of meaning back to himself—the author-narrator. In accordance with Kosta, however, he thereby still falls short of re-appropriating absolute meaning because "[b]y maintaining a signature, important extratextual references such as race, class, gender, ethnicity, and the cultural and historical background of the author are preserved as significant markers. The author, consequently, is read as one possible site of meaning, as a point of departure and not as the focus of absolute meaning or conclusion."[20] Kosta suggests that an author's influence, as well as the correspondence between signifier and signified, depends upon the reader's interpretation and varies on an individual basis. Holocaust scholar James Young, however, goes one step further in arguing against the ability of an author to preserve authorial command. According to Young, the author's withdrawal from a diary or autobiographical text upon publication is inevitable:

> The words in a reproduced Holocaust diary are no longer 'traces' of the crime, as they were for the writer who inscribed them; what was evidence for the writer at the moment he wrote is now, after it leaves his hand, only a detached and free-floating sign, at the mercy of all who would read and misread it. Once he withdraws from his words, the writer has in effect also withdrawn the word's evidentiary authority, the only link it ever had to its object in the world. The writer's absence thus becomes the absence of authority for the word itself, making it nothing more than a signifier that gestures back toward the writer and his experiences, but which is now only a gesture, a fugitive report.[21]

Whereas this notion finds an echo in Michel Foucault's question "What does it matter who is speaking?",[22] Hernán Valdés suggests that we read his work as a first draft of what he hopes will develop into a literary tradition of resistance. What such a tradition would characterize is the identity of the author as witness-survivor of the military Junta, and it is in this sense that Kosta's notion that an author's identity is "preserved as significant markers"[23] applies. Answers to the questions "what was the author's role during this period?" and "did the author partake as victim, perpetrator, or bystander?" may certainly influence a reader's approach to such a text, regardless of whether or not an author forthrightly exerts authorial command.[24] As I have previously argued in the context of *testimonio*, the identification of author / narrator as protagonist and witness aids to establish the link between literary representation and sociopolitical urgency. In this particular writing, the compliance with the authorial command is prerequisite to the achievement of the sociopolitical objectives; moreover, the entire narrative is built upon this adherence even by the anticipated antagonistic readership.

The authorial command here presupposes that the reader's judgement regarding the text's representation value, its authenticity and testimonial validity, resonates positively. "The possibility," suggested by Young, "that, once committed to paper, a witness's testimony could be perceived as a fabrication of reality and not the trace of it he had intended … seem to mock a witness's very raison d'être,"[25] would also shatter the very essence of Valdés' narrative strategy. In *testimonio*, the author is said to invoke an "erasure of authorial presence,"[26] by assuming the function of compiler and thereby procuring complicity between narrator and reader. Valdés, in contrast, reinforces the authorial presence and undermines the reader's role in assessing the text's testimonial validity by reinforcing the narrative's immediacy and authenticity effect.

Valdés does not emphasize a differentiation in the identities of narrator and author. This can be read as an indication of the author's continued struggle with the trauma originating in the camp experience, rather than as an indication of having surpassed it. It can also be read as a deliberate silencing of the traditional paradox in autobiographical writing on the part of the experienced author. In undermining the difference between the autobiographical I and the remembered as well as remembering I,[27] Valdés is able to enhance the immediacy effect, which, in turn, is linked to the representation value of the text.

As Helmut Peitsch explains regarding retrospectively created diaries of the Holocaust period, "the literary critic honored especially the evidently non-authentic diaries for providing the strongest sense of immediacy.[28] This immediacy and sense of actuality are created by way of an "authenticity fiction."[29] Nevertheless, *Tejas Verdes* serves to distinguish this authenticity fiction as a narrative strategy successful in hiding the illusion it creates: "The proscriptions against expression versus the demands for information, the imaginary worlds of the novelist versus the all too real world of political process, the semiconsciousness of the brutalized prisoner versus the eloquence of a personal testimony, the unreality of the experience of the moment versus the painfully vivid recall of a subsequent reflection" are, in Foster's words, "some of the juxtapositions Valdés' document uses to highlight the uniqueness of its narrative."[30] When a representation's strategic employment of authenticity reinforcing elements undermines an audience's recognition of the theoretical impossibility of representing a traumatic experience, as illustrated by *Tejas Verdes*, then the representation of the unrepresentable becomes—hypothetically speaking—possible.

The notion that "[e]ven though the time of life and 'time of narration' differ in autobiography ..., autobiography can nevertheless reflect the entire life time as a time fragment (in the sense of pars pro todo)"[31] is strongly reflected in Valdés' foreword. On the one hand, Valdés identifies *Tejas Verdes* as "the diary of one of the prisoners" who narrates his experiences utilizing an autobiographical I. On the other hand, Valdés also suggests that the diary constitutes "the writing of these memories." Such constitution would indicate that, rather than documenting the camp experience, the "diary" documents a recollection of the experience upon liberation. Yet, Valdés does not encourage such an interpretation. In his words, *Tejas Verdes* constitutes a "reconstitution" of a diary as it could have been written, and this is, according to David William Foster, precisely what makes Valdés' work stand out:

> What is singular about Valdés' narrative is the conjunction of his unquestionably true statements regarding his personal experiences and his use of a hypothetical diary to portray those experiences. The diary format, particularly when an author uses it to transmit alleged fact, presupposes that the author can transcribe events on a day-to-day basis, in moments of recollection and reflection. Such a document should possess the spontaneity of the moment and the accuracy provided by immediate recounting.[32]

The writing process of a reconstituted "diary" establishes an explicit interplay between factual and fictional,[33] with fictional here translating into reconstituted fact. This literary practice is built on the notion that an author-survivor of trauma can either reassume the autobiographical I's pre-trauma identity, or construct a literary recollection (memory) of traumatic experience uninfluenced by the closure of the traumatic event through liberation and survival. Such a process of recollection finds resonance not only in the context of *testimonio* but also in a perhaps more traditional understanding of memory "as a residue left in the mind by the ruins of time, and capable of retrieving and even restoring the past."[34] Valdés reinforces this concept of memory by implicating the reader's endorsement of the immediacy and authenticity effect, which aims at bridging the experience across the barriers of time and knowledge to autobiographical representation. The perhaps traditional approach to memory applied by Valdés has commonly been redefined to read that both perceived reality—which is traditionally considered object of a memory—and memory itself consist of artificial constructs. According to Klöss,

> the reversibility of time in autobiography has its borders...; because the autobiographical "retrospectivity" must necessarily be understood as a construction: The autobiographer loses with the "knowledge" of his past the point of view of the "Not-yet-knowing".... The known is irreversible, the condition of the tabula

rasa remains out of reach for the remembering person. Sartre calls this the "retrospective illusion"....[35]

Valdés does not contradict this understanding of history, rather he utilizes it strategically. He appropriates and reinforces the "retrospective illusion"[36] referred to by Klöss in identifying *Tejas Verdes* as a retrospectively created diary, yet, in accordance with an apparently deliberate narrative strategy, he falls short of establishing the reconstitution as an illusion.

In the Holocaust context, critic James Young suggests that the aim of providing "testimonial *proof*" is "unachievable,"[37] in that victims experienced the violence as a chain of discontinuous events although they were subjected to persecution, torture and extermination because of a strategic, continuous political agenda of annihilation. Young argues that the trauma experienced as a consequence of such a political agenda cannot be represented in literary form because "once written, events assume the mantle of coherence that narrative necessarily imposes on them, and the trauma of their unassimilability is relieved."[38] He identifies the excessive violence as a main reason for the impossibility of representing traumatic experiences and cites Friedländer's suggestion that "the terrain of the most extreme upheaval of our time [the Holocaust]...provides us with only shadows or myths."[39] Although Young and Friedländer essentially challenge the testimonial validity of Holocaust representations, neither one refutes the validity of survivor's discourse as an approximation of Holocaust experiences. Both build their observations on the victims' subjection to excessive violence and trauma. I think we can therefore also apply them to other experiences of trauma in history, such as the one enforced under the Chilean military Junta.

Valdés is aware of the problems entailed in the representation attempted in *Tejas Verdes*. He agrees that such a process of representation is difficult but, nonetheless, feasible: "Obviously, this is a reconstituted diary (nobody can conceive license such as to write and to safe-keep any type of text in those conditions), but in this process of reconstitution I have done everything possible to conserve the most faithful chronology of daily routine, which proves to be rather difficult if one considers the total absence of time and place references, which characterize these places [the concentration camps]."[40]

In *Tejas Verdes* Valdés chose to override the "total absence of time and place references" of the original experience by reconstructing not only a chronological diary but one whose individual chapters are entitled by exact date inscriptions. He refrains from issuing either comment or justification regarding the narrative's omission of three days,[41] which is only detectable by checking the completeness of these title dates. An inquiry into this practice has not yet been issued by literary critics, yet it would imply an analysis of the compatibility of narrative style, narrative content, and narrative agenda and eventually lead to an affirmation of the work as illusory writing. Because if the work indeed were to resemble a reconstitution of a diary as the author would have liked to have written while undergoing the experience, then the diary should be able to reflect the "total absence of time and place references" precisely, by not making any reference to such specific time references. Valdés merely affirms: "Due to obvious reasons, I have omitted or removed much information and experiences, but this does not imply an alteration of the content."[42] If the author hence invokes authorial command to establish the representation value of the work as a historically and autobiographically accurate account of experiences endured in Tejas Verdes, then the narrative's silent omission of three of the only 32 days may also be seen as warranting if not an explanation then at least an acknowledgement.

Critics have chosen not to ask these questions in observation, perhaps, of Valdés' command that "in these pages one should not be looking for any type of literary elaboration."[43] This writer, internationally acknowledged for his literary skills even prior to the initiation and publication of *Tejas Verdes*, utilizes the "Introduction" to inform the reader that all significance of this text lies in representing "the *current* experience of the Chilean people." At no point does Valdés identify his work as *testimonio*, yet in these comments he clearly appropriates Moreiras' observation that "the significance of testimonio... is more political than it is literary" for his own narrative.[44]

David William Foster responds in finding Valdés' observation quite reasonable and in agreement with the author's authenticity claim and sociopolitical agenda: "Because prisoners lose a sense of time, as well as a sense of identity, under the barrage of physical abuse at a place like Tejas Verdes," writes Foster, "the relative brevity of Valdés' internment lends credibility to his day-by-day recreation of events. The preface is dated May 1974; and the closeness of dates serves to validate further Valdés' claim to accuracy." According to Foster, "[s]uch a combination of circumstances testifies, of course, to Valdés' determination to bear personal witness to the terrible violation of human rights in Chile. His testimony speaks for the thousands who have died in places like Tejas Verdes or who have remained silent to avoid the risk of further persecution."[45]

It is not necessary to challenge Valdés' determination as defined by Foster, nor must we critique either *Tejas* Verdes or the genre of *testimonio* for its aim at "providing access to situations and modes of thought unknown or poorly understood by officially sanctioned culture"[46] due to the (pre-*testimonio*) voicelessness of the oppressed. Yet, given that this work comprises a very deliberate literary constitution, it is not clear how the representation can be separated from its own essence or how this essence could be ignored if the content is constituted by it. Instead, we can interpret even this apparent discrepancy between a void and overt presence of temporal consciousness as an explicit narrative strategy. This strategy is designed to illuminate the power of literary narrative to overcome barriers of time, space, and power by merging and, simultaneously, juxtaposing the literary and the oral, muteness and voice, the autobiographical personal-private with the sociopolitical public, the present and the past.

Tejas Verdes evolves on a present tense time line to represent a contemporary Chilean experience, challenging thereby a principle argument that literature may only construct and not reproduce reality. As Robert Scholes explains: "It is because reality cannot be recorded that realism is dead. All writing, all composition, is construction. We do not imitate the world, we construct versions of it. There is no mimesis, only poesis. No recording. Only constructing."[47] Valdés certainly identifies *Tejas Verdes* as a composed reconstruction of a hypothetical, yet realistic diary, at the same time, however, this text also assimilates a reproduction of reality in that the text is impregnated with numerous direct speech quotations whose echoes carry over to the reader. Nurturing an intense authenticity and immediacy effect, the text resounds a recording of torture chamber ambience engrained into the victim's memory. Rather than shielding the reader's experience, the narrator cites interrogators directly passing their insulting exclamations on to the reader:

- Hell, are you insolent, fucker, what a way to come in!
- We're having a conversation in here, you low life, what do you think you are?
- You got no manners, you motherfucker!
- Haven't they taught you to knock before entering a house?
- Do you think you're in the jungle, you sucker. You got no respect?
- You're gonna see what'll happen to you for being an intruder![48]

The prisoner does not absorb the literary bombardment of monological exclamations in this unequivocally harsh Chilean slang. Instead, his muteness allows the insults to reverberate through to the reader who, disengaged from the position of distant observer, is subjugated by the abrupt change of environment and language like an intruder him/herself. As Foster suggests, the "accurate descriptions of life inside the concentration camp" enable *Tejas Verdes* to emerge "as an ex post facto defiance of the silence and the loss of personal identity imposed by the extralegal prison system."[49] Even in translation the vulgarity and violence of the original wording does not lose but maintains its effect. The script-like recording may be read as a further attempt by the author to encourage the reader to take this intense actuality at face value.[50] Whereas Doris Sommer maintains that the testimonial I "neither presumes nor even invites us to identify with it,"[51] the autobiographical I in this scene has disappeared into a non-visual muteness. The only I conceivable in this interrogation scene would seem to be constituted by the reader him or herself.[52]

In the concentration camp setting, "the only legitimate forms of communication become the demands for information imposed by the interrogation and torture sessions." Through recreating this environment in literary representation, however, the text can be seen as "a defiant counterpoint to the real, Draconian circumscription of imprisonment."[53] On the one hand, the muteness of the protagonist enables the reader to relive the experience at the side of the prisoner. On the other hand, the "eloquence of the fictive day-by-day entries in Valdés' diary" also embodies a reversal of the silence imposed upon the victim "as a strategy to destroy political prisoners." As the mute protagonist hence regains his voice as narrator, the reader may find incentive toward joining the author's sociopolitical agenda and cry out against the injustice witnessed—thereby facilitating the work to accomplish *testimonio*'s ultimate objective of instigating awareness and promoting change.

Sergio Bitar's *Isla 10* consists of a retrospective, well contemplated and edited exposé of an autobiographical traumatic experience in a concentration camp under Pinochet's military rule, written, like *Tejas Verdes*, by an author-witness-survivor. In contrast to *Tejas Verdes*, *Isla 10* explicitly juxtaposes the dichotomous relationship between official and alternative representation, between author, narrator and protagonist, as well as addresses the issues of memory construction and trauma that are central to autobiographical representations of traumatic experiences in history.

Sergio Bitar identifies his "chronicle" as "testimonio/testimony."[54] In accordance with the literary genre of *testimonio*, which prescribes the sociopolitical function of denouncing official representation of traumatic events in history, Bitar explains that he felt obliged to relate and alert others of his experiences on Dawson Island: "I had undergone an experience that I never imagined possible in my homeland, and afterwards I had felt the obligation, the necessity to transmit this experience. Even if only one person read this account, it was my responsibility to describe and alert."[55] This drive to communicate the concentration camp experience, which is shared also by Valdés, may be said to originate out of the experience itself—like in the Holocaust—to prevent these experiences from becoming a never-to-be-written page in history.

In Chile, this urge to communicate did not reach the paramount significance of sole reason for survival. Rather, in Chilean autobiography of traumatic experiences in history, like in *testimonio*, this objective is more expressively future oriented. As Bitar declares with authorial command, it is tied to the sociopolitical understanding that "it is not possible to guarantee with silence the injustice and tragedy we live.... It is the responsibility of all Chileans to prevent that the events here pronounced be repeated to assure the freedoms of all. I do not want my children to live out something similar. That is only possible by clarifying the facts and making justice."[56] Like Valdés, Bitar exercises authorial command in soliciting judgment and action from his readership. He breaks the silence of the victim in publishing this testimony, intended to express solidarity and give recognition to the communal suffering: "This testimony," writes Sergio Bitar, "is also an expression of solidarity with those with whom I shared my prison on Dawson, as well as a modest contribution to and recognition of the thousands of Chileans who have suffered most during those years."[57]

Any literary representation of a traumatic experience entails a process of remembering, selecting, writing and editing, and it is noteworthy that Bitar addresses the change and development of memory and recollection both from the point of view of author as well as from the point of view as narrator. In accordance with Dale Porter (1993), it is the reader's task to evaluate a text's truthfulness and or plausibility. Sergio Bitar does not undermine this task but promotes it by addressing the issue of the reliability or unreliability of a victim's memory, in a similar way as he enunciates the contradiction between official and alternative representation.

Isla 10 addresses the notion of literature's inherent composition in challenging official accounts of political prison and camp experiences and illustrating the need to review, question, and denounce contradictory representation. The official accounts regarding Dawson Island events are exposed in the form of three quotations from newspaper reports published in Chile in October of 1973 on the two pages following the inside title page and preceding the author's introduction to *Isla 10*. The contradiction is self-sustaining; the discrepancy between these official statements and the narrative that follows is not directly addressed at any point, neither in the introduction nor in the narrative. Instead, in line with Porter's notion of judgement based on plausibility,[58] it is left to the reader to formulate an opinion, judge and take sides with either representation.

By way of juxtaposing official and alternative representation, as suggested before,[59] the question of an implicit point of view in representation moves into the foreground and culminates in an open challenge. The author / narrator denounces the official voice by implanting it into the framework of his own, alternative representation. He clearly anticipates the readership will take favorable sides with his account; as cited above, he appears confident that his objectives may be reached with a single reading experience.

Unlike Valdés, Bitar does address the distinction between the identities of author and narrator. He confines the narrator to the moment of narration and anticipates the author will undergo further change and development that incrementally distances the latter from the former. Consequently, he points to a change in memory regarding the Dawson Island experience and explains that nine years after the taped recollection and eleven years after the original experience, "I was rereading the pages and the initial recollection was very vague, only gradually would it be returning to my memory. At times, it was as if the text had been written by another."[60] By implication, Bitar affirms that the trauma experienced on Dawson Island is not contained in the corresponding time frame but continues to yield an influence in maintaining a conscious to subconscious post-Dawson presence and effect into the present. Aware of the manipulative powers of memory, the discrepancy between immediate post trauma and long term memory nevertheless does not lead Bitar to question the content of the tapes or narrative. He identifies the difference in memory as a type of survival technique manipulated by his own mind and observes: "It is curious how the mind blanks out those memories that could impede its functioning."[61]

In the process of identity formation, time and narrative engage in an interplay. In this interplay the different time lines can serve to distinguish between author, narrator and protagonist; indeed: "Autobiography is determined by the time distance in which the autobiographical I is divided into a remembered I (object) and a remembering I (subject) in order to recognize its identity beyond the time lines, that is in order actually to obtain an identity."[62] According to Bitar, *Isla 10* constitutes an edited version of the oral recollection recorded shortly after regaining his liberty, and it is in this characteristic that this *testimonio* is most closely linked to oral testimony, commonly considered a precursor to the literary genre. In accordance with the genre requirements, however, the author does clarify that "[i]n spite of the polishing, this book continues to be true to that first version dictated in 1975."[63]

Whereas Hernán Valdés insinuates the possibility of reconstituting experience and presents a narrative confined to a reconstituted present tense timeline of chronological experience, Bitar's narrative explicitly addresses the complexity and interdependence of knowledge, memory and representation. In contrast to *Tejas Verdes*, *Isla 10* evolves on a past tense time line, which, in addition, is frequently interrupted by the autobiographical narrator. These breaks in chronological narrative serve to identify unreliable memory as a primary handicap in achieving chronological and historical accuracy in representation.

By inserting temporal conjunctions, the narrator illustrates a discrepancy between awareness and knowledge at a point zero on the time line of the experience and that of a later point in time. In the following quote, for example, the protagonist lacks information at the moment of experience, which, when seen in retrospect, the narrator nevertheless considers pertinent: "*As we learned later*, several of the foreigners who presented themselves to these calls, disappeared or were found dead. Others barely managed to escape."[64] At the time of experience, the protagonist did not have access to this information. Its integration into the narrative emphasizes the silence that surrounds the dictatorship experience. It also aids the enhancement of the testimonial touch of this narrative in demonstrating the narrator's determination to provide a historically accurate representation. Even the instance, in which the narrator apprehends event-posterior information that contradicts his own memory, he does not silence but emphasize this discrepancy as a consequence of the anguish and confusion at the moment of occurrence:

> When I left the concentration camp after more than one year as a prisoner, my mother would tell me that when we arrived at the Military School, I had expressed to her not having any idea as to what was happening, but that this could well take one or two years. I don't remember this, but if this was so, it would show that the brain functions at different levels, like two parallel minds: one that is more cold and rational, that is located outside of the subjective, and another, in which that dominates what one wishes were the case.[65]

This narrative illustrates that the representation of an experience can, in retrospect, be contradicted. Moreover, it demonstrates that the experience itself is determined by concepts based upon available information and subjectively formulated conclusions. In accordance, the narrator also includes information obtained through friends and even pronounces surprise upon encountering contradictory evidence at a later time: "We climbed to the last floor of the building where there were a large number detained. My first surprise was to see several who in the days of the 11th, 12th and 13th had been considered dead or executed. … I imagined that until that moment when I saw them, their wives also didn't have any idea of the destiny they had run into and were suffering much anxiety due to their husbands' fate."[66] Through the voice of the narrator, Bitar thus enunciates the subjectivity entailed in the individual's experience and his/her understanding of the event in progress. As such discrepancies and corrections of information are affirmed within the narrative, the work acquires a perhaps less explicit and less direct but, nevertheless, an at least equally convincing ambience of authenticity and credibility as the one constructed by Valdés.

In addition to meeting specific genre requirements of *testimonio*, such as the urge to communicate, pronounce support, denounce and promote action against traumatic experiences in history, *Isla 10* and *Tejas Verdes* enunciate an element of autobiographical writing of such experiences rarely discussed in the theoretic discourse of this particular genre: the link between trauma, the experience, memory, the process of writing and the process of coming to terms with trauma. As exemplified in *Isla 10*, retrospective literary representation of traumatic experiences in history entails an understanding of a past that is shaped not only by a constructed memory, but also by the author's/narrator's present interpretation thereof. The narrative may consequently form part of a process of coming to terms with the traumatic past and, vice versa, the attempt to come to terms with the past may take the form of a testimonial representation. As Roy Pascal suggests: "Writing of autobiography is a new action of a person and [...] changes [...] in some respect the form of his life, afterwards the person is a different being."[67] Whereas it is difficult to detect if such a change applies to any one author, a narrative may nevertheless serve to illustrate whether or not such change is understood to form part of the process of memory construction and the process of writing and narrative constitution.

Holocaust and the Chilean dictatorship experiences do not permit us to assess and compare the extent of suffering accrued under each fascist regime. Yet we can ascertain trauma as a primary characteristic of both and, consequently, understand the individual experience as not limited to the timeframe of the event in history. Trauma may not be bracketed into a timeframe because it is difficult to assess and even more difficult to overcome. This interpretation of trauma concords with James Berger's who, in addition, links it with far reaching theoretical implications and possibilities. According to Berger,

> 'trauma' is not simply another word for disaster. The idea of catastrophe as trauma provides a method of interpretation, for it posits that the effects of an event may be dispersed and manifested in many forms not obviously associated with the event. Moreover such dispersal occurs across time, so that an event experienced as shattering may actually produce its full impact only years later. This representational and temporal hermeneutics of the symptom has powerful implications for contemporary theory. In its emphasis on the retrospective reconstruction of the traumatic event (for the event cannot be comprehended when it occurs), a traumatic analysis is both constructivist and empirical. It pays closest attention to the representational means through which an event is remembered and yet retains the importance of the event itself, the thing that did happen.[68]

The representational means applied in *Tejas Verdes* consists of a translocation into the sphere of memory as it may have been constituted in and by the traumatic event. In directing exclusive attention to the represented event, the text appears to silence if not to void the process of remembrance that would seem to precede it. However, this translocation may also be seen not as a hypothetical event or explicit narrative strategy illustrating what Susan Rubin Suleiman calls a "latency" period inscribed in the "very structure of trauma."[69] Based on the notion that "events, in so far as they are traumatic, assume their force precisely in their temporal delay,"[70] Suleiman concludes that "war memories, even more than ordinary memories, are layered: they 'bring back' the past, but a past perhaps truly experienced *for the first time* through the prism of the delayed present."[71] When literary representation of such a delayed present allows us to bridge the time gap caused by trauma (in the sense that "the event cannot be comprehended when it occurs" but requires a "retrospective reconstruction"), then we may wish to read a literary reconstruction of such an event as a first time experience. *Tejas Verdes* could hence be perceived not only as a representation of an original traumatic experience but simultaneously as a reconstitution of a memory suppressed in its traumatized predecessor.

When trauma theory is applied to representational literary means, it can serve to examine how a concept or awareness of trauma finds expression in literary strategy, form, expression and content.[72] In accordance, the narrative constitution of *Tejas Verdes* can be seen to support the notion that "the effects of an event may be dispersed and manifested in many forms not obviously associated with the event." This concept is also echoed by Sergio Bitar who addresses trauma in its effect on memory and also constitutes autobiographical literary representation as one means to initiate the process of healing.

Like many *testimonio* writers, Sergio Bitar writes that he felt obliged to relate and alert others to his experiences on Dawson Island, yet Bitar differs from these other writers in identifying a therapeutic complement to the writing process. The process of writing aided him to alleviate the personal anguish caused by the experience: "When I finished writing this chronicle, after recovering my liberty, I felt an enormous relief, as if I had relieved my senses of a great burden. I had overcome the most tragic period of my life...."[73] Whereas Bitar obviously welcomed the therapeutic complement of the processes entailed in the constitution of *Isla 10*, he also illustrates that trauma affects his memory as much as the traumatic experience itself.

Given that trauma surpasses the event in history, trauma may influence as well as achieve representation. Accordingly, an autobiographical representation of a traumatic event may provide explicit or implicit testimony of trauma itself. Whereas such representations tend to focus on the event itself, the sociopolitical ramifications of the event and the sociopolitical ramifications assigned to the representation of that experience, the speaker's or author's understanding and assessment of trauma, may find expression in the representational literary means, through which an event is reconstructed. As Berger suggests,

> a concept of trauma can be of great value in the study of history and historical narrative, and also of narrative in general, as the verbal representation of temporality. The idea of trauma also allows for an interpretation of cultural symptoms—of the growths, wounds, scars on a social body, and its compulsive, repeated actions.... Finally, a theory of trauma will intersect with other critical vocabularies which problematize representation and attempt to define its limits—discourses of the sublime, the sacred, the apocalyptic, and the Other in all its guises. Trauma theory is another such discourse of the unrepresentable, of

the event or object that destabilizes language and demands a vocabulary and syntax in some sense incommensurable with what went before.[74]

When trauma theory, as a discourse of the unrepresentable, is applied to another discourse of the unrepresentable, then emphasis may need to shift away from the unrepresentable and toward the represented. In a discussion of Menchú / Burgos-Debray's work Santiago Colás suggests that "the testimonio can be identical neither to her spoken testimony nor to the experiences of identity-formation that it relates."[75] In the context of Bitar and Valdés' works, this would correspond to a distinction between *testimonio* and the formulation of memory recollection or the experiences of identity formation of protagonist-narrator. Colás argues that genre specifications for *testimonio*, which call for such identification, may be challenged based on Laclau's notion of representation:

There is thus a double process: on the one hand, to exist as such, a representation cannot operate completely behind the back of the person represented; and on the other, to be a representation at all requires the articulation of something new which is not just provided by the identity of what is being represented. . . . [a]bsolute representation, the total transparency between the representative and the represented, means the extinction of the relationship of representation. If the representative and represented constitute the same and single will, the 're-' of representation disappears since the same will is present in two different places. Representation can therefore only exist to the extent that the transparency entailed by the concept is never achieved; and that a permanent dislocation exists between the representative and the represented."[76]

According to Berger's trauma theory, however, we can read such representation as a testimony of traumatic experience and memory construction. The text may be seen as constructing a delayed present of a trauma experience, which may serve to indicate a victim's concept of trauma and sociopolitical, as well as, possibly, literary agenda. A literary construct involving editorial intervention or authorship, would serve as testimony of an author / editor's explicit or implicit sociopolitical, literary agenda and understanding of the historical event and trauma implications. And, it is on the basis of this type of reading that a testifier's representativity and a text's construction of oral and literary testimony as identical may be examined as part of the generic requirements for *testimonio*, which must be upheld in order to achieve an agent's (author, editor or testifier's) narrative strategy, sociopolitical as well as literary agenda.

A study of *Tejas Verdes* and *Isla 10* reveals that both represent trauma as a central element of the experience.[77] In addressing the long term effects of trauma with regard to memory and survival technique, Bitar suggests that trauma supercedes the physical experience and continues to impact the victim's recovery as well as the (re)constitution of memory and narrative. And in the context of a merging historical narrative and reader consciousness, Foster points to one instance in *Tejas Verdes,* in which the narrator assimilates the identity of the author and merges the reconstituted experience of Tejas Verdes with its post event counterpart. In this scene, Valdés makes reference to a "here,"[78] which, according to Foster, "alludes to the problem of continuity between the 'situación histórica' of the narrator and of his colleagues and their imprisonment in Tejas Verdes" at the same time as it "signals the problem of continuity between the timeless and nebulous domain of miserable suffering and the commitment to bear witness of the individual ten thousand miles removed from Tejas Verdes."[79]

Although neither the representation nor the reading process may affect the experience retroactively, both can be linked to a society's understanding of the interplay between power, truth and representation. As official representation denies, challenges, discredits, undermines or silences trauma, it further enhances the effects of trauma and may hinder a victim's dealing with the experience in question. In contrast, when testimony expresses solidarity and recognition, it may directly impact other victims' recovery or sentiment. Moreover, literary representation of traumatic events in history may succeed in raising awareness and prompting a sociopolitical response from a readership as well as illustrate the inherent link between trauma and its representation.

Whereas clear references to the link between literary representation and the process of overcoming the trauma accrued under the ruling of the military Junta in Chile have yet to enter the literary debate, the overcoming of trauma has certainly emerged as a central issue in Holocaust related studies. And there, one argument suggests that in the context of traumatic experiences in history due to political persecution, torture and killing, coming to terms with the past is not only particularly complex but nearly impossible: the survivors are aware that their trauma can never find justification and that the trauma of others will never find a voice at all. Consequently, James Young, Elie Wiesel, Susan Rubin Suleiman and others suggest that due to the genocidal dimensions of the Holocaust experience, literary representations of the Holocaust must necessarily be incomplete because neither the number of the dead nor the mention of them can bring back their voices.

Even in the case of authors like Anne Frank, whose diary ends before her final demise, the deceased are considered "infinitely inscribable." Whereas Anne Frank has arisen to become "an omnipresent figure of postwar consciousness [that], like the war itself, means different things to different people,"[80] another dimension to Anne Frank consists in the fact that "off the page, the helpless girl with the blank book remains a fact beyond words, untranslatable into history."[81] Anne Frank's diary—honored above most other representations for its description of a Jewish experience under fascism, although it comes short of representing that author's horrific ending in the death camp, does, in spite of everything, represent the Holocaust by not representing the unrepresentable: that which no longer exists. Thus, Suleiman ends her brief discourse on War Memories on the note that "the only kind of autobiography I find truly essential, to read *or* write...is the kind that tries to recover, through writing, an irrecoverable absence."[82]

Whereas Holocaust victims have addressed the persistence of trauma and its multiple effects perhaps most vividly, this experience is not limited to Holocaust trauma but applies equally to victims of other traumatic events and experiences. In applying this scenario to the autobiographical representation of Chilean concentration camp experiences, the recognition that the irrecoverable absence in the Chilean context is not of as atrocious dimensions as the Holocaust, does not impede us from acknowledging that the many disappeared and killed under Pinochet may equally be identified as irrecoverable absences. Their experiences may be perceived as irrecoverable as well as unrepresentable. Survivor representations, on the other hand, are not free of obstacles in that survivor experiences are governed by a trauma whose paralyzing powers affect the traumatic experience, the post experience, memory and the literary (re)construction. Their representations may achieve no more than an approximation of trauma and its implications; whether or not this affects the representation value in terms of autobiographical and simultaneously historical accuracy will need to be determined by the individual reader. Perhaps, when official representation of history, authorized by political agents, is no longer equated with history, indeed, when such official representation is automatically challenged in and by the national and international arena, then a discourse may emerge and be acknowledged resulting in a timely, contemporary reaction in favor of humanity and human rights.[83] It is this sociopolitical literary objective that Sergio Bitar and Hernán Valdés aspire to achieve.

NOTES

1 Suleiman 1993, 563.
2 McAfee Brown 1986, v.
3 Suleiman 1993, 564.
4 Suleiman 1993, 564.
5 Suleiman 1993, 564.
6 Young 1987, 406.
7 Suleiman 1993, 564–5.
8 Kosta 1994, 19.
9 Robert McAfee Brown points out that Elie Wiesel, who today enjoys the privileges of renown writer and scholar, "had trouble finding a publisher" for *Night* due to the "depressing subject matter" (McAfee Brown 1986, v). Regarding Hernán Valdés' *Tejas Verdes*, María-Inés Lagos-Pope writes that the work narrowly escaped publication and circulation restrictions because the Spanish Government specifically sanctioned the text to retaliate against the cancelation by the Military Regime of a commercial contract designed under Allende see Lagos-Pope 1988, 123.
10 McAfee Brown (v–vi) reminding *Night*'s readers that "there are those today who—feeding on that wish [to treat *Night* as "the product of a diseased mind"], and on the anti-Semitism that lurks near the surface of the lives of even cultured people—are trying to persuade the world that the story is not true..." (McAfee Brown 1986, v).
11 "exterminar de raíz el marxismo en Chile...despolitizar el país" (Valdés 1974, 5). Given the statistics of the last democratic elections prior to the military coup d'état, showing a 44% in favor of the so-

cialist Allende government, Pinochet's aggressive agenda was designed to carry far reaching implications.

12 A comparison of the extent of individual suffering and persecution inflicted upon victims under the Holocaust and Chile's dictatorship neither is feasible nor is it necessary for a comparative analysis of survivors' literary representations.

13 This analysis of autobiographical representations of the Chilean dictatorship is limited to the works of victim/survivor accounts.

14 "...a toda prisa, 'al calor de la memoria'" (Valdés 1974, 6).

15 See Gugelberger 1996, 9 and Beverley 1989, 12–13.

16 Hoerning 1980, 679 quoted by Peitsch 1990, 23.

17 Gugelberger 1996, 9; Beverley 1989, 12.

18 "El lector tiene ante sí el diario de un prisionero en uno de los sectores del campo de concentración militar de Tejas Verdes.... La redacción de estas evocaciones me ha significado una profunda repugnancia, pero, si la he asumido, no ha sido con el objeto de exhibir o comunicar una desgraciada experiencia personal, sino para mostrar, a través de ella, la experiencia *actual* del pueblo chileno.... Este libro...está destinado principalmente a quienes, en Chile, quieren conservar la inocencia dentro de su complicidad y promiscuidad con el fascismo..., y a quienes en el extranjero piensan que el golpe militar que acabó con el gobierno de la Unidad Popular es ya un hecho del pasado. Este libro debe recordarles que el golpe continúa dándose, en otras formas, cotidianamente" (Valdés 1974, 5–6).

19 Kosta 1994, 3.

20 Kosta 1994, 5.

21 Young 1987, 413.

22 Foucault 1984, 101.

23 Kosta 1994. Also see Kosta's reaction to Foucault's question: "It makes a great difference, because to dismiss the author entirely not only undermines the struggle for presence and for a history and future which many socially and politically marginalized writers have fought, but also implicitly imparts traditional notions of authorship and textuality, prescriptively male and Western, to all subjectivities" (Kosta 1994, 4).

24 As Peitsch explains, the author's role in history can influence the amount of value attributed to his or her text: "Apologies, memoirs and portraits by military personnel, diplomats, ministers and chiefs of police were since 1949 attributed value as a historical source. Objectivity here meant matter-of-factness.... The idea was to 'let true witnesses speak who will increase our knowledge. Let us liberate them of the burden to justify themselves and let us encourage them to say how it really was.'" ["Den Apologien, Memoiren und Porträts von Militärs und Diplomaten, Ministern und Polizeichefs wurde seit 1949 ein historischer Quellenwert zugeschrieben. Objektivität hieß hier Sachlichkeit.... 'Lassen wir echte Zeugen sprechen, die unser Wissen vermehren. Befreien wir sie von der Last, sich selbst rechtfertigen zu müssen, und ermutigen wir sie, zu sagen wie es wirklich war'" (Peitsch 1990, 90; including a quote by Sieburg).

25 Young 1987, 413.

26 Beverley 1996, 29.

27 See Klöss' explanation: "An I cannot acknowledge itself in the present tense in which it lives, it recognizes itself only in memory, in reflection as a remembering I in the remembered I. That identity is obtained only in the form of paradoxical similarity.... I.e. recognition, experience, finally even identity are constructed paradoxically only by way of 'retrospectivity.' Based upon this 'retrospectivity' we can also explain what generally is understood by 'the subjective paradox of time'" ["Ein Ich kann sich in der gegenwärtigen Gegenwart, in der es lebt, nicht wahrnehmen, es erkennt sich erst in der Erinnerung, in der Reflexion, als erinnerndes Ich im erinnerten Ich. Jene Identität gelingt allerdings nur in Form paradoxer Aehnlichkeit.... D.h. Erkennen, Erfahrung, letztendlich auch die Identität, konstituieren sich paradoxerweise nur mittels der 'Nachträglichkeit'. Aus dieser 'Nachträglichkeit' erklärt sich auch, was allgemein unter dem 'subjektiven Zeitparadoxon' verstanden wird"] (Klöss 1989, 214).

28 "...die Literaturkritik [rühmte] gerade an den mit Sicherheit nicht authentischen Tagebüchern am stärksten die Unmittelbarkeit...." (Peitsch 1990, 293).

29 "Authentizitätsfiktion" (Peitsch 1990, 293).

30 Foster 1984, 48.

31 "Zwar divergieren Lebenszeit und 'erzählte Zeit' in der Autobiographie, da beispielsweise die wesentlichste Komponente der zurückgelegten Lebenszeit, der Alltag, fehlt, dennoch kann die Autobiographie als Zeitfragment (im Sinne des pars pro todo) die ganze Lebenszeit wiederspiegeln" (Klöss 1989, 212).

32 Foster 1984, 48.

33 See Sklodowska 1996, 85 quoted previously in the context of *testimonio*.

34 Hartman 1994, 1.

35 "die Reversibilität der Zeit in der Autobiographie hat ihre Grenzen...; denn die autobiographische 'Nachträglichkeit' versteht sich notwendigerweise als eine Konstruktion: Der Autobiograph verliert mit dem 'Wissen' um seine Vergangenheit den Standpunkt des 'Noch-nicht-Wissens'.... Das Gewußte ist irreversibel, der Zustand der tabular rasa für den Erinnernden nicht mehr erreichbar. Sartre nennt das die 'retrospektive Illusion'...." (Klöss 1989, 215).

36 Miething 1987, 179.

37 Young 1987, 403–4.

38 Young 1987, 404.

39 Friedländer 1984, 94–95 quoted by Young 1987, 405.

40 "Evidentemente, se trata de un diario reconstituido (nadie puede concebir licencias como las de redactar y guardar ningún tipo de texto en esas condiciones), pero en este proceso de reconstitución he hecho todo lo posible por conservar la más fidedigna cronología de la cotidianidad, lo que resulta harto difícil si se tiene en cuenta la total ausencia de referencias y plazos temporales que caracteriza a estos lugares" (Valdés 1974, 5).

41 Saturday, February 23; Thursday, February 28; Saturday, March 9. I find curious as well that this omission has not been commented on either by Valdés or by literary critics.

42 "Por razones obvias, he omitido o traspuesto muchas informaciones y experiencias, pero esto no significa una alteración de contenido" (Valdés 1974, 7).

43 "no debe buscarse en [estas páginas] ningún tipo de elaboración literaria" (Valdés 1974, 6).

44 Moreiras 1996, 195. Vice versa, considering the chronological order of these observations, Moreiras' observations may be seen based on Valdés'.

45 Foster 1984, 48.

46 Zimmerman 1996, 101.

47 Scholes 1975, 7 quoted in Young 1987, 406 and Foley 1986, 11.

48 "—¡Putas que soi insolente, huevón, manerita de entrar!—¡Estamos conversando aquí, desgraciado, qué te hai creído!—¡Pero soi muy mal educao, concha'e tu maire!—¿No te han enseñao a golpear antes de entrar a una casa?—¿Te creís que estai en la selva, culiao? ¿No tenías repeto por la gente?—¡Vai a ver lo que te pasa por intruso!" (Valdés 1974, 133).

49 Valdés 1974, 48.

50 Even in the following situation in which only the singular voice of a new commander can be distinguished, the direct speech asserts such intensity and immediacy that it outstrips the reconstitutionality of the discourse: "And this! What is this!... But you guys are a bunch of old hags!...And what is this? What's it good for?...The only thing missing here, you lazy bastards, are a bunch of sanitary napkins!...And this old bread, suckers? Are you raising rats? And this spoon, what's it doing here? And this can? And this stuff?...And this can? What the fuck is this can doing here?...And you, bastard, did you think this was a sanitarium?...You are gonna clean up this shit in five minutes. This dump is a temporary place. This is no motel, you fuckers!" ["—¡Y esto! ¡Qué es esto!...¡Pero ustedes son un lote de viejas basureras!...¿Qué es esto? ¿Para qué sirve esto?...¡Lo único que falta aquí, ociosos de mierda, son algunos trapitos regleros!...¿Y esos panes viejos, huevones? ¿Están criando ratas? ¿Y esa cuchara, qué hace aquí? ¿Y ese tarro? ¿Y esa muleta?...¿Y ese tarro? ¿Qué mierda hace aquí ese tarro?...—¿Y vos, huevón?, ¿te creís que esto es un sanatorio?...—¡Van a hacerme desaparecer todas estas huevá en cinco minutos! Esta huevá es un lugar de paso. ¡Esta no es una pensión, culiaos!"] (Valdés 1974, 162–3).

51 Sommer 1996, 146.

52 See Duchesne regarding a similar narrative strategy found in Omar Cabezas' *La montaña es algo más que una inmensa estepa verde* quoted previously: "the second person, which the repetitive 'you' of the monologue refers to, who never speaks and is not spoken of, only exists as a discourse polarity, a sole mold of a mediator in which the perspective of the reader may as well reside" ["La segunda persona a quien parece dirigirse el repetido 'tú' (o 'vos') del monólogo, la cual nunca habla y de la que nunca se habla, sólo existe como polaridad del discurso, puro molde de un interlocutor donde también puede alojarse la perspectiva del lector"] (Duchesne 1986, 117).

53 Foster 1984, 48.

54 Bitar 1987, 13. As Bitar pronounces this label in Spanish, the word "testimonio" may here translate both to *testimonio*, the literary genre, as well as to testimony, a testimonial utterance such as a victim of witness may offer during a judicial trial. Since the juxtaposition of these different meanings forms part of this analysis, I would like to leave it to the reader to choose the translation he/she may consider most adequate.

55 "había pasado por una experiencia que jamás imaginé podía darse en mi patria, y después de ella sentía el imperativo, la necesidad de transmitir esa vivencia. Aunque lo leyera solamente una persona, era mi deber describir y alertar" (Bitar 1987, 11). Unless otherwise stated, the translation of this and all other citations from this text is my own.

56 "No es posible avalar con el silencio la injusticia y la tragedia que vivimos. ...Es el deber de todos los chilenos evitar que se repitan los sucesos que aquí se relatan, para asegurar las libertades de todos. Yo no quiero que mis hijos vivan algo similar. Ello sólo es posible exclareciendo los hechos y haciendo justicia." No es posible avalar con el silencio la injusticia y la tragedia que vivimos. ...Es el deber de todos los chilenos evitar que se repitan los sucesos que aquí se relatan, paraa asegurar las libertades de todos. Yo no quiero que mis hijos vivan algo similar. Ello sólo es posible exclareciendo los hechos y haciendo justicia" (Bitar 1987, 13).

57 "Este testimonio es también una expresión de solidaridad con quienes compartí mi prisión de Dawson, así como una modesta contribución y reconocimiento a los miles de chilenas y chilenos que más han sufrido en estos años" (Bitar 1987, 14).

58 See Porter 1993, 318.

59 See my analysis of the notion of *testimonio* as an authentic narrative in the previous chapter.

60 "releía las páginas y el recuerdo inicial era muy borroso, sólo paulatinamente iba retornando a mi memoria. A ratos era como si el texto lo hubiera escrito otro" (Bitar 1987, 12–3).

61 "Curioso cómo la mente apaga aquellos recuerdos que podrían dificultar su funcionamiento" (Bitar 1987, 13).

62 "Autobiographie wird bestimmt von der zeitlichen Distanz, in der sich das autobiographische Ich in ein erinnertes (Objekt) und ein erinnerndes (Subjekt) Ich aufspaltet, um seine Identität über die Zeiten hinweg zu erkennen, bzw. sich Identität überhaupt aneignen zu können" (Klöss 1989, 214).

63 "Pero a pesar de su pulimiento, este libro sigue siendo fiel a aquella primera versión dictada en 1975" (Bitar 1987, 13).

64 "Como supimos después, varios de los extranjeros que se presentaron a estos llamados deaparecieron o fueron hallados sin vida. Otros apenas alcanzaron a escapar" (Bitar 1987, 21; the italics are mine).

65 "Cuando salí del campo de concentración, después de más de un año de preso, mi madre me contaría que, cuando llegamos a la Escuela Militar, yo le habría expresado no tener idea de lo que estaba ocurriendo, pero que aquello bien podía durar uno o dos años. No lo recuerdo, pero si así fue, ello estaría revelando que el celebro funciona en varios planos, como dos mentes en paralelo: una más fría y racional, que se sitúa fuera de lo subjetivo, y otra, dondo domina lo que uno desea sean las cosas" (Bitar 1987, 28).

66 "Subimos hasta el último piso del recinto...donde había un gran número de detenidos. Mi primera sorpresa fue ver a varios que en los días 11, 12 y 13 se los daba por muertos o fusilados.... Me imaginé que hasta ese momento en que yo los veía, sus mujeres, tampoco

tenían noción del destino por ellos corrido, y estaban sufriendo zozobra por la suerte de sus esposos" (Bitar 1987, 29).

67 "Schreiben der Autobiographie ist eine neue Handlung des Menschen und [...] ändert [...] in mancher Beziehung die Form seines Lebens, der Mensch ist danach ein anderer" (Pascal 1965, 213 in Klöss 1989, 216).

68 Berger 1997, 572.

69 Suleiman 1993, 571.

70 Caruth 1991, 8. See Suleiman 1993, 571.

71 Suleiman 1993, 571.

72 Also see Bruno Bettelheim who, regarding childhood trauma, suggests: "It seems that it requires a distance of twenty years or more, to understand how much a particular tragedy suffered in childhood can transform your whole sense of life" (Suleiman 1993, 571, quoted from Bruno Bettelheim, Postface to Vegh 1984, 164).

73 "Cuando terminé de dictar esta crónica, después de recuperar mi libertad, sentí un enorme alivio, como si descargara un gran peso de mi espíritu. Había terminado el período más trágico de mi vida...." (Bitar 1987, 11).

74 Berger 1997, 572–3.

75 Colás 1996, 169.

76 Laclau 1990, 38, in Colás 1996, 169.

77 Such an analysis, however, also needs to allow for the possible absence of any indicators of the speaker's traumatic awareness given the delay effect of trauma, which, in turn can not be determined for any particular individual.

78 The citation reads: "To talk about all this from here as though talking about a fuzzy reality, a unique historical situation decayed by terror, sounds like a nightmare. But even more so to recognize ourselves, as we talk, as survivors of that reality. Because if we are successful in finally getting out of here, what else will we be but survivors? The best we can expect is to be isolated individuals, obscurely concerned with sustaining our lives, melancholic about what we were incapable of doing with history." ["Hablar desde aquí de todo eso como de una realidad esfumada, como de una situación histórica única dilapidada

por el temor, suena a pesadilla; pero más todavía reconocernos a nosotros mismos, en la medida en que hablamos, como sobrevivientes de esa realidad. Porque, si logramos salir de aquí alguna vez ¿qué seremos si no? En el mejor caso, individuos aislados, ocupándonos oscuramente de mantener nuestras vidas. Melancólicos de lo que no supimos hacer con la historia" (Valdés 1974, 72)], translated by Foster 1984, 49.

79 Foster 1984, 49.

80 Rosenfeld in Morse 1993, 718.

81 Morse 1993, 718.

82 Suleiman 1993, 573.

83 It has been argued that the internet information highway has bridged many information gaps and multiple perspectives can relatively easily be accessed, opposed and evaluated. However, this highly improved and increased access should not give us reason to believe that we have finally facilitated a voice to all oppressed. To the contrary, the electronic information highway still remains accessible to only a small percentage of modern day society: Any information posted therein continues to be subject to much censorship and ought not be mistaken as representative. By far the majority of socially, politically and economically oppressed members of societies throughout the world continue to lack the linguistic, educational and technological skills and tools necessary for literary representation on the internet. Moreover, it is pertinent to recognize that we, who participate in national, international and cross-national discourse, and who recognize the theoretically unlimited horizons, applications and possibilities of intellectual and data exchange via electronic / satellite communication systems, continue to live a rather isolated existence.

Chilean Testimonio *in the Form of Monological Interviews*

The act of giving testimony is not limited to unsolicited, free speech oral testimony. Testimony may also be issued as a result of an interview process. Since the military coup by General Augusto Pinochet in the Fall of 1973, much oral testimony has been issued by victims and survivors in Chile and in exile. However, only a limited number of publications containing collections of testimonies have entered the literary arena. In this chapter, the analysis focuses on a type of literary narrative that I have named the monological interview.

The monological interview constitutes a form of *testimonio* that is based on oral testimony obtained by way of an interview process. It differs from a typescript of an interview in that it entails an extensive process of editorial intervention. The monological interview is authored by an editor who carries out the role of interviewer in the pre-narrative phrase and who, subsequently, removes the testimony from the interview frame. As a result of this editorial process, the monological interview constitutes a re-composition of the preceding oral testimony that omits to make reference to or include the questions, comments, silences and exclamations that interfere, influence and help shape the testimony in its interview setting. The Menchú / Burgos-Debray *testimonio*, which may be distinguished as a master narrative of *testimonio* literary practice because many genre delineations for *testimonio* are derived from this work, constitutes such a monological interview. Burgos-Debray obtained Menchú's oral testimony by way of an interview process and then edited and transformed it into one coherent narrative. The resulting narrative represents Menchú's voice but, as we are told, not the interviewer's voice, questions or comments.

This analysis compares and contrasts the narrative style and strategy of three of the most comprehensive volumes of monological interviews on the Chilean experience published so far: Samuel Chavkin's *The Murder of Chile* (1982), Emma Sepúlveda's *We, Chile* (1996), and Patricia Politzer's *Miedo en Chile* (1990). It examines the monological interview as a literary discourse that shares *testimonio*'s principle characteristics and that, in turn, provides a tool to test the applicability and sustainability of key components generically attributed to the *testimonio* literary practice. This analysis also serves to highlight some of the shortcomings of the *testimonio* genre delineation in demonstrating the significance of the sociopolitical agenda and intentionality of a text, and the difficulty in determining said intentionality.

This study of the monological interview as a form of *testimonio* literary practice is divided into two parts. First, it entails a comparative analysis of narrative styles and strategies discussing general attributes of the monological interview based on observations drawn from the three narratives specified above. It reviews the length specification and the reverse anonymity characteristic attributed to *testimonio*. It also examines the role of the author as interviewer and creator of the text, and discuss the link between giving testimony and the urge to gain a voice, to denounce human rights violations and to promote change. In a second part to this analysis, the focus shifts to Politzer's monological interview. Based on the narrative style and strategy exemplified by this text, the study discusses the significance of the sociopolitical agenda in the constitution of literary *testimonio* in accordance with its generic delineation. It examine the interplay between the author's sociopolitical agenda and the antithetical relationship between official representation (from a pro-dictatorship point of view) and alternative representation (from a victim's point of view) of the Chilean experience. This discussion entails an analysis of different monological interviews contained in Politzer's narrative in an effort to determine a testifier's intentionality in the face of the author's overriding agenda.

The three texts whose narrative styles and strategies are here compared represent multiple monological interviews, each of relatively short length and based on a separate personal interview within a comprehensive narrative framework. This multiplicity of voices, perspectives and experiences, combined with the relative shortness of the individual *testimonios*, distinguishes these Chilean monological interviews from the one modeled by Menchú / Burgos-Debray. I will now first address the length attribute and then later return to the issue of multiplicity of voices.

As part of his generic delineation of *testimonio*, Beverley describes this literary practice as a "novel or novella-length narrative … told in the first person by a narrator who is also a real protagonist or witness of the events he or she recounts, and whose unit of narration is usually a "life" or a significant life experience."[1] In applying this description to the Chilean monological interview, we can see that these texts comply with the desired identification of narrator as protagonist-participant-witness. However, we also see that the individual monological interviews do not meet the length suggested for *testimonio* literary practice. Should these monological interviews therefore be distinguished from the *testimonio* literary practice? I do not think so. Indeed, this study disputes the claim that the length of the text is central to the constitution of *testimonio*'s literary practice.

Much of literary critical discourse on *testimonio* has focused on novel or novella-length narratives (in particular on Menchú / Burgos-Debray's), and Beverley's description is clearly tailored to such narratives. However, the derivation of a literary genre based on a selected few literary practices can not be justified, if it leads to the exclusion of other *testimonio* narratives primarily because they have not been taken under consideration. A text that does not meet the novel-length requirement should not be excluded from this literary genre because of that characteristic alone. This observation finds support not only by critics like Rice-Sayre who maintain that *testimonio* may also give expression to suffering in the form of a poem or essay,[2] but it also accords with the concept of the monological interview here presented.

In order to meet the length requirement with Chavkin's *The Murder of Chile*, Sepúlveda's *We, Chile*, and Politzer's *Miedo en Chile*, we need to read these monological interviews not in isolation but in their collectivity. We need to identify them as decisive components, which, together with editorial commentary, help shape the comprehensive framework of the respective narratives. This can indeed be a useful approach to these texts and this chapter will later address the ramifications of such a reading in determining the identity of the agent who assigns the text's sociopolitical agenda. At this point, however, it is pertinent to point out that, in reading the Menchú / Burgos-Debray narrative, critics like Beverly detect a "sort of erasure of the function, and thus also of the textual presence, of the 'author.'"[3] This is because they define the *testimonio* as constituting only the text narrated by the protagonist / witness / participant. For example, Burgos-Debray's introduction is generally not considered part of the *testimonio*. In this study, however, I propose to challenge this dismissal unless it were to unveal the deceptive erasure of the textual presence and the function of the author as a narrative strategy that is linked to the sociopolitical and literary agenda of the author. When we read the *testimonios* issued by the Menchú narrator, or by any other protagonist-witness, as independent narratives or individual *testimonios*, then, we must also investigate the testifier's intentionality, if and as reflected by the narrator, as possibly distinct from that of the editor. As you will recall, Beverley distinguishes *testimonio* in that the text's intentionality corresponds to that of the narrator-protagonist-victim and not to the author. This is problematic.

In a challenge to Beverley's argument, this analysis will examine the monological interview by way of a dual approach. On the one hand, it will discuss the monological interview as a comprehensive narrative, in which the individual testimony presented constitutes, like a piece in puzzle, an interactive and dependent unit of a larger narrative web. Then, it will also approach the monological interview as a collection of individual, separate *testimonios* linked only by a common theme rather than a common intentionality or narrative strategy. This dual approach enables us to assess the power of the editor/intermediary, the power to complement or override the individual speakers' sociopolitical agenda with his/her own sociopolitical and literary agenda. It also enables us to discuss the possibility of determining the testifiers' sociopolitical agenda based on the literary *testimonio*. Finally, the dual approach highlights the need to dismiss the length specification for the *testimonio* literary practice as a generic attribute.

The three authors imprint their signatures onto these works in maintaining absolute control over the representation. They assume this control at a pre-narrative stage as they control the interview process, assign the sociopolitical literary agenda, solicit and carry out the interviews. In the process of narration, they appropriate the testifier's control over the oral testimony by extracting it out of the interview environment and submitting it to a different comprehensive narrative frame. Thereby each interviewer/author seizes complete power over the respective literary representation. He or she controls the narrative structure, organization, even the content and direction of the individual reports. In sum, the author's craft in the monological interview consists in setting the foundation and achieving the formation of a comprehensive narrative principally out of multi-representational, reconstituted testimonies.

In Chavkin's *The Murder of Chile*, the author's participation in the process of narration stands out in that the individual testimony feeds this coherent, narrative recapitulation of events. This text resembles a historiographical quilt with Chavkin's own comprehensive representation of Pinochet's coup and military ruling constituting the quilt's groundwork, and the witness' testimonies contributing a colorful, detailed patchwork. The content and structure of the narrative is determined by the author's text; the eyewitness statements serve as data and information to illustrate particular aspects, suffering and consequences of the coup. Although the testimonies are only seldom interrupted, Chavkin does not provide any indication as to their completeness. Clearly, he utilizes the different testimonies as evidence, as representative experiences, whose autobiographical representation enhances the authenticity claim of his own discourse.

Sepúlveda and Politzer demonstrate a different approach to their role and function as author/editor of the monological interview. They introduce their sociopolitical agenda and formulate their comments and observations regarding the testimony represented in an introduction, as does Chavkin. The editorial intervention differs, however, in that Chavkin's voice visually threads through the entire narrative, whereas Sepúlveda and Politzer reinforce what Beverley calls the erasure of the presence and function of the author. They propose reading their narrator's autobiographical *testimonios* as individual, separate representations of history. Neither Sepúlveda nor Politzer establishes a coherent editorial narrative that leads through the different testimonies. They construct the coherency mantle of the narrative in the "Introduction" or "Presentación," respectively. Sepúlveda's introduction consists of an extended, lengthy discourse, in which she presents the theme, her motives, project, and editorial procedure. The individual testimonies then follow without apparent editorial intervention or comment.

Sepúlveda concludes *We, Chile* with a brief "Afterword." In this, she reinforces the representativity of the testimonies presented, comments on the present state of affairs in Chile under democratic rule, and finally provides a contemporary update on the situation of the *arpilleristas* at the time of publication. In comparison, Politzer's "Presentación" is much shorter than Sepúlveda's. In less than four pages, she presents the narrative's title and underlying theme, *Fear in Chile*,[4] and states her objectives and motives. Politzer's presence and editorial comments reemerge as brief introductory paragraphs preceding each narrator's testimony. There she takes note of the interviewee's role, political affiliation and qualifications as testifiers, and her own impressions of and during the interview process.

Chavkin, Politzer, and Sepúlveda, reserve the final claim to authenticity in signing their works in the name of author, and share this characteristic with Burgos-Debray.[5] These authors hold in common that they undermine their influence and role in the representation processes by removing the oral testimony from the original interview setting. They deliberately exclude the questions that instigated and directed each testimony. Moreover, they silence their role in the transformation of the oral testimony into literary testimony, as they make no mentioning of editorial activities. These decisions are certainly linked to a narrative strategy. Indeed, it is of interest that the narrative technique of silencing the role of author/editor is, in turn, linked to the narrative's genre constitution.

It is based on such observations and underlying narrative strategies, that Sol Serrano Pérez identifies Politzer's *Miedo en Chile* as a *testimonio*. She explains, "the interview consists basically in one question: how each has lived, based on the own personal experience, this period of Chile's history. The questions do not appear in the text, due to which every interview is, in reality, a *testimonio*."[6] Considering that all of the texts studied here (including Burgos-Debray's and Viezzer's works) share these characteristics, this commentary can come to carry much weight. In identifying *testimonio* as a text that is devoid of the interview setting which precedes it, Serrano seems to imply that a literary representation of oral testimony transcribed in its original constitution, that is, accompanied by the questions upon which the testimony is based, disqualifies as *testimonio*. We should recognize this as problematic. Oral testimony provides an insight into the speaker's experience and interpretation of an event. As a result, oral testimony, which is issued in an interview setting, can provide insight into the frame of mind of both interviewer and testifier. By extension, literary *testimonio*, reproduced in its original interview setting (i.e. in the form of a direct literary transcript), can facilitate the reader to engage in the role of editor. The reader may hence base his/her understanding, judgment, and critique upon the verbal/literary interview experience and not on an edited version of that experience. However, the monological interviews by Sepúlveda, Politzer, and also by Burgos-Debray, invoke an erasure of the presence and function of the author.

By way of removing oral testimony from its original setting and editing this testimony to form part of a coherent narrative, these authors/editors seek to enunciate the speaker's sociopolitical understanding and agenda. They undermine their own role and presence in the interview exchange, but not until they have appropriated the oral testimony. They control the representation and determine the sociopolitical and literary agenda of the text. Consequently, we can maintain that the final literary product should also be viewed in the context of that authorship. Literary *testimonio* speaks of the experiences but also of the author/editor's sociopolitical and literary agenda.

In essence, it is not that we must challenge Serrano's identification of the monological interview as constituting a form of *testimonio*. To the contrary, we may share this identification. However, it important to recognize that the monological interview testifies not just on the narrator's experiences. It also testifies to the interviewer's understanding of the oral testimony and the significance attributed to particular aspects of this representation. Above all, it is the author/editor/interviewer's sociopolitical and literary agenda that determines the content, style, strategy and nature of the discourse. This applies equally to a monological interview that undermines the presence and function of the author as it does to a narrative quilt, in which a historiographical voice interweaves edited multi-representational autobiographical testimony.

The monological interviews discussed in this chapter each represent testimony based on personal interviews. The texts differ, however, in that Chavkin and Sepúlveda limit their sources to victims of the regime, and Politzer incorporates testimony by victims as well as perpetrators. This difference in sources targeted is linked to a difference in the authors' respective literary objectives and sociopolitical agendas. Chavkin seeks to expose and denounce human rights violations by military police and, thereby, to reveal an experience, which, in general, has been silenced and denied by pro-government representations. Consequently, he utilizes oral testimony as data and evidence to support an alternative, anti-government representation of Chile under the military dictatorship. With a similar agenda in mind, Sepúlveda interviewed Chilean *arpilleristas*.[7] She recorded their testimony, "so that the pain and suffering of so many human beings would not be totally in vain and so that, upon reading their testimonies, we might learn the immeasurable worth of human rights and teach future generations to defend them throughout the world."[8]

Unlike Chavkin and Sepúlveda, Politzer provides a voice to pro-government views as well as to victims' accounts in a counter complementary fashion. She aims at representing the dichotomy of the Chilean experience, perspective and reality. Her text constructs perspectivity and subjectivity as determining factors in the representation and understanding of history. Politzer invites the reader to greet both sides of the Chilean experience with an open mind. Consequently, she presents us with a dichotomous multiplicity of voices issuing harmonious, as well as antagonistic, representations and authenticity claims. The representation value of this work rests in the content and the dichotomous relationship of these antithetical portrayals. In opposition, the individual authenticity claims lose their strength; however, as this conflicting relationship finds repeated expression, the dichotomy itself gains representation value.

Based on Serrano's reading of *Miedo en Chile*, Politzer's editorial powers, interference and intervention are neatly confined to the introduction and the brief introductory paragraphs mentioned above. In accordance, Serrano suggests that Politzer's narrative strategy and practice permits a reading of *Miedo en Chile* as first-hand, live testimony:

> The author does not intervene; except for in a short introduction, in which she shows her motivation. Then she disappears, leaves us alone, and, suddenly, without realizing it, we are there, in the heart of the life of a southern village's former mayor, of the syndicate leader, of the militant communist, of a disappeared's mom, of a woman from the feminine volunteers, of the student leader, of the young executive, and we enter it with a profoundness that we can hardly accomplish with people who are closer to us.[9]

In accordance with this reading, each testimony contained in *Miedo en Chile* is issued the speaker's authorship. The speaker's subjective representation, understanding and interpretation of the experience move into the foreground and Politzer's own editorial activities and agenda appear to fade into a distant background. This reading is not unique or based solely based upon a theoretical understanding of the *testimonio* literary practice. To the contrary, it results from Politzer's narrative strategy; Politzer clearly anticipated and built her text to facilitate this type of interpretation.

Politzer's agenda and sociopolitical objective is spelled out in the "Presentación." It consists in facilitating the bridging of the gap of communication between adversaries: between people that are / were politically implicated with Pinochet and the military regime, and others who fell victim to the military dictatorship and continue to identify as such. According to Politzer, Chile's division is based upon this lack of communication, which, in turn, constitutes a threat to the country's peace efforts.[10] She wishes to expand the predominately one-sided, pro-dictatorship discourse to incorporate multi perspectivity—a step that she identifies as a likely requisite for initiating the turn toward democracy in Chile. In her words, "to begin to visualize a democratic solution, may require that we understand that Chile is us and also the others, those who we do not know but who we easily imagine, attributing to them the downside of humanity."[11] This reference to "us" and "the others" may be embraced from either side or leaves Politzer's own identification undefined.

In accordance with Serrano's reading and Politzer's agenda, it is significant that, in spite of her involvement as interviewer and author of the text, the reader does not perceive as prejudiced or in anyway implicated in the content organization or presentation of the discourse. It is in this aspect that Sepúlveda and Chavkin do not compare with Politzer. Both Sepúlveda and Chavkin clearly take sides with their interviewees and the sociopolitical objective that motivated the latter to participate in the interview process. Sepúlveda even provides personal data about her own experience during the military coup. Moreover, she explains the difficulty of establishing a mutual confidential relationship with the *arpilleristas* and of accomplishing an extended exchange with her subjects, their craft and sociopolitical cause. Chavkin, on the other hand, does not self-identify either his personal experience nor does he reveal details regarding the interview and investigation process. Nevertheless, his representation constitutes a historiographical account from an explicitly anti-governmental point of view. In his comprehensive representation of Chilean history, he utilizes individual testimony as evidence or to provide further or more personal details regarding the content matter. Clearly, his own substantial contribution to the book shares a relationship of mutual agreement and support with his testifiers; together they agree on the necessity to re-tell again and again their experiences during Allende's last moments and under Pinochet's military intervention and dictatorship. Theirs is a collective history, Chile's history, a history, they affirm, whose truth and authenticity value may not be disputed.

In contrast, Patricia Politzer suggests that perspectivity and subjectivity determine experience, personal and national history. In a challenge to absolute history, she calls on her readers to abandon their prejudices and to open their minds and hearts to diversity and difference in experience, in interpretation and understanding, in ideological, political and historical identification. In order to assure the author's and text's credibility as missionary intermediary between a divided Chile, Politzer and her work must be considered unprejudiced and representative. Consequently, Politzer herself must self-identify as an un-biased interviewer who manipulates neither her interviewees nor their testimony.

Serrano sees this requirement reflected in Politzer's conduct as author and interviewer, as well as in her representation of the testimony obtained. According to Serrano, the author interferes neither with the interview, the testimony, nor with the reading experience. Rather, she says, Politzer facilitates an unguided and unmanipulated encounter with unguided and unmanipulated testimony:

> Patricia chose one of many options: she opted to try to comprehend this country from the actual experience of actual Chileans and she opted not to intervene, to allow them to be so that they arrive to us in their full humanity. Patricia does not lead, does not strangle, does not manipulate her personages, but this is not all. Patricia does not conduct, does not indicate, and does not oblige her readers to any specific point of view. She only permits the meeting. And this, which seems so simple and easy, in reality requires a difficult maturity, humility, a sensitivity of spirit, and a severe respect. She opted not to have a privileged point of view on reality and that implies that, finally, by God!, somebody in this country opted to listen.[12]

In Serrano's terms, the text issues authenticity claims in and by itself, authenticity claims that apply not only to the interview content but also to its completeness. We are to assume that the work is void of censorship. Yet Politzer's involvement exceeds that of a patient audience. *Miedo en Chile* may well contain testimony: however, that testimony is the product of a deliberate process of selecting interviewees, soliciting specific testimony and, later, editing that testimony to invoke a specific narrative strategy. The same, of course, applies also to Chavkin and Sepúlveda. The difference, however, consists in that Politzer truly self-invested in her project. Her book serves her own explicit agenda, which may or may not have been explained to the individual testifiers prior to soliciting contributions. By extension, we can even suggest that this agenda may not necessarily find approval or coincide with testifiers' own sociopolitical objectives.

As interviewer, editor and author, Patricia Politzer may only pretend to assumethe role of an "objective," non-implicated agent representing multi perspective, contradictory, official and alternative testimony. Indeed, even Serrano suggests that one of the testimonies contained in this work is Politzer's own testimony, corresponding to her role and activities as interviewer and author, or rather, listener. This testimony is based on the form in which the book was conceived and then delivered. Serrano informs:

> And here is, in my opinion, the testimony, which is not listed in the index. I ask myself if the form, in which Patricia conceived her book, is not the fruit, no longer of the fear, but of the pain of her own experience in this country and of a

> pain that grew out of herself, in accepting the limitations of her own view to deliver us, as a delicate intermediary, fragments of life that we could not see.[13]

This observation then leads us back to the notion that Politzer's collection of testimonies may serve us to gain an understanding of the author's role, experience, intention and agenda that helped shape *Miedo en Chile*. Politzer's presence and influence is not limited to the lines of introduction. Rather her voice, personal experience and agenda are imprinted in and throughout the text as a whole, as well as in and throughout each individual testimony.

Let us note that Politzer makes no mention of her role as interviewer, editor or author, and that Serrano's identification of Politzer as audience mirrors this attitude. Neither does Chavkin, by the way. However, I see his interaction based on a mutual consensus regarding the validity and sociopolitical, as well as literary significance and agenda of *The Murder of Chile*. I suggest this does not apply to *Miedo en Chile* because Politzer's sociopolitical agenda does not accord with but contradicts the objective identified by victim narrators. When Politzer suggests in her introduction the possibility that any one of the alternative or pro-government testimonies may contain errors[14], she proposes to understand these as intrinsically linked to the speaker's experience, perception, interpretation and analysis of the event. Nonetheless, it is interesting that Politzer mentions the possibility of errors in the representation of history issued by her interviewees, but specifically refrains from identifying these misrepresentations. This lack of analysis or intervention may be linked to Politzer's agenda of presenting authentic testimony to present an uncensored, multi perspective representation of Chile's recent past. Yet, it also shows that Politzer attributes absolute subjective authenticity value to the individual testimonies.

Although she approached her task as interviewer with a specific agenda in mind, she does not appear to acknowledge that her interviewees may also have provided testimony to further their own agenda. Politzer openly attributes the mistakes in representation of history to ignorance or simply a tainted vision or experience on the part of the speaker. At no instance in her representation does she suggest the possibility that misrepresentations may have been utilized intentionally to provide false evidence in order to support a justification or denial of human rights violations. It is in conformity with the claim to provide authentic testimony, of course, that Politzer maintains absolute silence regarding her own interference and, or the lack of such interference, at the moment of receiving oral testimony. She makes no reference to her involvement in the process of transforming the oral precursors into literary testimony; finally, she refrains from engaging in an open interpretation of the contents represented. According to Politzer,

> In order to assure a stability of a future democracy, surely it will be necessary that we all assume our responsibility in the horror which we have lived, and that we accept and comprehend what has occurred in this period, in which Chile is afraid. This would help to construct a democracy in earnest, without absolute truths, without ideologies that go beyond the people, without killing, denigrating or disqualifying, simply because the other is different and does not think the same way.
>
> When we manage to see one another with all our qualities, our defects, our sufferings, our weaknesses, our mistakes and our accumulated experience, we will be able to respect each other truly, without anybody having reason to fear. In this context, the life experiences of my interviewees pretend to be an asset to the challenge, which implies to look at and to recognize ourselves for that what we are, neither as good nor as bad as we thought, neither as black nor as white as we prejudiced.[15]

As alternative representations of history, victims' eyewitness accounts in *Miedo en Chile* stand in fierce, direct opposition to statements issued by party liners or military personnel on the events in question. Each victim shares a personal experience marked by torture and suffering; one by one they denounce and accuse Pinochet's governing body of severe human rights violations. In contrast, *pinochetistas* and military personnel relate a very different perspective and understanding of the events in question. In presenting us with a representation of official and alternative history side by side, Patricia Politzer enunciates an inherent dichotomy. The validity or significance attributed to these contradictory representations needs to be questioned or determined by the reader. Politzer, on the other hand, suggests the reader take a different approach to these dichotomies. She does not focus on the truth or authenticity value or significance of each representation. Instead, as quoted above, she rejects the notion of absolute truth[16] and suggests that each person assume his/her responsibility with regard to the experience under Pinochet's military ruling.

As discussed earlier, critics consider *testimonio*'s representativity a distinguishing trademark. In *testimonios*, such as the ones issued by Menchú / Burgos-Debray, Valdés and Bitar, this representativity is created by way of a reverse anonymity effect. Accordingly, the testifier identifies as a spokesperson for a larger public. He or she claims to depict an experience that is particular due to its autobiographical nature, but, at the same time, also stands for of the trauma endured by other victims of the same sociopolitical constituencies of power. In the monological interview, the author / intermediaries and narrator / interviewees reinforce this effect in similar terms. Moreover, as author / editors reconstruct and bring together multiple *testimonios* in a contextual, comprehensive and larger discourse, the effected multiplicity of voices serves to broaden the representative value of the combined narrative. In comparison to more streamlined testimonies, like the ones mentioned above, the monological interviews studied feature a wider range of points of view and experiences and, consequently, multiple authenticity claims. In these narratives, each testimony differs in content, tone and character; yet, it is the multiplicity of voices pronounced that reinforces the validity of the personal history.

The conjunction of multiple harmonious representations with individual authenticity claims, this reinforced collectivity and choir of a multiplicity of voices, enables Chavkin to pronounce a pluralistic, representative forefront against misrepresentation and denial, above all, against the military regime's continued human rights violations. Chavkin's interviewees express the hope that justice will prevail and that change is imminent. This hope is intrinsically linked to their voluntary, yet, painful cooperation in the interview process. It serves as principle motive for providing oral testimony and, most certainly, cannot be read as an attempt to assume personal responsibility for the crimes suffered. That responsibility clearly rests on the shoulders of the guilty and those who have chosen to look the other way. The responsibility the testifiers are willing to assume is that of setting history straight by making the crimes be known. Chavkin explains:

> Recalling their suffering, and the brutality their relatives and friends underwent at the hands of the Junta, took courage; indeed, it was a searing experience. Nevertheless, they [the interviewed] took part in this project in the belief that the epic story of Allende and the Popular Unity government, as well as that of the Fascist orgy of sadism that followed, should be told again and again. This book is a collection of personal accounts by the victims and resisters of the putsch, which when pieced together gives perspective to the drama of the Chilean tragedy. Though many of the survivors of this group have been hurt psychologically and maimed physically after years of terror in concentration camps, they remain astonishingly optimistic, confident that the Chilean Junta will not continue to rule for long.[17]

Chavkin's narrators identify their experiences under Pinochet as principally traumatic. The ordeal endured by one individual differs from that of another. Many continue to suffer significantly. The trauma inflicted still weighs them down. However, the urge to combat the military regime, to put an end to fear, terror and persecution, torture and murder, gives them the strength to endure the interview process. They reconstruct mentally the torture and suffering and pronounce it to make history be known. They seek to construct a social conscience that will give the country the strength to stand up against the military regime and to tear it down. They are optimistic that they will succeed.

Sepúlveda's *arpilleristas* do not necessarily continue to share the same optimism expressed by Chavkin's narrators. They have now invested more than two decades in their quest for justice and in their search for detained and disappeared family members. For some *arpilleristas,* the terror and horror intrinsically tied to the detainment and disappearance of a loved one in Chile began with the military coup in 1973. For others, the unforgettable military intervention into the private, family sphere did not occur until three to four years later. Like Chavkin's interviewees, all of these women have been psychologically hurt in their endeavors to locate their family members. Many have themselves been detained by military or local police in response to their persistent public outcry and demands for justice.

The *arpilleristas* formed in 1975 out of one of the many workshops organized and sponsored by the National Vicariate of the Catholic Church,[18] in an effort to provide both psychological and financial support to political, social and economic victims of the dictatorship. The *arpi-*

lleristas thus came to constitute a support group that enabled them to share and express their trauma for the duration of their meetings at the Vicariate. They also organized public events, such as several hunger strikes and musical and theatrical performances, to promote their cause.[19] Above all, however, they created the "*arpilleras* of denunciation,"[20] which enabled them to make their protests be heard, touched and felt in the international arena as well. As Sepúlveda informs,

> from the outset, their works carried a clear political message. Some members of the *arpillera* workshop also belonged to the Association of Families of the Detained-Disappeared. The majority of these women of all ages had met in the long lines at the jail or in the detention centers where they awaited news of a family member. The *arpilleras* were begun in those years to express what Chilean media could not say. This utterly silent social art was soon converted into the most effective clandestine means of communication to resist the military dictatorship of General Augusto Pinochet.[21]

The "reading" of the *arpilleras* requires a certain familiarization not only with the thematics but also with the significance of specific images, colors, landscapes and symbols. Of the many *arpilleras* produced to this date, no two are identical. Each *arpillera* articulates a personal experience, struggle and suffering. Each constitutes an *arpillerista*'s testimony of highly personal significance and investment. The setting and colors recreate the sociopolitical and geographical environment. Onto this background, cloth-dolls come to embody family members relocated into history. They are dressed in their customary attire that, as narrator Inelia Hermosilla Silva explains, is handmade "with little pieces of our own disappeared children."[22]

Sepúlveda sought to provide another medium through which *arpilleristas* could spread their message. This, she says, is her sociopolitical literary agenda. This is why she set out to interview these women, asked them to share their trauma orally so that she may transform it into literary testimony. The *testimonio* presented in *We Chile*, enunciates a unique choir of voices with each individual voice relating a very personal, yet also similar, experience. Together the eight *arpilleristas* denounce a past and present in Chile that Chile still tends to greet with silence and denial. Like Chavkin's interviewees, they did not enter the process of giving oral testimony to Sepúlveda with ease. However, for them it was less a struggle of overcoming the personal barriers in pronouncing the trauma inflicted upon them and their beloved. Rather, they struggled to overcome a staggering fear that as a result of their quest to be heard, their videotaped testimony would reach the wrong hands. Sepúlveda explains,

> I know that the *arpilleristas* told me their experiences fearfully, but behind that terror was the tremendous desire to have someone hear their stories and re-tell them in other countries with the hope that others, after hearing these women's lives, would help those in Chile defend their basic freedoms, without which human dignity can never exist. Often they feared the very words they pronounced, a fear compounded by the fact that someone with a camera recorded their faces together with their words. They knew that both records would leave with me, fulfilling their desire to have others receive their individual messages sent from Chile.[23]

Unlike Chavkin's interviewees, hence, the *arpilleristas* are working not in isolation but as a group. Together, they provide mutual support, denounce their suffering, and empower their fight for justice. As Sepúlveda informs, these women still have not overcome their fear, the terror of the past continues to haunt and affect them in the present. Yet, despite more than twenty years of continued oppression and terror, these women have not turned their backs to Chile. The title, *We, Chile*, pronounces a plural self-identification with Chile. In accordance, the *arpilleristas* continue to live, craft, struggle and fight from within their national boundaries. Through song, dance and metaphor, they maintain a visible presence in Chilean society. With the support of the Vicariate, Sepúlveda and others, they manage to bypass national censorship restrictions and to introduce their cause and concerns to the international arena through the *arpilleras* and their testimony in *We, Chile*.

Whereas the *arpilleras* also serve as a commodity, facilitating the *arpilleristas'* economic survival, their testimony still smacks of political censorship. To decipher these testimonies requires an interpretive process and familiarity with theme and medium. Although the dolls and images resemble the *arpilleristas'* families and personal experiences, in retrospect, this personal significance and authorship may only with difficulty be verified. On the other hand, the literary *testimonio*, *We, Chile*, serves to decipher the underlying message of the *arpilleras*, as well as to establish the link between these testimonies and their authors. *We, Chile* articulates a nearly unequivocal manifestation of joint denunciation and accusation: photos, multiple authenticity claims and verifiable authorship accompany the testimony contained herein. By way of this complementary relationship and coexistence, the *arpilleras* and the *testimonios* proffered in *We, Chile* may join forces, verifying each other's validity and augmenting their common, sociopolitical purpose.

As Chavkin suggests, "when pieced together," the personal accounts represented in *Murder in Chile* give "perspective to the drama of the Chilean tragedy." [24] We can view his text as a comprehensive narrative, in which the individual testimony contributes a piece to the whole. The same applies to Sepúlveda's *Fear in Chile*. These texts entail complementary representations of trauma and terror in Chile. They give no cause to dispute that both agents share the sociopolitical agenda issued by the text: the editor/interviewer and the testifier/narrator.

This is different in Politzer's case. Therefore, I will now approach the interplay between editorial intent and the monological interviews contained in her narrative. By way of a dual approach, reading, on the one hand, the testimonies as constitutive elements of a comprehensive narrative, narrative strategy and agenda, but on the other as individual statements, we can investigate and try to assess the testifiers' intentionalities. For this purpose, we will need to understand the literary *testimonio*, in accordance with the author and Serrano, as real-life testimony. The individual narrators express antithetical intentionalities that, consequently, suggest being, at least in particular cases, distinct from the agenda manifested by the author. This analysis should enable us to assess the power of the editor/intermediary, the ability to complement or override the individual speakers' sociopolitical objective with his or her own agenda. As a result, I believe, we will be able to confirm the "sort of erasure of the function, and thus also of the textual presence, of the 'author'"[25] as a narrative strategy that is linked to the sociopolitical and literary agenda of the author.

In her introduction, Politzer suggests that victim, perpetrator and onlooker alike need to assume responsibility for Chile's traumatic past. In this way, she nearly echoes pro-dictatorship testimony by Coronel Juan Deichler Guzmán, who she cites explaining, "the moment that it is a matter of war, everybody assumes his/her responsibility and...he who dies dies....”[26] From a sociopolitical critical point of view, of course, we can question if the military coup and the dictatorship imposed upon Chile indeed constitutes a war, or if it this interpretation does not rather correspond to a military strategy seeking to justify violence and crimes committed.[27] We can also question whether this assignation of responsibility in a crime to the victim of the crime does, as suggested, correspond to a mere question of difference in belief or, to the contrary, if it indicates a perpetrator’s rejection of responsibility and denial of guilt. Deichler Guzmán expands his ideas explaining that it is “therefore,” i.e. due to the previously cited argumentation, that

> ...in what refers to the disappeared, I do not give anybody the blame...I think it was a stupidity, like in the dirty war in Argentina. But there were more than 35 thousand disappeared and in Chile, had there been some 600? Moreover, I think that all of those disappeared people were like rabid dogs, with rabies! And one has got to eliminate rabies, although I do not justify it for any motive. Neither in the Military, nor in any institution of the National Defense the disappeared are justified.[28]

It is curious that in this quote Deichler Guzmán chooses to point to the Military and National Defense’s lack of justification for the disappeared people, but refrains from making a similar comment regarding their disappearance. Deichler Guzmán strongly refrains from assuming any concrete responsibility for the human rights violations he refers to. Above all, he suggests that all parties share the blame and that, perhaps, no one will be able to justify the crimes committed. Deichler Guzmán’s and Politzer’s attitude regarding shared responsibility is clearly echoed by Chile’s archbishop Raúl Cardenal Silva Henríquez.

Politzer’s book opens with a letter by the archbishop that, preceded only by the title and the acknowledgments, seems programmed to receive special attention. In this letter, the archbishop proclaims the value of diversity in beliefs in a peaceful context and writes: “This work by the journalist Patricia Politzer has the value of reminding us of that, which we should never forget: we can think distinctly without the necessity to consider each other enemies. We can have differences in our ideas, but it is not necessary that we seek the destruction of the adversary.”[29] Politzer’s work is certainly set up to serve as an illustration of different interpretations and perspectives regarding the Pinochet dictatorship and related events. Moreover, it is constructed in the intention to aid a peaceful, sociopolitical mission by uniting antagonistic experiences and interpretations in a harmonious, comprehensive representation.

Rather than pointing a finger, any and all Chileans are encouraged to open their minds and hearts to differences in opinion and recognize that they need not kill adversaries in response to difference in ideology. The killing and torture form part of the past; the division into perpetrators and victims continues to divide the country, entire neighborhoods and families, yet tragic history ought not find repetition. Chile is supposed to be shaping its path toward reunification and democracy, and Politzer and the Archbishop alike suggest interpreting the division as a question of opinion and belief.

Sol Serrano's introduction to *Miedo en Chile* appears more supportive and receptive of the trauma proclaimed. According to her, the text requires neither introduction nor commentary. She explains:

> When I finished reading Patricia Politzer's book, I was invaded by such a profound silence, that the mere idea of making a commentary seemed superficiality: not a single word had to be added. I continue to believe that that silence, filled with pain and hope, is the best commentary, and I think that you, when you read it, will share this first and primordial sensation with me.[30]

The pain Serrano refers to may be the pain shared with the victims upon reading their accounts of suffering. It may also be the pain linked to the realization that Chilean society continues to be divided into victims and *pinochetistas*, as well as the pain linked to the recognition that fear has become a common experience among Chileans. The hope Serrano refers to, however, is more difficult to interpret. Clearly, Politzer suggests that better times may lie ahead for Chile when communication is reinstated and society learns to understand and accept its differences and embarks on a joint project of constructing a harmonious and peaceful future.

Whether or not *Miedo en Chile* truly does not require a preface may still need to be determined; what this text does need, however, is an explanation. The problem here is that the difference in experience, interpretation and representation of Chile's past as exposed in *Miedo en Chile* cannot well be reduced to a question of belief and ideology. As stated before, the crimes have been committed and justice has not been served.

A hope shared by many victims certainly consists in bringing justice. Politzer, the archbishop, as well as perpetrators, on the other hand, seem to suggest that victims share a responsibility in the crimes they suffered.

In her introduction, Politzer explains the book's title in her observation that fear constitutes a common experience in Chile not just in the past, but also in the present. My observation is that the author's own fear is mirrored in and by the book, as it exposes Politzer's lack of support for the victims' rights and fight for justice. For justice is THE human right that Politzer neither suggests nor solicits; yet, the victim testifiers in *Miedo en Chile* do explicitly cry out for justice. Politzer on the other hand proposes that victims and perpetrators alike learn to treat each others' differences in experience and understanding of Chile's history with respect rather than demand justice. In other words, so that torturers, killers and victims may learn to live in harmony, they are to shake hands and listen to each other open-mindedly, the victims to their torturers and vice versa. Yet, as a mirror reflection of alternative and official representations of history, the victim's and perpetrator's representations in *Miedo en Chile* are so contradictory that they void each other. We may read *Miedo en Chile* as an indication that the wrongs of the past prevail and are reinforced in and through the present.

In presenting the voice of the perpetrator next to the voice of the victim as a mere illumination of difference in ideology serves only to widen the victim's trauma, mental and physical scar. The human rights violations under the Pinochet regime continue to be greeted by righteous downplay and denial. In attributing equal value and validity to victim's and perpetrator's interpretation of the past, both are legitimized; in spite of their contradiction, they are said to enable the foundation for peaceful relations among Chileans. With a firm stamp of approval, the Church sanctions Politzer's narrative and sociopolitical strategy. Politzer requests the reader, victim and perpetrator alike, to acknowledge and assume responsibility for Chile's history.

Politzer's text is constructed in such a way that the individual testimonies are attributed exclusively to their speakers. They are presented as complete, comprehensive and non-interrupted testimonies, missing, at the most, the quotation marks. With above analysis, I challenge the testifier's authorship of these testimonies in pointing to the authorial signature of the text and to the non-commented transformation of an interview dialog into the representation of a monological speech.[31] The study addresses Politzer's role in instigating and directing content and structure of these representations and the lack of acknowledgment of her editorial intervention. At the same time, selected citations from these *testimonios* serve to invoke a critique of Politzer's agenda and sociopolitical purpose.

In this analysis, I have identified the testifier (i.e. Deichler Guzmán, and others) as author or speaker of the testimony rather than attributed authorship to Politzer, in accordance with her role as editor and author of *Miedo en Chile*. This difference in reading and authorship attribution is linked to a dual reading and interpretation of the text. On the one hand, I critique Politzer's literary and sociopolitical agenda as well as narrative strategy. On the other hand, I also consider it important to engage in an analysis of the narrative as constructed by the text's own framework.

In *Miedo en Chile*, this framework is based upon the traditional understanding of literary *testimonio* that assigns authorship to the spokesperson the moment a statement is labeled testimony, or presented as such. In her introduction, Politzer emphasizes that her intention is to present unfettered testimony to enable an insight into different experiences and interpretations regarding the Pinochet regime. In accordance with her literary and sociopolitical objective, the reader is encouraged to enter the discourse unprejudiced. At the same time, one is to enter with the understanding that the multi-perspectivity, which is constructed through contradictory representations and interpretations of events and experience, is equally valid rather than mutually exclusive. In accordance, the reader may find a higher incentive to focus on the testifier's narrative content and strategy, on his or her construction of memory and understanding and interpretation of the experiences in question, as well as on the sociopolitical purpose of the individual testimony.

The first testimony presented in *Miedo en Chile*, corresponds to Blanca Ester Valderas Garrido and is entitled "La alcadesa fusilada," "The executed mayor." It is not clear who chose this contradictory title for Valderas' testimony.[32] According to Politzer's brief preface to this chapter, "[It] is a story of horror and of sadness, of fear, of loneliness, of abandoned children, of hunger, of poverty, of anguish and of much pain. But, at the same time, it is the story of a villager who Allende named mayor of Entre Lagos. And —for her— this is more important than having been executed."[33] This contradiction in terms, that an executed person may provide testimony about her own execution, lies at the center of this testimony. Politzer clarifies,

> [Her execution] was no simulation. She was executed with bullets of war on a bridge over the river Bueno, near Osorno. Her husband and three other companions died as they fell toward the water, but she miraculously saved herself. 'If God did not want to take me—she says— it was because of my children.' Or perhaps it was so that someone could tell this story.[34]

An authorial stamp of approval and credibility is hence issued even prior to the testimony. Politzer even explains the title's underlying significance: the testifier has taken her executioners to court. Perhaps justice was slanted or her testimony too improbable or shocking, Valderas' literary *testimonio* suggests. She has yet to win her case:

> I know that the judge believed me, that she realized that I was speaking the truth, but even though they are judges, these men also have a limit, and that's as far as the thing goes....I don't know what type of a law they have now, because the true law is the truth, is what I have declared and have told, but they have not wanted to recognize it.[35]

As Politzer facilitates Valderas a new chance to testify in *Miedo en Chile*, the reader may be tempted to assume the role of the judge and call for justice. However, in accordance with the "Presentación," Politzer hopes that the reader will instead be able to overcome the now typical Chilean judgment. She wants Chileans "to look at each other and recognize each other as we are, neither as good not as bad as we thought, neither as black nor as white as we prejudiced."[36] To understand Valderas' experiences and representation not as absolute truths also invites a different interpretation of the title "The Executed Mayor." Although the military's attempt to execute Valderas failed, in that she survived and lives to give testimony, their endeavor did succeed to the extent that the suffering, marginalizing and denial that followed and prevailed left her permanently scarred.

As she testifies on that most dramatic and traumatic moment of her life, Valderas makes reference to her feelings, her thoughts, and even the absence of thought. The interplay between narrative timelines in this testimony serves to illustrate the timeless limitations of the experience, the overreaching dimension of trauma:

> I knew that they were going to kill us. I know it because all of their movements were indicators for that. I did not say anything to them, nothing. They did not see me either crying to them or moaning to them, or anything. I did not have reason to cry to them! I was not afraid. Why was I not afraid? Because I knew that I did not owe anything. I had not committed any crime. I did not think anything, I only kept telling myself: "If it is God's wish, I will have to die and they will kill me. But I don't owe anything, I am not an assassin because I have not ordered anybody to kill, nor have I killed." I was pretty calm. What hurt me the most...and bothered my conscience...was that they would kill my husband. Why will they kill him? He did not have any blame either. They did not have a reason for having killed him! I found myself more to blame, because I had the position....[37]

In accordance with her retrospective point of view, the narrator employs the past tense to describe her state of emotion at the moment of execution. As a result of an imaginary repositioning into the past, her narrative mirrors the actual timeline of the event: she utilizes the future tense to question the reason's for her husband's capital punishment, as she might have done in the moment prior to the execution. She then reflects on his innocence and expresses, two sentences later, the lack of justification for her husband's now completed execution. The grammatical construction, consisting of a combination of past and past perfect tenses, serves to locate this conclusion either in the moment immediately following execution or in the moment of giving testimony.

Valderas' testimony on the possibly most dramatic experience of her life, her execution, is combined with a testimony on past as well as post trauma experiences. Throughout her personal account, Valderas provides background information as necessary for the comprehension of events. The chronological order is thereby interrupted or reversed. In accordance, the testimony regarding the moment of execution precedes the representation of her election to town mayor, even though this election, in her own reasoning, is linked to the execution. She identifies her holding office as Allende's mayor as primary cause for having been singled out by the military regime and for having been made a victim.

This free conjunction of tenses also includes the present tense timeline of giving testimony as it emerges sporadically throughout the narrative. This tense then reaches a climax in the last chapter as the narrator turns to her current state of affairs, her present suffering due to the economically critical situation, etc. In integrating the present experience into the testimony, this experience is translated into recent history. It forms part of and shapes the construction of this *testimonio* and our image of her understanding and interpretation of history. The narrator evidently shares an experience in which she still takes part, an experience that is still valid today:

> Here there has been happiness between my children, daughters-in-law and grandchildren. We are fifteen, now, and I have been able to feel calmer. But times are becoming sadder every day. When I see that the children cry and ask me for a piece of bread, that makes me very bitter. I get sick and can't stand the nerves.[38]

As she tells about her present experience, her narration continues to denounce the misery and suffering brought to her family under Pinochet. We may ask whether or not she does not indeed tell of the moment, in the moment and for the moment. The process of giving testimony may aid her in dealing with the trauma. It may also aid her to address and search for an answer to her own questions: "For ten years now I am trying to forget what has happened to me, and I have not been able to do so. Will it be possible to forget the child who was left, thrown into the street, without father or mother? How can we forget this!"[39]

Valderas' testimony ends on this question and exclamation. In *Miedo en Chile*, her testimony is then followed by that of Colonel Deichler Guzmán, entitled "El alcalde del régimen," "The Regime's Mayor." As the title indicates, his testimony corresponds to a regime-friendly correspondent. It also contradicts or belittles her testimony. Set next to each other, her testimony denounces official history; his testimony answers her alternative representation with ridicule and laughter.[40]

Politzer does certainly not limit *Miedo en Chile* to these two antagonistic accounts; rather she includes the testimony all together of fourteen different subjects. Only four of these express pro-Pinochet views like Deichler Guzmán's. The other ten denounce human rights violations in the form of political persecution, detainment, torture, and murder, explicitly like Valderas or they speak out against other forms of social, economic, and political oppression. Given the quantity of testimonies and multiplicity of voices represented, the negative experience in *Miedo en Chile* clearly outweighs the positive.

Whether or not Politzer understands this imbalance of negative and positive experience as representative of the Chilean experience under Pinochet is not clear. She anticipated the testimonies to facilitate the contemporary Chilean "challenge that implies to look at and to recognize ourselves for that what we are, neither as good nor as bad as we thought, neither as black nor as white as we prejudiced."[41] However, no testimony in *Miedo en Chile* models this type of behavior or attitude. To the contrary, *pinochetistas* continue bashing victims and holding them responsible for the crimes committed against them. Likewise, victims and their supporters are as steadfast as ever in their characterization of the perpetrators. Whereas Elena Tesser de Villaseca suggests that the victims became victims "because of something bad they have done,"[42] in Damián Acuña Jarpa's words, the perpetrators are men who

> thought that in order to save the country it was necessary to get rid of the adversaries and proceeded with brutality and with exaggeration against anybody who could have been thinking a different way, even though he had been mislead with false promises. He who carried a weapon had the right to judge the others and, what is worse, to take decisions about other people's life. I would say that it resulted in a true massacre against humble people who, many times, had nothing to do with anything at all.[43]

Such indisputable characterization does not allow much leeway for differentiation into different shades of black and white (to apply the color scheme so frequently used in these testimonies). Moreover, the perpetrator's identification of victims as guilty of the crimes committed against them does not create a strong motive for victims to change their attitude with regard to a Christian pardon or a trial invoking an amnesty law. Elsa Esquivel Rojo, for example, would surely agree with Acuña Jarpa's characterization. Nonetheless, this would certainly not give her any motive even to consider a pardon:

> Some say that one day we will have to know how to pardon, I don't agree with that. If I knew who took my son away, I am not going to take a weapon and I am not going to kill him because I don't believe in the death penalty, but I would not pardon him. I would see to it that they go through the same as we have, I would be capable of taking one of his children away —for a few days— so that he'd learn what it means to suffer.... There will have to be a trial for the guilty, but a trial without amnesty so that the responsible are punished and this

> not come to happen again. This will have to take place when democracy returns, when this returns to be a free country as it was years ago. I would like if we had a government without dead, without tortures, without massacres and that we could be a country of brothers and sisters.[44]

Politzer and many others evidently share a similar hope of a more peaceful future. The difference only lies in whether or not justice should be called for and whether or not it should be served. For if we truly identify the antagonism of these representations, as based solely upon a difference in point of view, then, perhaps, the past could be forgotten in a similar way as modeled by Andrés Chadwick Piñera. Reciting his successful elimination of his socialist past shortly before joining the *Gremialistas* (with the opposite ideology) at the University of Chile, Chadwick Piñera explains: "in that moment, in which I burned my books, I burned everything and wiped out an entire phase."[45] But Blanca Ester Valderas Garrido's testimony, in which she cites her inability to forget the horror and terror that she was brought to experience under Pinochet, of course, challenge this.[46] Valderas is certain that the responsible will never find pardon: "Jesus said that one had to pardon, but those men, who are governing, I think that neither God nor we is ever going to pardon. Although we cannot judge them, I know that God is going to judge them and punish them."[47]

When conceived as one solid *testimonio*, *Miedo en Chile* is, in accordance with Beverley's understanding of *testimonio*, constituted by the collective intentionality of the speakers and not by the intermediary. However, the individuals' intentionalities are contradicting. This exposes the collective intentionality as a deliberate overriding of the antagonistic intentionalities and their absorption into an involuntary harmonious whole, that is determined less by the individual speaker than by the intermediary who controls the power of the representation.

As Beverley points out, *testimonio* informs its "unit of narration" as "usually a 'life' or a significant life experience." The modifier "usually" indicates that Beverley views these characteristics not as required but as common features of *testimonio*. Given that the designation of an external referent as a "significant life experience" may be authored differently by any literary agent, witness, and reader, significance is attributed here less to the content of the experience than to the designation itself. I suggest extending this observation beyond the literary framework of *testimonio*.

In order for *testimonio* to maintain and achieve its sociopolitical paradigm and agenda, a reader must recognize *testimonio*'s content as significant and also come to understand the *testimonio* itself as a significant component of the sociopolitical paradigm, out of which it grows and which it aims to influence. This applies to the individual monological interview that is perceived as a *testimonio* on its own. But it also applies to the comprehensive *testimonio* that is constituted by editorial or honorary comments and the multiple monological interviews. The novel- or novella-length attributed to *testimonio* thereby loses significance. Likewise, the identification of *testimonio*'s intentionality as corresponding to the narrator/testifier is also challenged because it is and remains the author/editor who controls the representation, its content and literary agenda.

Whereas the antithetical statements in Politzer's monological interviews appear to pronounce their speaker/narrator's intentions, this can not be taken for granted. Politzer invokes the sort of erasure of her editorial intervention, but she still intervenes. This we should not ignore. Whereas Chavkin, Sepúlveda, and Politzer each emphasize their intent to give a voice to the voiceless, in essence each author appropriates the informants' voices by removing them from the interview environment and submitting them to a vigorous process of interpretation, reconstitution and editing. Above all, the oral testimony is inserted into a larger contextual and comprehensive narrative whose sociopolitical and literary dimension overrides the oral testimony's constituency and objective.

NOTES

1 Beverley 1989, 12–3 in Gugelberger 1996, 9.
2 See Rice-Sayre 1986, 5.
3 Beverley 1996, 29.
4 Miedo en Chile.
5 Also see Viezzer 1977.
6 In Spanish, her comments read: "la entrevista consiste básicamente en una pregunta: cómo ha vivido cada uno, desde su propia experiencia personal, este período de la historia de Chile. Las preguntas no aparecen en el texto, por lo cual cada entrevista es, en realidad, un testimonio" (Sol Serrano Pérez 1985, 4). My translation exposes a problem in terminology. In Spanish, testimony translates as testimonio. However, critics have utilized this same Spanish term to designate the literary practice, *testimonio*. Since Solano does not elaborate on the connotation of her use of the term, I chose to translate it, in accordance with my reading, as *testimonio*, connotating the literary practice.
7 Political prisoners, mothers and wives of the disappeared, who created *arpilleras*, which Sepúlveda describes as "appliquéd and embroidered cloth rectangles...like gigantic books that sought to depict the multiplicity of experiences of daily life...compact records of the misery and suffering of all Chileans" (Sepúlveda 1996, 21).
8 Sepúlveda 1996, 36.
9 "La autora no interviene, salvo en una pequeña introducción en que muestra su motivación. Luego ella desaparece, nos deja solos, y, de repente, sin darnos cuenta, estamos allí, en el corazón de la vida de la

antigua alcaldesa de un pueblo sureño, del dirigente sindical, de la militante comunista, de la mamá de un desaparecido, de una señora del voluntariado femenino, del dirigente estudiantil, del joven ejecutivo, y entramos en ella con una profundidad que difícilmente logramos con las personas que nos son más cercanas" (Sol Serrano Pérez 1985, 4).

10 In her introduction, Politzer explains: "Since several years ago, Chile is divided into two clearly defined countries which don't look at each other, don't touch each other and don't know each other; but which recognize each other intuitively and fear each other. This situation encloses—without doubt—an enormous risk, because the step from fear to hatred and from hatred to aggression is an almost natural evolution, which brings us inevitably to the logic of war, as happened in September 1973" ["Desde hace varios años, Chile está dividido en dos países claramente definidos que no se miran, no se tocan y no se conocen; pero se intuyen y se temen. Esta situación encierra—sin duda—un enorme riesgo, porque pasar del miedo al odio y del odio al la agresión es una evolución casi natural que nos lleva inevitablemente a la lógica de la guerra, como sucedió en septiembre de 1973"] (Politzer 1990, 11).

11 "Empezar a visualizar una salida democrática, quizás requiere que entendamos que Chile somos nosotros y también los otros, esos que no conocemos pero que imaginamos fácilmente, atribuyéndoles los males de la humanidad" (Politzer 1990, 11–2).

12 "Patricia tomó una opción de entre muchas: ella optó por tratar de comprender a este país desde la experiencia concreta de chilenos concretos y ella optó por no intervenir, por dejarlos ser para que llegasen a nosotros en su plena humanidad. Patricia no conduce, no ahoga, no manipula a sus personajes, pero eso no es todo. Patricia no conduce, no indica, no obliga a sus lectores a ninguna mirada específica. Ella solamente permite el encuentro. Y esto, que parece tan simple y sencillo, requiere, en realidad, de una difícil madurez, de humildad, de gran fineza de espíritu y de un severo respeto. Ella optó por no tener una mirada privilegiada sobre la realidad y eso significa

que, al fin, ¡Dios mío!, alguien en este país optó por escuchar" (Sol Serrano Pérez 1985, 4–5).

13 "Y aquí está, a mi juicio, el testimonio que no aparece en el índice. Me pregunto si la forma en que Patricia concibió su libro no es el fruto, ya no del miedo, sino del dolor de su propia experiencia de este país y de un dolor que germinó en salir de sí misma, en aceptar la limitación de su propia mirada para entregarnos, como delicada intermediaria, retazos de vida que no podíamos ver" (Sol Serrano Pérez 1985, 5).

14 Politzer writes: "By way of these 14 interviewees I have tried to give a realistic and ample vision of that which has happened over the last years. There may be historical errors in some testimonies, but this is how the people perceive the events and its is based on that vision that they analyze the past and project the future" ["A través de estos 14 entrevistados he tratado de dar una visión realista y amplia de lo que nos ha pasado en los últimos años. Puede haber errores históricos en algunos testimonios, pero es así como las personas perciben los acontecimientos y es a partir de esa visión que analizan el pasado y proyectan el futuro"] (Politzer 1990, 3).

15 "Para asegurar la estabilidad de una futura democracia, seguramente se requerirá que todos asumamos nuestra responsabilidad en el horror que hemos vivido y que aceptemos y comprendamos lo que ha ocurrido en este período en el que Chile tiene miedo. Esto ayudaría a construir una democracia en serio, sin verdades absolutas, sin ideologías que estén por sobre las personas, sin que se mate, se denigre o se descalifique, simplemente porque el otro es diferente o no piensa del mismo modo.

Cuando logremos vernos unos a otros con todas nuestras cualidades, nuestros defectos, nuestros sufrimientos, nuestras debilidades, nuestros errores y nuestra experiencia acumulada, podremos respetarnos de verdad, sin que nadie tenga por qué sentir miedo. En este contexto, las vivencias de mis entrevistados pretenden ser un aporte al desafío que implica mirarnos y reconocernos tal cual somos, ni tan buenos ni tan malos como creíamos, ni tan negros ni tan blancos como prejuzgábamos" (Politzer 1990, 12).

16 In accordance with my analysis of truth and knowledge or rather non-truth and non-knowledge, as construed by Foucault and others, I certainly agree with Politzer in the negation of absolute truth. Yet, by understanding any formulation of a truth, as in the case of testimony regarding experiences under Pinochet, a construction of truth, the construction of this truth may then be examined with regard to a literary or sociopolitical agenda. It is this function or application of a construction of truth, which Politzer does not address in her discourse.

17 Chavkin 1982, 7.

18 The Vicariate of Solidarity of the Catholic Church is generally heralded for the support provided to victims of the Pinochet regime. Oppenheim writes in this regard: "Many of the grass-roots organizations formed under the protection of the Vicariate of Solidarity of the Catholic church. The church, virtually the only institution that the military could not openly attack or dismantle, played a very significant role in fostering these local groups. It provided the physical space for organizational meetings, as well as other forms of support and protection" (Oppenheim 1993, 184).

19 Violeta Morales explains, "We were desperate to get our message out, we wanted, like our people had done so many times, to turn to other art forms—we wanted to express ourselves in our song and dance. We wanted not only to embroider and shout our pain, we also wanted to sing our message of denunciation" (Violeta Morales in Sepúlveda 1996, 55).

20 Violeta Morales in Sepúlveda 1996, 52.

21 Sepúlveda 1996, 24–5.

22 Inelia Hermosilla Silva in Sepúlveda 1996, 70.

23 Sepúlveda 1996, 33–4.

24 Chavkin 1982, 7.

25 Beverley 1996, 29.

26 "desde el momento en que se trata de una guerra, cada uno asume su responsabilidad y...muere el que muere..." (Politzer 1990, 67).

27 In an interview with by David Albala entitled "Aquí no hubo guerra," Edgardo Enríquez, former president of the University of

Concepción, comments in this regard: "There was no war in Chile but an occupation of the national territory by its own Military Forces. First, in order to have a war, there must be two armed militaries. Here these did not exist. Secondly, the Military Forces dominated the situation completely. There were shoot-outs, but they were the same soldiers who were shooting to give the impression that there was a war. And, third, if there had been a war, they did not respect the laws of warfare. One does not massacre prisoners of war, one does not kill them. They, for example, killed many who left La Moneda [the presidential palace] with their hands up. So that there was no war!" ["En Chile no hubo una guerra, sino que una ocupación del territorio nacional por sus propias Fuerzas Armadas. En primer lugar, para que haya una guerra tienen que haber dos ejércitos armados. Aquí no los había. En segundo lugar, las Fuerzas Armadas dominaron completamente la situación. Hubo tiroteos, pero eran los mismos soldados que disparaban para dar la impresión de que había guerra. Y, en tercer lugar, si hubiera habido una guerra, no se respetaron sus leyes. A los prisioneros de guerra no se les masacra, no se les mata. Por ejemplo, mataron a muchos de los que salieron de La Mondea con las manos en alto. ¡Así que no hubo una guerra!"] (Verdugo 1994, 14–5).

28 "Por eso, en lo de los desaparecidos yo no le echo la culpa a nadie.... Pienso que fue una estupidez, como en la guerra sucia de Argentina. Pero allá pasaron de los 35 mil desaparecidos y en Chile, ¿habrá unos 600? Además pienso que toda eas gente desaparecida eran como perros rabiosos, ¡con rabia! ¡Y hay que eliminar la rabia, aunque yo no lo justifico por ningún motivo. Ni el Ejército, ni en ninguna institución de la Defensa Nacional se justifica a los desaparecidos" (Politzer 1990, 67).

29 "Este trabajo de la periodista Patricia Politzer tiene el valor de recordarnos lo que nunca debimos olvidar: podemos pensar distinto sin necesidad de considerarnos enemigos. Podemos tener divergencias en las ideas, pero no es necesario que busquemos la destrucción del adversario" (Raúl Cardenal Silva Henríquez in Politzer 1990, 1).

30 "Cuando terminé de leer el libro de Patricia Politzer me invadió un silencio tan profundo, que la sola idea de hacer un comentario me

pareció una superficialidad: no había ni una sola palabra que agregar. Sigo creyendo que ese silencio, lleno de dolor y esperanza, es el mejor comentario y creo que ustedes, cuando lo lean, compartirán conmigo esa sensación primera y primordial" (Serrano Pérez 1985, 3).

31 In this regard, it may be of interest to point to out the manner in which Politzer divides the presentation of the individual *testimonios* into four parts. First comes the *testimonio*'s title in capital letters; second, the testifier's name in italics; third, Politzer's brief introductory paragraph in the same italic font applied to the testifier's name; and, finally, fourth, the actual testimony printed in standard font. This order and font selection does not facilitate an indisputable designation of authorship or identity construction. The testifier's name seems to indicate authorship of the title and that, which follows. However the matching special font applied to the name and Politzer's introduction can be seen to support a dispute of authorship. By extension, we can read this to endorse a redefinition of the testifier as an identity construction that is linked to the author's agenda. On the grounds that the testifier's name (may it reflect an external identity construction or not) and the author's voice follow the title (whose authorship may be attributed to either testifier or author) and, jointly, precede the testimony, that testimony's authorship may be questioned. Hence, we may also question the testimony's authenticity. And this can then result in its redefinition as a deliberate discourse construction that is administered by the author and her editorial intervention.

32 Unlike Sepúlveda's titles for the individual testimonies which, like Politzer's subtitles are extracted from the actual testimony and wording to provide additional emphasis, the title of Valderas testimony does not appear to correspond to Valderas' self-identification, indeed, she never applies it throughout her testimony.

33 "Es una historia de horror y de tristeza, de miedo, de soledad, de niños abandonados, de hambre, de pobreza, de angustia y de mucho dolor. Pero, al mismo tiempo, es la historia de una campesina a la

que Allende nombró alcaldesa de Entre Lagos. Y—para ella—eso es más importante que haber sido fusilada" (Politzer 1990, 13).

34 "[su execución] no fue un simulacro. La fusilaron con balas de guerra en un puente del río Bueno, cerca de Osorno. Su marido y otros tres compañeros murieron mientras caían al agua, pero ella se salvó milagrosamente, 'si Dios no me quiso llevar—dice—fue por mis hijos'. O quizás fue para que alguien pudiera contar esta historia" (Politzer 1990, 13).

35 "Sé que la jueza me creyó, que se dio cuenta que yo hablaba lo justo, pero aunque sean jueces esos señores también tienen un límite, y hasta ahí llega la cosa.... No sé en qué forma tienen la ley ahora, porque la ley verdadera es lo justo, es lo que yo he declarado y he dicho, pero ellos no lo han querido reconocer" (Valderas Garrido in Politzer 1990, 33–4).

36 "mirarnos y reconocernos tal cual somos, ni tan buenos ni tan malos como creíamos, ni tan negros ni tan blancos como prejuzgábamos" (Politzer 1990, 12).

37 "Yo sabía que nos iban a matar. Sabía porque todos sus movimientos eran indicados a eso. No les dije nada, nada. Ellos no me vieron llorarles, ni gemirles, ni nada. ¡No tenía por qué llorarles a ellos! No tenía susto. ¿Por qué no me dio susto? Porque yo sabía que yo nada debía. Ningún crimen había cometido yo. No pensaba nada, solamente me decía: 'si es la voluntad de Dios, tendré que morirme y me matarán. Pero no debo nada, no soy una asesina porque a nadie he mandado matar, ni he matado.' Estaba bien serena yo. Lo que más me dolía...y me molestaba la conciencia...era que mataran a mi marido. ¿Por qué lo matarán? El no tenía ninguna culpa tampoco. ¡No tenían por qué haberlo muerto! Más me encontraba culpable yo, porque yo tenía el cargo..." (Blanca Ester Valderas Garrido in Politzer 1990, 15–6).

38 "Aquí ha habido alegría entre mis hijos, mis nueras y mis nietos. Somos quince, ahora, y he podido sentirme más tranquila. Pero el tiempo se va poniendo cada día más triste. Cuando veo que los niños lloran y me piden un pedazo de pan, eso me amarga mucho. Me en-

fermo y los nervios no los soporto" (Valderas Garrido in Politzer 1990, 35).

39 "Hace diez años que estoy tratando de olvidarme de lo que a mí me ocurrió y no he podido. ¿Se podrá olvidar el niño que quedó botado en la calle, sin padre ni madre? ¡Cómo vamos a olvidar esto!" (Valderas Garrido in Politzer 1990, 38).

40 See Guzmán's comments regarding the coup's fatal victims: "When they speak of so many fatalities, they make me laugh. I could assure—and sign before a notary—that September 11 and the days which followed in the year 73, if in Chile there were five thousand dead bodies—on both sides—is a lot. I have had to travel through Latin-America and other parts, and in El Salvador, for example, in one year there are 36 thousand dead. So that I don't loose my sleep, nor does it keep me up thinking about this. Chile was very calm. Very calm!" ["Cuando hablan de tantas muertes a mí me da risa. Podría asegurar—y firmo ante notario—que el 11 de septiembre y los días que siguieron el año 73, si hubo en Chile cinco mil cadáveres—por ambas partes—es mucho. Me ha tocado viajar por Latinoamérica y por otras partes, y en El Salvador, por ejemplo, en un año hay 36 mil muertos. Así que no me quita el sueño ni me desvela pensar en esto. En Chile fue muy tranquilo. ¡Muy tranquilo!"] (Deichler Guzmán in Politzer 1990, 45–6).

41 "ser un aporte al desafío que implica mirarnos y reconocernos tal cual somos, ni tan buenos ni tan malos como creíamos, ni tan negros ni tan blancos como prejuzgábamos" (Politzer 1990, 12).

42 "por algo mal que han hecho" (Elena Tesser de Villaseca, "Pinochetista hasta el final" ["Pinochetista Until the End"] in Politzer 1990, 156.

43 "creyeron que para poder salvar al país había que deshacerse de los contrarios y procedieron con brutalidad y con saña frente a cualquiera que pudo haber pensado de otra manera, aunque fuera un engañado por falsas promesas. El que cargaba un arma tenía derecho a juzgar a los demás y, lo que es peor, a tomar determinaciones sobre la vida de otros. Yo diría que se produjo una verdadera masacre contra gente humilde que, muchas veces, no tenían nada que ver."

(Damián Acuña Jarpa, "Rebeldía de un cura a la antigua" in Politzer 1990, 226–7). Also see Deichler Guzmán's comment: "Here, those who are afraid are so because of some sin they'll have committed. If it is not so, then why are they going to be afraid of the Police?" ["Aquí los que tienen miedo es porque algún pecadillo tendrán encima. Si no es así, ¿por que le van a tener miedo a Carabineros?"] (Deichler Guzmán in Politzer 1990, 68).

44 "Algunos dicen que un día tendremos que saber perdonar, yo no estoy de acuerdo con eso. Sí yo supiera quién se llevó a mi hijo, no voy a tomar un arma y lo voy a matar, porque no creo en la pena de muerte, pero no lo perdonaría. Haría que ellos pasaran lo mismo que hemos pasado nosotros, sería capaz de raptarle un hijo—por unos días—para que supiera lo que es sufrir.... Aquí tendrá que haber un juicio para los culpables, pero un juicio sin amnistía para que se castigue a los responsables y esto no vuelva a ocurrir jamás. Eso tendrá que ser cuando vuelva la democracia, cuando éste vuelva a ser un país libre como lo fue años atrás. A mí me gustaría que hubiera un gobierno sin muertes, sin torturas, sin masacres y que pudiéramos ser un país de hermanos" (Elsa Esquivel Rojo, "Desaparecer no es morir" [To Disappear is not to die"] in Politzer 1990, 268).

45 "...en ese momento en que quemé mis libros, quemé todo y borré una etapa" (Andrés Chadwick Piñera "Al gremialisma por la razón" in Politzer 1990, 207).

46 She informs: "For ten years now I am trying to forget what happened to me and I have not been able to do so" ["Hace diez años que estoy tratando de olvidarme de lo que a mí me ocurrió y no he podido"] (Valderas Garrido, "La alcadesa fusilada" ["The Executed Mayor"] in Politzer 1990, 38).

47 "El Señor Jesús dijo que había que perdonar, pero a estos señores que están gobernando yo creo que ni nosotros ni Dios los va a perdonar jamás. Aunque nosotros no los podemos juzgar, yo sé que Dios los va a juzgar y los va a castigar" (Valderas Garrido, "La alcadesa fusilada" ["The Executed Mayor"] in Politzer 1990, 38).

"What is What?" in Historical Fiction

"I had learned a tremendous amount from fictional works, not only about how novelists construed their reality, but also (do I dare to say it?) about the reality itself."

Foley 1986, 16

In his historical novels, the Argentinean writer Tomás Eloy Martínez asks "What is what?" as he challenges our ability to distinguish between truth and fiction in literary narrative, in particular in his latest novel, *Santa Evita*. Eloy Martínez is convinced that this is a challenge indeed. "Historical documents" and "sources" served as a solid foundation for his work of fiction, which resulted in an intricate, elaborate web of "history, biography, and myth" whose separate twines have fused into a multi-leveled yet solid string of narrative. What is truth and what is fiction in this or any literary narrative?, we may ask. At the same time, we should take a moment to contemplate who, indeed, can author a judgment of truth and fiction and what, if anything, can this judgment be based upon?

Historical fiction, a sub-genre of literary fiction, aims at representing a reality that simultaneously is and is not. A form of literary fiction, in which a fictional representation of the human experience is placed into a historical context, historical fiction is, according to Dale Porter, "an elusive child of mixed parents. It claims the right of invention reserved for fiction, it claims, also, to be based on historical reality."[1] In Barbara Foley's words, fiction can be understood as "intrinsically part of a binary opposition" in that "it is what it is by virtue of what it is not."[2] By extension, any attempt to define fiction in opposition to nonfiction would seem to lead us no further than a similarly vague definition.

As we identify perception, experience, knowledge, fact and representation as compositions and challenge the theoretical distinctions between fiction and fact, we also challenge historical references commonly considered factual data. We can distinguish historical fiction from other works of fiction precisely because historical references in the form of data (names, places, dates, etc.), or in the form of the setting, tend to form an integral part of these narratives.

These historical data and setting serve as common denominators: In the form of data they aim at identifying historical events (Holocaust, Pinochet dictatorship); in the form of settings, they attribute historical validity to an experience without pinpointing it to one identifiable event (persecution, torture). Although any number of individuals may perceive a particular point of reference (historical event or experience) differently, in the past, critics have traditionally assigned these points of reference a non-fiction (fact) status even as they are inserted into an explicitly fictional narrative. The traditional genre definition for historical fiction is based upon this assertion in that the distinguishing characteristic of historical fiction is identified as the interplay between fiction and fact within a narrative.

According to Nancy Partner, the differentiation between historical fiction and non-fictional history ought not be approached either from the historical situation, or from the text, but from the claims of the author: Whereas the author of non-fictional history "*claims* the status of objective truth for an account," the author of historical fiction "*claims* the privilege of invention."[3] As the task of assigning a genre is thereby attributed to the author of the text, and the author's claim as well as an individual's understanding of 'objective truth' are subjective in essence, reader reception plays a role. And there the discussion tends to focus on verosimilitud rather than truth.

Whereas the inclusion of historical data may support the notion of a text's historical validity, it is, according to Dale Porter, the text's plausibility that most affects the judgment of a text as historical fiction or nonfictional history. And, as Porter explains, that "question of plausibility arises from the conjuncture of public historical fact with private historical experience."[4] Accordingly, a text would be considered fiction when it seems based on the author's imagination and nonfiction when it is considered to be based on factual information. This emphasis on plausibility and claims offers support to the identification of genre definitions as subjective in essence. Nevertheless, the incorporation of either recognizable data or setting into a text indicates that a strategy of different layers of fiction may be intended and an analysis of these common denominators in the relevance or relation to the development of theme may be warranted.

Oja and Porter argue that through fiction, the author manipulates the representation of history in such a way that it is more entertaining than other texts, such as documentaries. Oja explains: "Fiction intends to engage readers morally and emotionally to a greater degree than nonfiction. A reader can follow non-fiction arguments and re-experience, if not the original events, at least an author's adventure in discovering and recreating them."[5] Moreover, it is assumed that fiction enables the author to enunciate particular characteristics or experiences over others and to represent official history from a point of view of a particular individual or group of individuals.

In taking advantage of the distinguishing characteristic of historical fiction by inventing protagonists and events alongside historical figures and occurrences, the interplay between what is traditionally considered fiction and history can, according to Porter, be construed in such a way that it suggests a particular message or simply makes the text more appealing. "The interplay and tension between what's real and what's invented, what's public and what's personal, what's strange and what's familiar," Porter writes, "have given historical fiction more influence and popularity than either non-fiction or legend."[6] The popularity factor of fiction over nonfiction can be influential in an author's choice of narrative style as an economic consideration.[7] It also may be distinguished as a means to reach out to a larger readership.

The theoretical definition of literature suggests subjective representation, and composition, construction, and consequently fictional discourse suggests a theoretical re-categorization of non-fictional discourse under the rubric of fiction. Nonetheless, the tendency in reader reception is to prefer, in accordance with Oja and Porter, what traditionally has been considered historical fiction over that what traditionally has been considered non-fictional history. This preference would not seem to disappear when both texts are theoretically redefined as composition and, hence, as fiction. Barbara Foley (1986) suggests that historical fiction has been distinguished favorably from non-fictional history based on the argument that "it uses language in a concentrated manner prohibited to nonfiction; it arouses the emotions and liberates consciousness from the constraints of ideology; it carries the reader into another world; it offers none of the commitments of statement and all of the joys of pseudo-statement."[8] In her analysis, Foley turns against this claim arguing that the "hypostatization of elements such as linguistic texture, ontology, and affective response results from a textual fetishism that insists upon fragmenting mimetic communication into its component parts and divesting it of social significance."[9] With the distinction between historical fiction and non-fictional history thus disputed, the readers' tendency to prefer the former to the latter may be more due to marketing techniques than content matter or traditional distinctions. However, they may also be due to the intensity, in which a text and its marketing identify and reinforce the sociopolitical literary agenda.

There has been a tendency in literary criticism to treat a text in isolation (and consequently not consider the range of motives influencing writer or reader favorably toward a particular narrative style, i.e. fiction). Yet Foley explicitly warns against removing the process of writing and reading, and the texts themselves, from their respective (and varying, changing) sociopolitical, cultural, historical, literary environments. She proposes to understand fictional and non-fictional discourses not as "immutable essences" but as "historically varying types of writing, signaled by, and embodied in, changing literary conventions and generated by the changing structures of historically specific relations of production and intercourse."[10] Foley suggests one view historical discourse like Barthes "as saturated in ideology as ... mimetic discourse" but warns against concluding that "historical and mimetic discourse adopt equivalent representational procedures or constitute equivalent modes of cognition."[11] Whereas a complex history of philosophical discourse has established a system of cognitive oppositions "that, in the guise of reflecting transcendent essences, naturalize dominant ideology," Foley argues "all inherited cognitive oppositions are [not] equally ideological and equally fallacious. Some oppositions—between fact and fiction, for instance—

describe very real (and, I believe, necessary) cognitive operations, in which actual historical people engage and have engaged."[12]

Barbara Foley hence proposes a "qualitative approach to defining fictionality"[13] involving a classification of fictional and non-fictional discourses "not in degree but in kind." Since human intelligence, according to contemporary studies in the fields of the social sciences, "characteristically operates in a configurational and—indeed—binary manner," Foley suggests that "[p]articulars must be grasped as functional components in qualitatively defined totalities—and excluded from other possible totalities—if they are to be grasped at all."[14] Rather than subsuming non-fiction into the rubric of fiction, Foley maintains that fictional and non-fictional discourse make qualitatively different use of totalizing frames, at the same time, both fiction and non-fiction depend on these frames so that their meaning(s) can be deduced.[15]

Erving Goffman and others speak of a "primary framework" that is constituted by narrative. They suggest the framework facilitates "its user to locate, perceive, identify and label a seemingly infinite number of concrete occurrences defined in its terms" while the reader "is likely to be unaware of such organized features as the framework has and unable to describe the framework with any completeness if asked."[16] In accordance, a text could be seen as guiding a reader nearly clandestinely toward the derivation of a self-inscribed cognitive meaning, i.e. a meaning predetermined by the author and inscribed into the form, content and structure of the text.

As in the foregoing analysis of the autobiographical *testimonio* and the monological interview, a narrative framework can be seen to include a preface but also not necessarily require one. A narrator's voice can establish a framework for a reading experience, complementary to any other framework intersected in the process of reading. Extra-, intra- and intertextual frameworks may hence influence a reading in complementary but also in harmonious as well as antagonistic manners. Therefore Foley questions the ability of texts to self-determine cognitive meaning and suggests—and I agree with her argument—that facts may not be created by "interpretations if they are bound by them." Any given textual paradigm may only fall short of constituting "innate or transhistorical knowledge."[17] Instead of assigning all cognitive powers to the text, we need to accredit the reader's highly active role in the reading experience.

It is the reader who facilitates the reading experience to emerge within and out of a particular intertextual exchange with a sociopolitical, cultural, linguistic, present and historically changing subjective framework. Constituted by multiple frameworks of intertextuality facilitating distinct interpretations, each reading experience is different, and each reading too. A reader may place any given framework(s) under consideration or even scrutiny based on interplay of a wide arena of private-public frameworks. Consequently, we also need to grant the reader a voice in the determination of fact and fiction in literary representation. Moreover the power over the distinction between these elements may, according to Foley, not be attributed exclusively either to the author (see Nancy Partner), to the reader (see reader reception theory), to the text's exclusive referentiality, nor to a specific socio-linguistic-political, spacio-temporal or cultural environment. Instead the fiction / nonfiction identification of any particular element in and of the narrative may be seen as determined by a contract agreement between writer and reader, a contract that need not be formulated but merely presupposed. Foley explains:

> any given element in a narrative ... must be scanned and interpreted as either fact or fictive in order to be read and understood. There is no specifically linguistic essence of fictionality that is immediately perceptible in the particulars of a text.... The writer assumes that the reader will possess the 'competence' to know how to understand each particular, and that the 'tacit knowledge' undergirding this competence is the knowledge of generic conventions shared by writer and reader alike.... I am arguing, in short, for a definition of mimesis as a contract, wherein writer and reader share an agreement about the conditions under which texts can be composed and comprehended. Even when writers take quantitative steps toward altering the terms of this agreement, they do so in the context of qualitatively defined discursive conventions. And the essence of mimesis—for it has an essence, pace Derrida and company—is that it is a social practice, whereby authors impart cognition of a particular kind to their readers. [18]

In the following analysis of Isabel Allende's *La casa de los espíritus*, I will approach the text by way of an intertextual exchange of different frameworks and reading experience(s). I seek to approximate the complex network of meanings due to author, text, reader and varying sociopolitical, historical environments in the differentiation between fiction and fact in historical fiction, and discuss the relationship / role of the processes of writing and reading and the (re)appropriation of the power of representation.

Unlike Ellie Wiesel, Valdés and Bitar, Isabel Allende does not identify *La casa de los espíritus* as an autobiographical work. Although "it's been said that all first novels are autobiographical," Allende clarifies, "that is not exactly true for me, because I do not take part in it, I am not one of the characters, but I don't deny that I knew some of them and that their passions and pains touched me closely. Some of the anecdotes in those pages I heard from the lips of my mother and grandfather or I read them in my grandmother's journals of her life. I could say that they are part of my family's tradition."[19] The autobiographical element in *La casa de los espíritus* hence consists in the family tradition of writing life journals as modeled by the protagonists Clara and Alba, as well as in the author's personal familiarity with some of the characters and their experiences. An autobiographical element may consequently also be extended toward the role and experience of the reader who may share some of the author's experiences by way of the reading experience.[20]

Allende does not distance herself from the literary world created in *La casa de los espíritus* due to the lack of an explicit autobiographical presence in the novel. Instead, she underlines the text's representativity and contradicts autobiographical constituency in suggesting that in order to speak about the novel, "I should refer to my family and the events in my country."[21] Nonetheless, Allende does not limit this representative constituency to her own native environment. She deliberately refrains from fixing the locus of the narrative to any particular country (such as Chile) because of the many similarities shared across the Latin American continent in spite of much inherent diversity. She cites support for the pluralistic representativity value of the novel, based on a positive autobiographical identification with the characters by a diverse reader community:[22]

> The Truebas could exist in any place on this continent and their turbulent passions, their accumulated and shared sufferings, their victories and their defeats would have been the same. That is true to the extent that I frequently receive correspondence from readers from diverse cities of the continent who manifest

> having identified with those characters and with that story which is similar to their own.[23]

Nonetheless, in the last two chapters *La casa de los espíritus* eventually does turn exclusive and explicit attention toward Chile and it is then that the sociopolitical dimension of *testimonio* comes to dominate the narrative most vividly.

Allende is clearly aware of the discrepancy between Chilean official history and Chilean reality under Pinochet's military Junta. Consequently, she merges the roles of narrator and author, identifying her journalistic activities as primary sources for the denunciation of persecution, torture and death: "Thanks to my work as journalist I found out exactly what was happening in my fatherland, I saw it close up and those tortured dead, widows and orphans, left non-erasable imprints in my memory. The last chapters of *La casa de los espíritus* tell those events. I based myself on what my eyes say and on the direct testimony of those who saw the brutal experience of the repression."[24] The sociopolitical function of this denunciation is directed primarily toward the Chilean community to bridge the abyss from official representation to a representation of Chilean reality. Whereas outside of Chile "it is enough … to read the international media to learn the details,"[25] within the national boundaries truth is censored "because the control of the public opinion is indispensable"[26] for the dictatorship.

Allende did not experience torture and persecution first hand; nonetheless, she acknowledges a period of trauma due to the witnessing of human rights violations under Pinochet but also due to closing the door on family, friends and homeland by moving into voluntary exile. The writing process served her to rebuild the bridge from the past to the present. It enabled her to rescue memories from the world of oblivion to her own attention, that of Chile, the Latin American continent and other international communities: "I thought that if I would put into writing what I wanted to rescue from forgetting, I could reconstruct the lost world, resuscitate the dead, reunite the dispersed, detain the memories for ever and make them mine. Then nobody could take them away from me. … I remembered the words of my old journalist friend: tell the truth. I wanted to speak of my people's suffering and that of other people on this tormented continent, so that the truth would touch my readers' heart."[27] Surely the dead may not find representation even in this novel, nor can life be returned to those from whom it was taken.

Nevertheless, the text does convey a pluralistic approach toward the life experience through a polyphony of voices. According to the narrator, the principal foundation to the story is provided by Clara's life journal, in which she initially recorded only important and later also trivial events and observations.[28] Clara's granddaughter Alba serves in the role of narrator, compiler and commentator. She recounts the generations of life experiences in the presumptuous voice of a third person omniscient narrator who overrides the journal's (presumed) autobiographical "I," changing it into a distant "she." This distancing serves to enunciate the separation of the narrative and its precursor; although the journal is established as a primary text, the narrative absorbs it, modifies and outgrows it. Despite a brief self-reference in the form of a first person indirect object and a possessive adjective in the opening paragraph, the narrator does not reveal her identity at this point. Alba approximates the role of a rhetorical narrator who, "situated outside of the story," according to Lubomír Dolezel's definition, "assumes the functions of representation and interpretation but not those of action, so that [she] can appear in the narrative as a protagonist but always unfolded in a [she]."[29]

Although Alba enters the story as a protagonist in Chapter IX, entitled "The Child Alba,"[30] the narrator and the protagonist Alba do not merge voices until the "Epigraph"[31] when she concludes the narrative from the point of view of an autobiographical "I." This singular voice sets a sharp contrast to the polyphony of voices pronounced throughout the preceding narrative. It enhances the division between the fourteen chapters and the "Epilogue" established in the index by this name only rather than as a chapter in sequence.[32] Prior to the "Epigraph," the third person narrative is routinely interrupted by short subchapters,[33] in which Alba's grandfather Esteban Trueba provides an autobiographical insight into experiences he considers relevant and decisive in the development of family events and the course of their destiny.[34]

As narrator, Trueba serves, in part,[35] the role of counter balancing the point of view of the unimposing[36] narrator constituted by Alba. It is Alba's unimposing attitude as narrator, which permits her role to resonate with the attributes corresponding to a rhetorical narrator. Yet I suggest she merely approximates these characteristics, because I do identify Alba as a rhetorical narrator who participates in the action, not in the form of a visual protagonist but in the form of an intermediary. This is where my reading is different from that of Mario Rojas. The narrative suggests that Trueba constructed his contributions parallel to Alba's rewriting of Clara's journal; protagonist-narrator Alba also suggests that Esteban Trueba and Clara assisted her in the writing process, yet it is her narrative that surpasses and encompasses all. The "Epilogue" meets the present tense timeline of the moment of narration, the grandfather rests, "sailing the tranquil waters[37], smiling and calm, while I write at the blond wooden table that belonged to my grandmother."[38] Yet it also catches us, who have come to mistake the narrator as an omnipotent anonymous entity, somewhat off balance. Prior to the "Epilogue" the narrative meets the neutral point of the timeline of narration only twice: once in the very first lines of the text and once more in Chapter IV.[39] The hundreds of pages that lie in between carefully shield the narrator's presence and the present tense.

The "Epilogue" brings the polyphony of voices together and also the times, the past the present and the future. It concludes the narrative and hands it over the reader, suggesting, at the very least, a turning of pages back to the beginning to continue the sentence that links the last to the first and to reinitiate the process of reading, which will, like any other reading, never be quite the same as the first. It is in the "Epilogue" that we come to understand and appreciate the intertextuality and polyphony of voices that constitute the text: Alba's roles as third person narrator (chapters 1–14), protagonist (birth until torture chambers, chapters 9–14), and first person narrator-protagonist (concentration camp survivor); Esteban Trueba as third person protagonist and first person protagonist-narrator (issuing a retrospective account and commentary), and Clara as protagonist and author of the primary text that is reconstituted by the narrative, as well as spirit-protagonist and narrative collaborator. With the tripartite identification of Alba reinforced through the "Epilogue," a second reading will reveal, at the very least, a continuous presence of Alba as intermediary between differences, times and people. The story comprises more than just this family's share of history, it stands out as a testimony, representative of a larger experience, it stands out as an attempt to mediate between ignorance and knowledge, across cultures and across times.

Marcelo Coddou characterizes Isabel Allende's novel *La casa de los espíritus* as a transgressive work due to the sociopolitical criticism it issues "against an official version of history which wants to be considered unitarian" in the intent "to transform, at the level of language, the social conscience."[40] According to Coddou, this literary work

> offers neither any adjustment nor harmony with the discourse about the world and History that is imposed by the sectors who hold the power over the environment that it refers to and that now lacks the transgressions that the novel exerts upon it. What is important to underline is that it is a non fictitious code, which rejects the established discourse at a level that we can call political-philosophical—that assumes an ideological body as the 'fictitious' of the text, both in an unmarked relationship.[41]

Coddou thus points out several issues of interest to this analysis. The sociopolitical function of a literary work, a feature otherwise attributed to the genre of *testimonio*, is here identified in a work of historical fiction. The text strongly denounces an oppressive sociopolitical environment in which traditional means of representation do not surface and are not accessible. Its female protagonist Alba is urged to make use of resources that no one can take away or censor: "Clara brought her the life-saving idea to write with her thought, without pencil nor paper, to keep the mind busy, to escape the cell and to live."[42] Thought is here empowered by a dual capacity.

On the one hand, thought facilitates the victim to transcend the physical world of torture, to leave the present behind and retreat into the past constituted by the memories of her experience. Her mental universe thereby serves as a medium for survival; it constructs or constitutes a world, to which she can retreat when the real world fails her. At the same time, this realm of memories also serves to transmit a world of experiences that is silenced and denied by official history. Thought may host the representation of that what some people do not wish to confront. It may thereby assume the function of providing a safe haven in which the groundwork necessary for instigating the process of transforming social conscience may be laid. Consequently, Clara suggests Alba channel her strength toward her mental powers and

> write a testimony that some day may serve to expose the terrible secret that she was living, so that the world would learn of the horror that was occurring parallel to the pleasant and ordered existence of those who did not want to know, who could live the illusion of a normal life, who could deny that they were on a raft in a sea of tears, ignoring, in spite of all, the evidence, that at a few blocks distance from their happy world were the others who survive or die in the dark.[43]

A mental testimony denouncing official history[44] and exposing the real, is here established as a precursor for the literary testimony constituted by the novel. It is based on the presumption that the differentiation between fiction and non-fiction determining the reading experience resonates with the mimetic contract issued by the writer, as suggested by Foley. The function of Alba's mental testimony, like Clara's life journal and Alba's rewriting of this life journal, is "to rescue the memory of the past and to survive the horror," "to see the things in their real dimension and make fun of bad memory" because "by assigning a name to the problems these materialize and it is no longer possible to ignore them."[45]

Yet there is a decisive difference in how grandmother and granddaughter confront life and problems. Clara deliberately refrains from assigning names to problems in public and thereby avoids having to confront them publicly as well. At any given problematic circumstance in her life, Clara retreats from the critical world by elevating herself into the fantastic realm governed by her mental powers alone. However, this retreat does not imply that she ignores the problems; rather, she appears to address them, and thereby confront them, in her private journal. When Alba is imprisoned in solitary confinement, Clara suggests that Alba engage in the same behavior that in her own life repeatedly enabled her to survive her own horrors. In retreating into her mental universe, Alba does not physically depart from her torture cell, nor does she protect her physical health. She does, however, confront the problems mentally, forcing herself not to ignore but to deal with them. Her mental arena allows her to work herself through her experiences and suffering and to come to understand their relations.

Clara's journal and Alba's testimony bear fruit in that they assist their creators' survival. The difference lies in Alba taking to heart Clara's suggestion to write testimony. Whereas both Clara and Alba address problems in the private sphere (journal and thought, respectively), it is

Alba who enables these testimonies to transcend into the public sphere. In integrating Clara's, Esteban's and her own testimony into one representation, she articulates problems that hence may no longer be ignored. She exposes dichotomous representations of reality without mediating between them. Thereby she confronts the reader with the task of deriving their underlying relationships, to see the real dimensions and to construct a future, in which such history does not repeat itself. Given that the imaginary world constructed by Clara and Alba to survive their horror dominates the narrative, this imaginary world must be seen, in accordance with Coddou, as a "metaphorical substitute for reality."[46]

Esteban's testimony often contradicts the primary text constituted by Alba. It silences the terror he embodied, the crimes he enacted and the suffering he produced. Yet the contradictory representations enhance rather than diminish the testimonial effect of the narrative. The discrepancies in the opposing testimonies are limited to the depiction of Esteban's criminal activities. His voice, aggressive arrogance and attitude resonate in his autobiographical testimony. Her story, in contrast, is the story of the victim who, in solitary confinement when her physical resources have lost the power to relieve her pain, takes refuge in the vast metaphysical arena of thought and memory. And it is there that she witnesses, as prophesized by Clara, that once a problem is named it materializes and cannot be ignored: by pinpointing the very first of her thoughts, Alba spurs the eruption of a volcano filled with testimonies of a near century of injustice, crimes and denial. Alba's story is constituted by her own voice, by Clara's, and by that of "the characters of her story, who entered overhasty and enveloped her in their anecdotes of their vices and virtues, crushing her documentary objectives and throwing her testimony onto the ground, beleaguering her, demanding from her and urging her."[47]

Yet Alba stands her ground; the time has come for the story to be told. Urgency governs her testimony, the story is hers, yet it is also fed by her characters' anecdotes. The question is who are they, these characters who intrude into Alba's mental haven. Could they be the voices that provide steady opposition to the patriarch's autobiography, which contradict his make-believe and false pretense, his denial and abuse? Or are these the voices, which belong to her torturers, in particular to Esteban García, her grandfather's illegitimate grandson. Alba does not elaborate further on these characters, yet the testimony of her torture and imprisonment is kept well on target; it neither wavers from its determination nor brooks any interference.

Rather than becoming anecdotes of vices and virtues, Alba's testimony of the inhumane suffering inflicted upon her at the hands of her torturers joins the testimonies represented throughout the book as merely one further chapter of "The Hour of Truth." It joins them also as one further voice that is absorbed, among many others, by the narrator's voice. From the hidden presence of the all-knowing narrator, these voices and testimonies join forces in the battle against official history and the lack of social conscience. Only when the reader heeds the writer's mimetic postulate and understands the testimony as a non-fiction work, i.e. only when the reader understands the imaginary, which dominates the text, as a "metaphorical substitute for reality," may the text assume the function of a sociopolitical literary tool aimed at (trans)forming social conscience.

Close reading of the Clara's suggestion[48] to Alba will reveal the interplay of tenses, past and present. This interplay assigns the testimony not only historical but contemporary validity, as well as a sense of futuristic (conditional) positivism (that may be considered, to a certain extent, typical of Allende's writing). The employment of the Spanish conditional tense of the verb *poder*, which translates into the English "may" (my translation), "could," or "would be able to," serves to enunciate the hypothetical function Clara attributes to testimony, i.e. the denunciation and exposing of a silenced reality. This conditional function is directed toward a readership that, in past progressive or imperfect tense—parallel to the past tense time line of narration—, which chose to remain ignorant of the suffering and death occurring on its side at the time of Alba's torture. However, the sociopolitical urgency entailed in the testimony finds added emphasis in the shift to the present tense antagonistic reality of those who "survive or die." This tense spells out the sociopolitical objective that, by heeding the sociopolitical purpose of Alba's *testimonio* in a timely fashion, readership may succeed to intervene in favor of the victims of the regime.

This futuristic positivism enunciated in *La casa de los espíritus* but also in *De amor y de sombra* finds an echo in Allende's own attitude toward society: "I have great faith in the capacity of mankind to construct a better future. I think we are advancing toward a wonderful goal, distant and difficult to reach, but we are heading there. I don't think society is going to self-destruct, that we are walking in bad circles, that the cycle of history repeats forever. I think it is a spiral that rises."[49] As Clara explains, problems named can no longer be ignored. When social conscience (trans)forms as a result of problems being named in *La casa de los espíritus*, then Alba / Allende's objective seem one step closer to realization.

Having survived the worst of her torture at the hands of Esteban García, Alba is transferred to a concentration camp for women. There her best friend inspires her to write her story, to tell of her experiences, which are identical and representative of those of so many others: "If you want I'll tell you my case so that you can write it," her co-inmates tell her, "laughing and jokingly complaining that all cases were the same and that it was better to write a love story because they are liked by everybody."[50] Pluralistic representation value, a key component in *testimonio*, finds articulation in this novel through protagonist prisoners who ought be taken as real figures. In this autobiographical "Epilogue," Alba carries out the role of informant who, like Menchú, presents her autobiographical experiences as representative of those of a larger population. Alba exceeds this function in issuing her representation without the intervention of an intermediary. Indeed, it is she who serves as intermediary between reader and family history, as well as between Clara's life journal and Esteban's autobiographical narrative. Alba credits Clara's journal with an intermediary function in facilitating communication between events of the past and the experience of the present; she also credits Clara's spirit with illuminating the dark spots of life and humanity, making it possible for life to sprout where death and torture govern. Likewise, we may credit Alba for opening the door of textual representation and mediating between the different voices that cry out to us today and yesterday.

Whereas the sociopolitical purpose of Allende's writings is not as explicitly directed toward promoting change as the testimonial works by Valdés, Bitar and others, Allende nevertheless specifies her objective as conveying her truth about Latin American society and reality, in particular, about Chile. Juan Manuel Marcos and Teresa Méndez-Faith link Allende to a group of post boom writers called "contestors of power,"[51] according to Angel Rama. These writers not only protest against twentieth century oppressive systems of power in Latin America but also "share a search for the appropriate means to integrate history in fiction … with an interrogatory and dialectic attitude aimed at understanding the actual problematic of the present conflictive reality."[52]

Indeed, Alba's narrative is proceeded by a reading process that reminds us of Elie Wiesel's extensive reading engagement prior to formulating his own narrative. Like Wiesel who is still trying to "understand what happened," narrator-protagonist Alba approaches the construction of her narrative like the assembling of a complex puzzle, whose dispersed pieces must be examined and arranged carefully to obtain meaning and purpose: "In the prison cell, I had the idea of constructing a puzzle, in which each piece has a specific orientation. Before arranging them all, it seemed incomprehensible, but I was certain that if I managed to complete the work, it would give each a meaning and the result would be harmonious. Every piece has a reason for being just as it is…."[53] Yet the justification Alba attributes to each event is not suggested to determine the development and direction of a life's path nor to serve as an excuse or justification for the crimes enacted. Instead, Alba presents the significance in each event as of cognitive relevance. Precisely to avoid the repetition of history, each event and interrelation must be comprehended in its "true dimension" so that humanity may advance in its spiral path.

Intertextuality forms the basis of this narrative. It is shaped "with the help of my grandfather whose memory remained intact until the last moment of his ninety years," with the memory engraved into her thoughts while in prison, with the assistance of the old albums and … a heap of pictures," with "Clara's notebooks, my mother's letters, the administrative books from Las Tres Marías and so many other documents that are now on the table and within reach." [54] This narrator-protagonist not only looks at the writings of others, in her efforts to deduce meaning from history she also studies her own notes on significant and insignificant events and experiences. Yet *La casa de los espíri-*

tus is not just a text that "has first been read and written afterwards," a text, as Juan Manuel Marcos and Teresa Méndez-Faith suggest, written by an author who "instead of saying and writing new things has done nothing more than copy faithfully what others have already said and composed."[55] On the contrary, *La casa de los espíritus* is a text that entails and promotes a continuous process of reading and writing, rereading and rewriting, a text whose meaning changes from the moment it was first written to the moment it is read by one and then by another:

> Sometimes I feel like I have already lived this and written these same words, but I understand that it is not I but a different woman who wrote in her notebooks so that I could use them. I write, she wrote, that memory is fragile and the course of a life is very short and occurs at great pace, so that we don't get to see the relation between events, we can't measure the consequences of actions, we believe in the fiction of time, in the present, the past and the future, but it can also be that everything happens simultaneously like the three sisters Mora said, who were able to see the spirits of all ages in space. That's why my grandmother Clara wrote in her notebooks to see things in their real dimension and to escape poor memory.[56]

It is in and through text that the present, the past and the future can merge and join forces. Alba writes, yet in having written, the text is no longer hers. It tells of memories, experiences and events, its purpose lies in facilitating meaning to those who seek it: to the author who takes a step back and looks at her words, to the reader, to us. The memories Alba formulates in *La casa de los espíritus* are hers and, at the same time, they are Allende's and ours. In entering the mimetic contract we may share these memories, learn of people's torments and suffering and deduce meaning from them. Indeed, we may allow ourselves to be touched by the experiences portrayed and the knowledge we obtain. We may feel inspired to participate in the struggle to move humanity one step further on the eternal spiral toward peace,[57] to turn, once again, to the first page and acquire the knowledge that can serve us to prevent history from repeating itself. To remain active, to read and to write, like Alba, not hatred and fear but life and for life:

> I want to think that my craft is life and that my mission is not to extend hatred but only to fill these pages while I await Miguel's return, while I bury my grandfather who now rests at my side in this room, while I wait for better times

> to come, carrying to term the child I hold in my womb, daughter of so many rapes, or perhaps Miguel's daughter, but, above all, my daughter.[58]

Waiting, so patiently, it seems as if Alba's role in reading and writing were void of real action indeed. Yet it is this activity, which generates text, perception, thought and understanding, and which, as such, generates the basis for change: "The epilogue concludes with what turns out to be the generating moment of the text, not the last but the first phrase of the novel."[59] The "Epilogue" serves not, as the title suggests, as a conclusion or afterword, nor, in accordance with its location, as the last of many chapters. Instead it may be read as the opening chapter of a new book, in which we are to contribute and participate, a book that can grow out of an understanding and conception of reality that does not silence the silenced but pronounces that which official history does not, a book in which traditional fact is turned into fiction and fiction may emerge as fact, a book that is built not on a concept of charity but on a call for justice.[60]

NOTES

1 Porter 1993, 315.
2 Foley 1986, 28.
3 Porter 1993, 316.
4 Porter 1993, 318.
5 Oja cited in Porter 1993, 339.
6 Porter 1993, 346.
7 At least in modern times it has been possible for some authors of popular fiction to sustain themselves economically by their work. Consequently the economic advantage entailed in choosing a popular form of narration over a not so popular one may well influence an author's choice of narration.
8 Foley 1986, 42.
9 Foley 1986, 43.
10 Foley 1986, 27.
11 Foley 1986, 35.
12 Foley 1986, 35.
13 See Foley's analysis of arguments against a qualitative approach in Foley 1986, 28–35.
14 Foley 1986, 40.
15 In this argument, Foley draws support from "most twentieth-century theories of cognition—in fields from psychology to the philosophy of science to linguistics—[who] have found it necessary to postulate that the human mind characteristically uses polarity as an essential device in gaining understanding. Any given particular must be understood as part of a larger scheme, these theories tell us, if it is to be

considered at all." Applied to the context of "defining fictionality" the argument hence reads that "the genres of fictional discourse engage informing paradigms qualitatively different from those of the various genres of nonfictional discourse, and even a presumably verifiable fact must be framed and contextualized before its signification can be determined" (Foley 1986, 36).

16 Goffman 1976, 21 in Foley 1986, 37.

17 Foley 1986, 39.

18 Foley 1986, 40–1.

19 "Dicen que toda primera novela es autobiográfica.... En mi caso no es exactamente así, porque no figuro en ella, no soy ninguno de sus personajes, pero no niego que a varios de ellos los conocí y que sus pasiones y dolores me tocaron de cerca. Algunas anécdotas de esas páginas las escuché de labios de mi madre y mi abuelo o las leí en los cuadernos de anotar la vida de mi abuela. Podría decir que conforman una tradición en mi familia" (Allende 1986, 15).

20 René Campos assigns the reader an even more active participation in the narrative. According to Campos, the reader approximates Alba's role not only in observing and re-experiencing the life experiences presented but also in approximating the role of a narrator or writer, constructing the text parallel to Alba. Campos sees Alba's rewriting of Clara's life journal as "the parallel operation to a reader who writes him/herself into or onto the text" [la operación paralela de un lector que (se) escribe en / sobre el texto"] (Campos 1986, 21).

21 "Para hablar de ella, debo referirme a mi familia y a los acontecimientos de mi país" (Allende 1986, 16).

22 Nonetheless, the majority of critics maintain that the location references, which Allende perceives as vague and non-implicit, may easily be identified as the author's native country. See Marcos 1986, 62.

23 "Los Trueba podrían existir en cualquier lugar del continente y sus turbulentas pasiones, sus sufrimientos acumulados y compartidos, sus victorias y sus derrotas habrían sido las mismas. Tanto es así, que con frecuencia recibo cartas de lectores de diversas ciudades del

continente, que manifiestan haberse identificado con esos personajes y con esa historia, que es similar a la suya" (Allende 1986, 17).

24 "Gracias a mi trabajo de periodista supe exactamente lo que sucedía en mi patria, lo viví de cerca y esos muertos torturados, viudas y huérfanos, dejaron huellas imborrables en mi memoria. Los últimos capítulos de *La casa de los espíritus* relatan esos acontecimientos. Me basé en lo que vieron mis ojos y en los testimonios directos de quienes vivieron la brutal experiencia de la represión" (Allende 1986, 18).

25 "Basta en el extranjero, con leer la prensa internacional para conocer los detalles" (Allende 1986, 18).

26 "...porque el control de la opinión pública es indispensable para ella" (Allende 1986, 18).

27 "Pensé que si ponía por escrito lo que deseaba rescatar del olvido, podría reconstruir el mundo perdido, resucitar a los muertos, reunir a los dispersos, aprisionar para siempre los recuerdos y hacerlos míos. Ya nadie me los podría quitar. ... Recordé las palabras de mi viejo amigo periodista: decir la verdad. Deseaba hablar del sufrimiento de mi pueblo y de otros pueblos de ese atormentado continente, para que la verdad tocara el corazón de mis lectores" (Allende 1986, 18–9).

28 The narrator explains in the book's opening paragraph: "Even then [the girl Clara] already had the habit of writing the important things and later, when she was mute, se also wrote the trivial, without suspecting that, fifty years later, her notebooks would serve me to rescue the memory of the past and to survive my own horror." "Ya entonces [la niña Clara] tenía el hábito de escribir las cosas importantes y más tarde, cuando se quedó muda, escribía también las trivialidades, sin sospechar que cincuenta años después, sus cuadernos me servirían para rescatar la memoria del pasado y para sobrevivir a mi propio espanto" (Allende 1982, 1987, 11).

29 "situado fuera de la historia asume las funciones de representación e interpretación pero no la de acción, de tal manera que puede aparecer en la narración como personaje pero siempre desdoblado en un él" (Rojas 1986, 89 with reference to Dolezel 1973).

30 "La niña Alba."

31 "Epílogo."

32 The index lists fourteen chapters numbered in order and titled in accordance with each section's central focus. In contrast, the epilogue is not identified as the last of the chapter sequence; it is listed only under the title "Epilogue."

33 Pages 27–30, 36–40, 100–105, 153–157, 174–178, 249–256, 259–260, 266–270, 317–320, 351–356 Allende 1982, 1987.

34 In accordance, protagonist and narrator Esteban Trueba explains his decision to include a visit to a brothel: "I would not have mentioned this episode if Tránsito Soto had not played such an important role for me much later because, as I already said, I am not a man of prostitutes. But this story could not have been written if she had not intervened to save us and to save, in passing, our memories." ["No habría mencionado este episodio si Tránsito Soto no hubiera jugado un papel tan importante para mí mucho tiempo después, porque, como ya dije, no soy hombre de prostitutas. Pero esta historia no habría podido escribirse si ella no hubiera intervenido para salvarnos y salvar, de paso, nuestros recuerdos"] (Allende 1982, 1987, 105).

35 I say "in part" because his words constitute only little more than ten percent of the narrative.

36 I utilize the adjective "unimposing" ironically because the narrator hides (rather than elaborates on) her identity, her consciousness, and her role in the process of narrative construction from the reader's eyes until the "Epilogue."

37 This is a metaphoric reference to Clara's bed.

38 "...tendido en el velero del agua mansa, sonriente y tranquilo, mientras yo escribo sobre la mesa de madera rubia que era de mi abuela" (Allende 1982, 1987, 357).

39 Explaining the lack of information in Clara's diaries regarding aspects of her twin brothers' adolescence, the narrator writes: "... Clara never found out about this, so that she could include it in her notebooks so that *I* would read it one day. *I* learned about it otherwise" ["... Clara nunca lo supo, de modo que no pudo anotarlo en

sus cuadernos para que yo lo leyera algún día. Me enteré por otros conductos."] Allende 1982, 1987.

40 "...disuena frente a la versión oficial, que se quisiera única;" "asume el rol de transformar, en el nivel del lenguaje, la conciencia social" (Coddou 1986, 9).

41 "...no ofrece ajuste ni armonía algunos con el discurso sobre el mundo y la Historia impuestos por los sectores que detentan al poder en el ámbito al que remite y que padece ahora las transgresiones que la novela sobre él ejerce. Lo importante de ser subrayado es que es desde un código no ficticio aquel que rechaza en un nivel que podemos llamar político-filosófico el discurso establecido—que se da cuerpo ideológico a lo 'ficticio' del texto, ambos en relación indeslinable" (Coddou 1986, 9).

42 "Clara trajo la idea salvadora de escribir con el pensamiento, sin lápiz ni papel, para mantener la mente ocupada, evadirse de la perrera y vivir" (Allende 1982, 1987, 350).

43 "que escribiera un testimonio que algún día podría servir para sacar a la luz el terrible secreto que estaba viviendo, para que el mundo se enterara del horror que ocurría paralelamente a la existencia apacible y ordenada de los que no querían saber, de los que podían tener la ilusión de una vida normal, de los que podían negar que iban a flote en una balsa sobre un mar de lamentos, ignorando, a pesar de todas las evidencias, que a pocas cuadras de su mundo feliz estaban los otros, los que sobreviven o mueren en el lado oscuro" (Allende 1982, 1987, 350).

44 It should be noted that *La casa de los espíritus* does not issue only an alternative representation of official history under the dictatorship but, as discussed by René Campos, also pronounces a "voice against the official vision of facts imposed by the conservative paradigm" ["contra-voz frente a la visión oficial de los hechos impuesta por el paradigma conservador"] prior to the Allende government. See Campos 1986, 22–8.

45 "rescatar la memoria del pasado y para sobrevivir el espanto" (Allende 1982, 1987, 11); "para ver las cosas en su dimensión real y

para burlar la mala memoria" (365); "al poner nombre a los problemas, estos se materializan y ya no es posible ignorarlos" (147).

46 "un sustituto metafórico de la realidad" (Coddou 1986, 14).

47 "los personajes de su historia, que entraron atropellándose y la envolvieron en sus anécdotas en sus vicios y virtudes, aplastando sus propósitos documentales y echando por tierra su testimonio, atosigándola exigiéndole, apurándola..." (Allende 1982, 1987, 350).

48 Allende 1982, 1987, 350.

49 "Tengo una gran fe en la capacidad del hombre y la mujer para construir un futuro mejor. Creo que avanzamos hacia una meta maravillosa, lejana y difícil de acceder, pero para allá vamos. No creo que la humanidad se vaya a autodestruir, que caminemos en círculos malditos, que el ciclo de la historia se repita incansablemente. Creo que es una espiral que sube" (Allende Sept. 6, 1983 quoted from Coddou 1986, 12).

50 "'si quieres te cuento mi caso, para que lo escribas,' me decían se reían, se burlaban alegando que todos los casos eran iguales y que era mejor escribir cuentos de amor, porque eso gusta a todo el mundo" (Allende 1982, 1987, 360).

51 "los contestatarios del poder" (Marcos 1986, 61).

52 "los une una comun búsqueda de los medios apropiados para integrar la historia a la ficción ... con una actitud cuestionante y dialéctica destinada a la comprensión de la problemática actual, de la conflictiva realidad presente" (Marcos 1986, 62).

53 "En la perrera tuve la idea de que estaba armando un reompecabezas en el que cada pieza tiene una ubicación precisa. Antes de colocarlas todas, me parecía incomprensible, pero estaba segura que si lograba terminarlo, daría un sentido a cada una y el resultado sería armonioso. Cada pieza tiene una razón de ser tal como es..." (Allende 1982, 1987, 364).

54 "con la ayuda de mi abuelo, cuya memoria permaneció intacta hasta el último instante de sus noventa años" (364), "los viejos álbums y ... un montón de retratos" (364), "los cuadernos de Clara, las cartas de mi madre, los libros de administración de Las Tres Marías y tan-

tos otros documentos que ahora estan sobre la mesa al alcance de la mano" (Allende 1982, 1987, 365).

55 "...ha sido leído primero y escrito después. En lugar de decir y escribir cosa nueva, no ha hecho nada más que copiar fielmente lo ya dicho y compuesto por otros" (Roa Bastos 1974, 467, quoted and applied to Allende's text by Marcos and Méndez-Faith in Marcos 1986, 65).

56 "En algunos momentos tengo la sensación de que esto ya lo he vivido y que he escrito estas mismas palabras, pero comprendo que no soy yo, sino otra mujer, que anotó en sus cuadernos para que yo me sirviera de ellos. Escribo, ella escribió, que la memoria es frágil y el transcurso de una vida es muy breve y sucede todo tan de prisa, que no alcanzamos a ver la relación entre los acontecimientos, no podemos medir la consecuencia de los actos, creemos en la ficción del tiempo, en el presente, el pasado y el futuro, pero puede ser también que todo ocurre simultáneamente, como decían las tras tres hermanas Mora, que eran capaces de ver en el espacio los espíritus de todas las épocas. Por eso mi abuela Clara escribía en sus cuadernos, para ver las cosas en su dimensión real y para burlar a la mala memoria" (Allende 1982, 1987, 365).

57 Rather than viewing history as an eternal repetition of events, in accordance with Allende's own notion of history, the past is seen as constituting a spiral chain of events. In it each event builds and links up with another as in an infinite number of stepping stools organized not necessarily chronologically but contextually. Clara's journals may serve to exemplify the importance of the content of the event over the time of the event. Shortly before her death, she bound the notebooks with colored ribbons, separating them by event and not by chronological order because the only thing she had forgotten to include in them were the dates and in the hurry of her last hour she decided she could not lose time guessing them" ["Los ató con cintas de colores, separándolos por acontecimientos y no por orden cronológico porque lo único que se había olvidado de poner en ellos eran las fechas y en la prisa de su última hora decidió que no podía perder tiempo averiguándolas"] (Allende 1982, 1987, 245).

58 "Quiero pensar que mi oficio es la vida y que mi misión no es prolongar el odio, sino sólo llenar estás páginas mientras espero el regreso de Miguel, mientras entierro a mi abuelo que ahora descansa a mi lado en este cuarto, mientras aguardo que lleguen tiempos mejores, gestando a la criatura que tengo en el vientre, hija de tantas violaciones, o tal vez hija de Miguel, pero sobre todo hija mía" (Allende 1982, 1987, 365).

59 "Dicho epílogo concluye con lo que resulta ser el instante generador del texto, no la última sino la primera frase de la novela" (Marcos 1986, 66).

60 As Clara explained to Blanca, the poor "don't need charity but justice" "No necesitan caridad, sino justicia" (Allende 1982, 1987, 119).

CLOSURE?

In defining *testimonio* we have to recognize considerable diversity and plurality in the experience, the process of remembering, representation, narrative style and strategy, and, finally, sociopolitical implication. The preceding study shows *testimonio* as a signifier for a developing rather than a fixed literary practice. It demonstrates the need to modify the genre definition to approximate better the literary body to which it refers; delineation for the genre must focus, above all, on this literature's socio-political dimension.

Authoritarian regimes and, specifically, Pinochet's military rule, give rise to contradictory truth paradigms. In Chile, the dominant form of representation is issued in the form of official history, which remains sympathetic to the dictatorship. Its truth paradigm is challenged by alternative history, which denounces human rights violations, oppression and repression under the dictatorship. This alternative representation is the focal point of this study. It assesses Chilean alternative history as a form of *testimonio* and, at the same time, reviews the genre delineation for *testimonio* in its applicability to the Chilean literary practice.

The analysis of Chilean alternative representation of Pinochet's dictatorship and its consequences manifests that official (or regime sympathetic) and alternative representation assign equal authenticity and representation value to contradictory informing truths of a common socio-political historical experience. The fact established by the former is challenged by the latter. In instigating this challenge, *testimonio* brings into question the traditional understanding of fiction and fact in representation of oppressive regimes of power. Traditionally, *testimonio* and official history have been distinguished as non-fictional representations. The investigation demonstrates, however, that in challenging the truth claim of official history, *testimonio* also challenges our concept of historiography. By acknowledging the subjectivity and composite nature of experience, perception, reason, knowledge and representation, we can approach the distinction between fictional and non-fictional discourses and between fiction and fact in literary representation of history as a narrative strategy and tool. The distinction between fiction and fact corresponds to a denial of experience versus a denunciation of such a denial, or a silencing of experience when literature is commissioned to represent a society at a time when victims and perpetrators undergo a dichotomous sociopolitical experience.

In the Chilean context, the relationship between official and alternative history mirrors the antagonistic relationship shared by perpetrator and victim. Their representations clash, manifesting the abyss that separates the "truth" of one from that of another and also the abyss that distances the underlying sociopolitical objective of the former from that of the latter. Official and alternative histories constitute sociopolitical literary tools that emanate out of distinct sociopolitical urgencies and steer toward different goals.

Authoritarian rule determines official history; it strives to maintain political dominance and its control over representation. The narrative voice in dictatorship sympathetic discourse emphasizes neither its own nor another's subjectivity. It claims to represent truth; it does not propose a dialogic discourse on history; it does not openly link its truth claims to a sociopolitical objective. Instead, it completely undermines its literary constituency. Official history does not perform these narrative strategies because they would weaken the veracity claim assigned to it by the ruling voice. By undermining its literary constituency and promoting unquestioned adoption of the ruling sociopolitical paradigm as the only valid, truthful constitution of external referents, official history guards against alternative representation.

The study identifies *testimonio* as a contestant to this application of official history under authoritarian rule. In contrast to official history, *testimonio* emphasizes its literary constituency, addresses its subjectivity, initiates a dialogic discourse on history and identifies a sociopolitical, literary objective. *Testimonio* performs these narrative strategies in order to challenge the truth paradigm of the ruling voice and to demonstrate its own paradigm and discourse as superior and more truthful than that of the former. *Testimonio* utilizes the narrative tools and strategies which official discourse undermines and silences in order beat the former at its own game and to re-appropriate the power of representation that official history has reserved for itself.

The question arises of what happens to *testimonio* the moment that the sociopolitical purpose of provoking change is obliterated. The research provides only a partial answer to this question. In the Chilean sociopolitical context, the dictatorship has come to an end, but investigation shows that the dictatorship alone does not comprise the sole focal point of Chilean *testimonio*. The *testimonios* discussed in this study constitute a literature of trauma that represents the dictatorship experience as traumatic by nature, and that provides evidence that trauma maintains continuing impact upon survivors' experiences and their memory construction. This literature affirms that the trauma did not dissolve with the change to a democratic form of government in 1989. It addresses the problematic condition of Chilean society today, which is divided into victims of the regime and perpetrators or others, sympathetic to the dictatorship. Chile has yet to acknowledge the crimes committed under military rule; it has also yet to acknowledge the trauma and suffering that victims faced and that survivors continue to perceive.

In Chile, *testimonio* continues to provide an alternative representation to dictatorship representation. It raises awareness of human rights infractions and thereby affects the formation of a social conscience. In particular, in addressing the need to come to terms with the past on an individual and also a communal basis, Chilean *testimonio* reinforces the immediacy, if not temporal simultaneity that links it to the sociopolitical event and condition that it condemns and seeks to change. It establishes a counterbalance to official history and maintains its sociopolitical purpose and relevance for as long as the antagonistic relationship prevails.

We can see this *testimonio* as an actual participant and activist in the struggle which it represents, and we can see that it constitutes, in accordance with Cavallari, "simultaneously a 'message' and a 'model' of resistance against fascist violence."[1] The joint literary and sociopolitical essence of *testimonio* poses a challenge to the traditional separation of literary representation and its underlying perceived external referent. The impact of trauma and the prevalence of the sociopolitical situation of repression enable *testimonio* to form part of an external referent while constituting it textually. Chilean *testimonio* establishes itself not only as a literary production that is relevant to a socio-politically, persistent experience but requires that it be seen within the context of this experience. It is designed as a disclaimer of official history and the ruling voice that controls the latter's representation, and demands to be acknowledged as a sociopolitical tool in literary form. I think we can heed this self-identification, together with the reservation that we do not overlook the hypothetical basis upon which *testimonio* must place the achievement of its sociopolitical literary goal.

The theoretical discussion of the genre delineation for *testimonio* serves as a point of departure for the analysis of two types of narratives that have commonly been identified as *testimonio* literary practices, the autobiographical *testimonio* and the monological interview. The findings of this comprehensive text and genre analysis suggest that *testimonio* is intended as a sociopolitical, literary tool and emerges out of the need to include literature in the sociopolitical struggle of modern day. It serves the role of an alternative representation that challenges a regime-sympathetic truth paradigm and a representation of a sociopolitically, problematic situation.

Testimonio originates in this situation and represents it in accordance with survivor-witness accounts in order to provoke a change in the sociopolitical environment. *Testimonio* seeks to aid the formation of a social conscience aware of the injustices, crimes, oppression and repression that inform the survivor-witness experience. *Testimonio*'s authenticity claims are linked to its sociopolitical, literary agenda and provide evidence that the author of *testimonio* informs his or her text with survivor-witness accounts. On the other hand, analysis also reveals discrepancies between the literature and the genre delineation for *testimonio*, in particular, with regard to the non-fiction designation, the identification and function of the speaking subject, and the authorship of the text's sociopolitical literary agenda and intentionality.

The discussion of Isabel Allende's historical novel, La casa de los espíritus, as a form of alternative history re-addresses the truth and fiction paradigm of sociopolitical writing. The novel suggests that we acknowledge this text as a *testimonio* despite its identification as a work of fiction. The analysis points out that even in the autobiographical and monological interview *testimonios*, which have traditionally been distinguished as non-fictional works, the authors' claim to non-fictional representation issues no guarantee. Valdés, Bitar, Chavkin, Sepúlveda and Politzer issue truth statements similar to those formulated by Isabel Allende; each claims to portray the truth personally experienced, observed and comprehended.

Clearly, these authors selected the literary styles and strategies most adequate for the sociopolitical literary project that each intends. That their texts differ in narrative style and strategy comes as a direct result of the author's experience and approach to literary representation in and of the socio-politically oppressive and repressive environment. Isabel Allende's novel can be distinguished from the autobiographical and the monological interview *testimonios* in that it is not limited to the attributes of either type of narrative, but brings together the sociopolitical and literary strategies and agendas exercised in both. La casa de los espíritus embraces the sociopolitical dimension characteristic of *testimonio*. It also offers support for a challenge of the contemporary genre delineation for *testimonio* based on the discrepancies encountered in the analysis of the former.

Testimonio forms part of a larger sociopolitical and literary context that constitutes *testimonio* and is constituted by it. Valdés, Bitar, Chavkin, Sepúlveda, Politzer, and Isabel Allende utilize preface, epilogue or other editorial commentary to address the narration and pre-narration process, to identify the source of information, and, above all, to establish the authenticity and sociopolitical paradigm of the text. In order to evaluate the sociopolitical dimensions of the text, we must consider the editorial comments and extended sociopolitical framework as an implied and constituting element in *testimonio*.

Valdés, Bitar, Chavkin, and Sepúlveda state their intent to inform the reader of a silenced and denied experience resulting from political persecution, imprisonment, torture, and repression. Their texts aim at raising awareness and forming a social conscience apt to change the sociopolitical situation and prevent its recurrence. In addition, they address the trauma tied to this situation and also to the process of giving testimony. Politzer's sociopolitical, literary objective is different in that she aims at providing the reader with access to dichotomous experiences and representations. She wants to reach a common denominator that can serve as a basis for the construction of a peaceful reunification of Chile's divided society.

Isabel Allende addresses the pre-narration and narration process of her first novel not in intratextual editorial commentary but in post-publication academic exchanges. In this extended sociopolitical and literary framework of the novel, Allende also identifies her narrative as a sociopolitical tool. She wrote the novel with the knowledge that Pinochet's regime censored the representation of history. She thought it necessary to represent the truth she experienced and witnessed through a literary work that would serve to denounce the Chilean experience, an experience official history had silenced and denied. Thereby, she hoped to aid the formation of a social consciousness aware of the human rights infractions under dictatorship rule and the struggle of the underrepresented, the oppressed and repressed in Latin-America in general. Like Politzer's Miedo en Chile, Isabel Allende's *La casa de los espíritus* pronounces the dichotomous relationship between the ruling powers and the oppressed, the perpetrators and the victims and witnesses of human rights infractions. It enunciates the role of alternative history in Latin-American society and the interplay in which it involves official history while giving voice to its own *testimonio*.

The antagonistic relationship between alternative and official history is central to *testimonio*, but is reinforced differently in the works studied. Tejas Verdes, Murder in Chile, and We, Chile, are seen to give voice only to alternative history. In these texts the challenge to official history is exposed in the larger framework of the novel, specifically in the preface and the sociopolitical and literary context into which the *testimonio* enters upon publication. In their editorial commentary, Valdés, Chavkin, and Sepúlveda suggest that their exposés set straight the distorted picture of the Chilean experience perpetuated by the ruling voice. These authors do not perceive the need to include the junta's perspective in a discourse on alternative history, because the latter exercised control over all statutory means of communication in Chile and also censored the information leaving Chile. They aim at forming a national and international social consciousness aware of the human rights violations, persecution and repression experienced.

In contrast, Sergio Bitar, Patricia Politzer, and Isabel Allende enunciate the opposing truth paradigms by giving voice, predominately, to anti-government perspectives but also to regime sympathetic points of view. Bitar precedes his autobiographical exposé with brief excerpts taken from official, pro-dictatorship newscasts in the outer framework of the narrative. The antithetical relationship between his alternative history and the official accounts cited is thus enunciated intratextually, even though the author does not address or react to this discrepancy directly. Politzer pronounces the discrepancy more strongly in placing monological interviews with opposing truth paradigms side by side. Her comprehensive narrative gives voice to a multiplicity of personal histories in order to facilitate a more panoramic glance at the contemporary and recent Chilean experience. Her informants are victims and also perpetrators of Pinochet's military regime. Their accounts share an antithetical relationship that mirrors the relationship shared by alternative and official history principally in that the different accounts present contradictory truth-paradigms. Politzer acknowledges that one or other issues a distorted image of the Chilean experience, but leaves it to the reader to evaluate the discrepancy entailed.

More so than any one of these narratives, Isabel Allende's novel *La casa de los espíritus* exposes the essence of alternative and official history, and intratextually exemplifies the function which alternative history seeks to serve in Latin American society under authoritarian rule. Like Bitar's autobiographical *testimonio* and Politzer's monological interview *testimonio*, Isabel Allende's historical fiction also gives voice to opposing truth paradigms. However, in her narrative it is the interplay between these paradigms that mirrors the prototype of the relationship between official and alternative history under dictatorship rule. Like the other *testimonios* discussed, this text reveals the composite, subjective nature of the representation intratextually in that the process of writing is distinguished as a deliberate, purposeful reconstruction of memory. We can read this text as a metaphorical substitute for Latin American reality, and specifically, for the Chilean experience under authoritarian rule. As explained in Chapter V, Isabel Allende did not first hand experience torture and persecution; however she witnessed human rights violations while continuing her work as a journalist in Chile during the first few years after the coup.

Within the textual framework of La casa de los espíritus, it is not the author but the fictional narrators, Alba and Trueba, who constitute the narrative. Alternative history in this novel is informed by a diary written by a grandmother who has supernatural powers, and by the voices of the victims, the oppressed and repressed in Chilean society that intrude into narrator-protagonist Alba's subconscious world in the torture cell. Official history in *La casa de los espíritus* is issued by the voice of protagonist-narrator, patriarch and republican senator, Esteban Trueba. His autobiographical account silences and denies the crimes denounced in the former representation and thus unfolds as a misconstruction of a personal/public history that mirrors the dictatorship's own denial of human rights infractions.

The narrative strategy and style of Isabel Allende's novel approach the editorial processes exemplified in the monological interview *testimonio*. As the study indicates, in both literatures the voice and editorial intervention of the narrator is nearly invisible. In La casa de los espíritus, the narrator autobiographically addresses her role and function in the process of narration and the sociopolitical situation related in the epilogue. Here she informs the reader of the perspectives from which the text is written, pronounces the sociopolitical, literary agenda that she strives to achieve, and also testifies on her own traumatic imprisonment and torture at the hands of the regime's military police.

As the text's main constituent, the narrator appropriates the power of representation in issuing this autobiographical *testimonio* in epilogue form. Her alternative representation of history seizes the power to define its own essence and that of the narrative, which precedes it while constituting the individual components of this comprehensive narrative as composition. In this act, the narrator does not discredit her ability to represent. To the contrary, the analysis shows that she promotes a strong authenticity, which emerges as an even stronger speech act than the representation it surpasses. Her narrative encompasses a confrontation of alternative and official history, whereby both are drawn into the discussion of what it means for a representation to have a sociopolitical cause, function and agenda. Her autobiographical *testimonio* concludes the novel in suggesting a return to the beginning, giving us to understand, thereby, that the narrative's content and sociopolitical agenda remains prevalent.

La casa de los espíritus illustrates the mechanism and essence of *testimonio* in its own act of narration. It shows what the study indicates to be characteristic of *testimonio* in general. It demonstrates that, in contrast to official history, *testimonio* emanates out of a challenge and constitutes a challenge. It manifests that as an alternative representation of history, *testimonio* seeks to invalidate the external referent, which the dictatorship's official voice generates as truth. Alternative representation must "summon truth," because pro-dictatorship discourse presents as truth what the former identifies as misrepresentation, distortion, denial, or silencing of a perceived external referent. Like the other *testimonios* discussed, this work exposes subjectivity in the representation of history, in particular, the subjectivity of the discourse it juxtaposes. It challenges official history by transgressing the truth paradigm of the ruling voice. It aims at liberation and is commissioned to re-appropriate the power of representation, which military rule has appropriated. It resists the oppression imposed by authoritarian ruling power. At the same time, it defies the rules of literary standards by avoiding a strict genre definition. Valdés, Bitar, Chavkin, Sepúlveda, Politzer and Allende, in particular, are seen to demand a reevaluation of history, and, by extension, also of our concepts of historiography and representation in general. *Testimonio*, as modeled by these texts, "suspends the literary at the very same time that it constitutes itself as a literary act,"[2] it identifies as a sociopolitical literary activity and, by way of its inherent juxtaposition to official history, exposes the latter in similar terms.

The identification of the narrator as protagonist-witness and the identification of the autobiographical voice as a genre characteristic of *testimonio* are clearly identified as problematic. Chavkin, Sepúlveda, Politzer, and Burgus-Debray identify the narrators of the respective monological interviews as protagonist-witnesses of the external referents represented. The identification of the autobiographical narrator / protagonist as survivor-witness is complemented by the invisibility of the author's textual presence and function in the monological interview. This narrative strategy reinforces the link between the survivor-witness' experience and sociopolitical urgency, its representation and sociopolitical, literary agenda and to enunciate the proximity between *testimonio* and oral testimony provided in an interview setting. It enables the author/editor to highlight the authority of the speaking agent as a witness/survivor who pronounces his/her own authenticity claims and sociopolitical agenda.

As shown, this strategy may be successful when the monological interview is read in isolation, that is, when read independent of its larger narrative framework, which may include editorial comments as well as other monological interviews. Within the immediate parameters of the individual *testimonio*, the speaking narrator omits reference to the presence and function of the author. However, this undermining of editorial intervention is by no means limited to or requires the implementation of autobiographical narrators in the monological interview. Clearly, these narrators are presented as sole informants of their narrative, but the larger framework contradicts this, showing it to be less a "true" feature than a deliberate narrative strategy.

On the intratextual level, Burgos/Debray, Chavkin, Sepúlveda and Politzer retract the autobiographical 'I' of the monological interview narrator and place the strategic invisibility of the own voice and presence into a different light. In their prefaces, they identify themselves as interviewer and subsequent transcriber of the oral testimony obtained. They clarify that from the interviewer- author's point of view the autobiographical voice disguises a third person: A 'she' referring to Menchú in Burgos-Debray's case and a 'he' or 'she' referring to the speaker of the individual monological interviews in, for example, Politzer's text. The first-person narrators in these *testimonios* consequently emerge as pretentious autobiographical voices that are designed to override the third-person perspective from which they are constituted. They undermine the extensive process of editorial intervention by which an author extracts oral *testimonio* from the interview setting, assumes control its representation while undermining his/her self-presence. Allende's narrator, Alba, achieves the same effect in transcribing her informant's autobiographical diary in biographical form and augmenting it with information drawn from multiple sources, protagonists, victims and witnesses, including her own autobiographical experience in the sociopolitical relations that she depicts. This transcription is also told in autobiographical form. However, the extensiveness of the narrative emphatically overshadows the only two brief pronominal self-references voiced that this representation appears to be reinforcing a similar silencing of the role and function of the text's constituent as we have seen in the monological interview.

Literary critics have pointed to an implied reverse anonymity as a narrative strategy in *testimonio*, by which a narrator/protagonist's experience is conferred plural representation value. A pluralistic validity is implied in the identification of the speaker as a spokesperson for a larger public. It enhances the authenticity effect's functionality by underlining the significance of the sociopolitical agenda and urgency shared by many. Whereas Valdés, Bitar, and the individual speakers in the monological interviews each emphasize the pluralistic validity of the traumatic experiences represented, the analysis also shows that the implicit reverse anonymity in *testimonio* may be complemented by an explicit plurality of voices. Bitar, Valdés and Burgos-Debray limit themselves to one source (the two former to their own autobiographical experience and the latter to testimony given by Menchú). However, Chavkin's, Sepúlveda's, and Politzer's monological interview, and also Isabel Allende's novel, bring together a multiplicity of *testimonios* to provide an extended panoramic insight into a sociopolitical context. Although these narratives reinforce applicability even here of the reverse anonymity construction, in that the individual interviewees identify themselves as representative spokespersons, the texts also illustrate that trauma affects and is experienced by individuals differently and that, consequently, each *testimonio* provides different insights into the larger sociopolitical experience. This explicit multiplicity of voices serves to enhance the sense of authenticity through an augmented representativity, which, in turn, correlates with the identification of these texts as alternative representations that aim at raising consciousness and provoking change.

The discussion of the author-narrator relationship—their perceivable presence and identity—is significant to the analysis of *testimonio*'s sociopolitical intentionality and agenda. Critics have suggested that *testimonio*'s narrator-protagonist determines the text's intentionality. My study provides evidence that this relationship does apply to the autobiographical *testimonio*, however, it is not seen applicable to the monological interview. In this literature, a plural perspective informs the text's intentionality. In order for the monological interview to be determined by the intentionality of the native informant, it must either complement or override the agenda of the intermediary who controls the representation.

At first sight, some of these *testimonios* are seen to exhibit a sympathetic relationship between interviewer and testifier. Chavkin and Sepúlveda, for example, proclaim the text as a result of a project shared by testifiers and transcriber who harmoniously coincide with the text's and project's sociopolitical intentionality and agenda. However, this does not give cause to belittle the role of the author who controls the literary representation. The analysis shows that the intentionality and the sociopolitical agenda of the testifier can be different from that of the author and compiler. At the same time, the latter's intentions may also not be explicit to the speaker. For the most part, the reader does not gain access to the testifiers' retrospective reactions to the literary *testimonio* derived from the oral interview exchange. This is because oral testimony is indeed issued by people who otherwise are under-represented in contemporary discourse due to a prevailing oppressive and repressive system of government. Menchú poses an exception due to her subsequent celebrity. Yet, the fact that other testifiers' interpretations and opinions, regarding the *testimonio* issued on their behalf, have not found representation and may not even have been solicited, does not give reason to dismiss the possibility that they may disagree with either narrative style, content matter or the sociopolitical literary agenda announced.

Chavkin, Sepúlveda and Politzer assume authorship of their texts' sociopolitical intentionality. Chavkin and Sepúlveda make clear that this agenda received the informants' approval prior to the interview process, with Sepúlveda making detailed reference to the difficult process of establishing a relationship of confidentiality and trust with her informants. Politzer does not inform the reader that she shared her agenda prior with her informants prior to obtaining their interviews. She merely notes the difficulty experienced in obtaining certain interviews deemed necessary for the panoramic view of the sociopolitical experience. Based on the analysis of Politzer's text, we can see her text as an example of a monological interview in which the transparency of the sociopolitical literary agenda at the time of the interviews can be questioned. As a result of such questioning, we can find evidence that the power of representation rests, principally, with the author/compiler and not with the individual speaker. It is the author/compiler who selects the interviewee, edits the interview, transforms it into a monological interview, and then assigns it a location and sociopolitical literary function that complements, and, in Politzer's compilation, also contrasts with and contradicts, the surrounding multiplicity of voices and *testimonios*.

Interlocutors link the under-representation of the speaker to the sociopolitical dimension of the text. Accordingly, an intermediary gives voice in *testimonio* to a previously "voiceless and anonymous collective popular subject."[3] In many ways, *testimonio* can be seen as an attempt to re-appropriate the power of the representation of history from the grasp of the socio-politically, dominating force, i.e. from the hands of the oppressors. On the other hand, mediated *testimonios*, such as the ones issued by Burgos-Debray, Sepúlveda, Chavkin, and Politzer, still do not invoke a re-appropriation of the representation of history by the victims. In these texts, we should not mistake a silencing of the function of the author as a pretentious "sort of erasure" of that function. The study suggests that *testimonio* constitutes an intricate narrative web that interpolates witnessing with biography and autobiography, which we should also not misconstrue as "a verbal recording of the real"[4] because *testimonio* constitutes itself differently. These intermediaries may well pretend or even aim to give voice to a voiceless public. Above all, however, they show to give voice to their own sociopolitical and literary agenda. The investigation makes evident that the larger sociopolitical and literary framework of *testimonio*, in particular editorial commentary and accompanying monological interviews significantly influence the constituency of the individual testimony.

Critics have identified a lack of aesthetic intentionality in *testimonio*, distinguishing this literature from other literary works.[5] This study does not find support for this assertion. Whereas certain texts issue an explicit disclaimer of literary finesse to emphasize the sociopolitical dimension of the work, the analysis reveals these disclaimers as inherently linked to an underlying literary-sociopolitical narrative strategy. The literalness of *testimonio* must be seen as a tool aimed at facilitating the text's sociopolitical agenda. It is in accordance with this notion that *testimonio* may entail elaborate, as well as deliberately "less" refined, literary constructs; however, the investigation shows, that we can hardly speak of an underachievement of aesthetic literary standards in Chilean *testimonio*. On the contrary, in particular in the case of Hernán Valdés's Tejas Verdes, the study shows that what the author describes as a possible under-performance in literary standards can well be read as a highly elaborate and refined narrative strategy and performance.

Testimonio, as a literary genre, can be distinguished, above all, based on its sociopolitical dimension. Within its literary-political constituency, the literary embodies, primarily, a textual sociopolitical tool whereas the political is understood, principally, to make up the cause and objective of the representation. Each of the narratives discussed reinforces a socio-political agenda. The achievement of this agenda, in all cases, suggests that readers heed the writer's mimetic postulate and understand the *testimonio* as a non-fiction work. This applies to Valdés, Bitar, Chavkin, Sepúlveda, Politzer and Allende alike. Each differs in the narrative strategies and tools employed to pronounce and reinforce the mimetic postulate and to advance the sociopolitical agenda specified. Consequently, I renew the call to modify the genre delineation for *testimonio*. The definition needs to absorb the key components of the sociopolitical dimension of *testimonio* but omit the non-fiction designation and specifications regarding the identity and functions of the speaking subject and the authorship of the text's sociopolitical literary agenda and intentionality.

NOTES

1 "...a la vez un 'mensaje' y un 'modelo' de resistencia a la violencia fascista" (Cavallari 1986, 162.
2 Moreiras 1996, 195.
3 Moreiras 1996, 195.
4 See Rice-Sayre 1986, 52.
5 See Prada Oropeza 1986, 19, 20.

Bibliography

Adorno, T. W. (1986). *What Does Coming to Terms with the Past Mean?* Bloomington, Indiana University Press.

Alexander, E. (1979). *The Resonance of Dust: Essays on Holocaust Literature*. Columbus, State Ohio University Press.

Allende, I. (1982, 1987). *La casa de los espíritus (CE)*. Bogotá, Colombia, Editorial La Oveja Negra, Ltda.

———(1986). Los libros tienen sus propios espíritus. *Los libros tienen sus propios espíritus*. M. Coddou. Xalapa, Ver., México, Universidad Veracruzana: 15–20.

———(Sept. 6, 1983). "Carta de Isabel Allende. No hay angustia que dure cien años." *El Mercurio*: 26.

Aman, K. a. C. P., Ed. (1991). *Popular Culture in Chile—Resistance and Survival*. Oxford, Westview Press.

Amnesty International (1996). CHILE: Transition at the Crossroads, Human Rights Violations under Pinochet Rule Remain the Crux. Online posting, http://www.web.amnesty.org/ai.nsf/index/.

———(2001). Chile. Chile Legal Brief on the Incompatibility of Chilean Decree Law No. 2191 of 1978 With International Law, AI Index AMR 22/002/2001, January 2001).

———(2001). Chile: Commitments must be fulfilled. Online posting http://www.web.amnesty.org/web/news.nsf/weball/.

Barthes, R. (1970). Historical Discourse. *Introduction to Structuralism*. M. Lane. New York, Basic.

Bayer, O. (1997). "El Día de la Memoria." *La Patagonia Rebelde.*

Berger, J. (1997). "Trauma and Literary Theory." *Contemporary Literature* XXXVIII(3): 569–582.

Beverley, J. (1989). "The Margin at the Center: On *Testimonio* (Testimonial Narrative)." *Modern Fiction Studies* 35(1): 11–28.

———(1996). The Margin at the Center. *The Real Thing: Testimonial Discourse and Latin America*. G. M. Gugelberger. Durham, Duke University Press: 23–41.

———a. M. Z. (1990). *Literature and Politics in the Central American Revolutions*. Austin, University of Texas Press.

Bitar, S. (1987). *Isla 10*. Santiago, Chile, Pehuen.

Burgos-Debray, E. (1984). *I, Rigoberta Menchú - An Indian Woman in Guatemala*. Thetford, The Thetford Press.

Campos, R. (1986). *La casa de los espíritus*: Mirada, espacio, discurso de la otra historia. *Los libros tienen sus propios espíritus: Estudios sobre Isabel Allende*. M. Coddou. Xalapa, Ver., México, Universidad Veracruzana: 21–28.

Carrasco Moya, R. (1991). *PRIGUE: Prisionero de guerra en Chile*. Santiago, Chile, Aquí y ahora.

Caruth, C. (1991). "Introduction to Psychoanalysis, Culture and Trauma." *American Imago* (Special issue).

Cavallari, H. M. (1986). Fernando Alegría y la deconstrucción del fascismo. *Testimonio y Literatura*. R. a. H. V. Jara. Minneapolis, Society for the Study of Contemporary Hispanic and Lusophone Revolutionary Literatures: 162–169.

Chavkin, S. (1982). *The Murder of Chile: Eyewitness Accounts of the Coup, the Terror, and the Resistance Today*. New York, Everest House.

Coddou, M. (1986). *La casa de los espíritus:* De la historia a la historia. *Los libros tienen sus propios espíritus: Estudios sobre Isabel Allende*. M. Coddou. Xalapa, Ver., México, Cuadernos Del Centro: Centro de Investigaciones Lingüístico-Literarias, Instituto de Investigaciones Humanísticas, Universidad Veracruzana: 7–14.

Colás, S. (1996). What's Wrong with Representation? *The Real Thing: Testimonial Discourse and Latin America*. G. M. Gugelberger. Durham, Duke University Press: 161–171.

Dolezel, L. (1973). *Narrative Modes in Czech Literature*. Toronto, University of Toronto Press.

Duchesne, J. (1986). Las narraciones guerrilleras: configuración de un sujeto épico de nuevo tipo. *Testimonio y Literatura*. R. a. H. V. Jara. Minneapolis, Society for the Study of Contemporary Hispanic and Lusophone Revolutionary Literatures: 85–137.

Felman, S. a. D. L., M.D. (1992). *Testimony: Crises of Witnessing in Literature, Psychoanalysis, and History*. New York, London, Routledge.

Foley, B. (1986). *Telling the Truth: The Theory and Practice of Documentary Fiction*. Ithaca and London, Cornell University Press.

Foster, D. W. (1984). "Latin American Documentary Narrative." *Publications of the Modern Language Association of America (PMLA)*(1): 41–55.

Foucault, M. (1970). *The Order of Things: An Archaeology of the Human Sciences*. New York, Vintage Books.

———(1980). *Power /Knowledge: Selected Interviews and Other Writings, 1972–77*. New York, Pantheon.

———(1984). What Is an Author? *The Foucault Reader*. P. Rabinov. New York, Pantheon Books.

Gearhart, S. (1984). *The Open Boundary of History and Fiction: A Critical Approach to the French Enlightenment*. Princeton, Princeton University Press.

Goffman, E. (1976). *Frame Analysis: An Essay on the Organization of Experience*. Cambridge, Harvard University Press.

Guevara, E. C. (1969). *Pasajes de la guerra revolucionaria. Obra revolucionaria*. Mexico, Era.

Gugelberger, G. M. (1996). Introduction: Institutionalization of Transgression. Testimonial Discourse and Beyond. *The Real Thing: Testimonial Discourse and Latin America*. G. M. Gugelberger. Durham, Duke University Press: 1–19.

———, Ed. (1996). *The Real Thing: Testimonial Discourse and Latin America*. Durham, Duke University Press.

Jameson, F. (1996). On Literary and Cultural Import-Substitution in the Third World. The Case of the Testimonio. *The Real Thing: Testimonial Discourse and Latin America*. G. M. Gugelberger. Durham, Duke University Press: 161–171.

Jara, R. a. H. V., Ed. (1986). *Testimonio y Literatura*. Minneapolis, Society for the Study of Contemporary Hispanic and Lusophone Revolutionary Literature.

Klöss, S. (1989). *Die "Zeit"-Problematik in der Deutschsprachigen Schriftsteller-Autobiographie des 20. Jahrhunderts unter spezieller Berücksichtigung von Klaus Mann*. Augsburg, AV-Verlag.

Kosta, B. (1994). *Recasting Autobiography—Women's Counterfictions in Contemporary German Literature and Film*. Ithaca, London, Cornell University Press.

Laclau, E. (1990). *New Reflections on the Revolution of Our Time*.

Langer, L. (1975). *The Holocaust and the Literary Imagination*. New Haven, Yale University Press.

Marcos, J. M. a. T. M.-F. (1986). Multiplicidad dialéctica y reconciliación del discurso en *La casa de los espíritus*. *Los ibros tienen sus propios espiritus*. M. Coddou, Universidad Veracruzana.

Maza, G. d. l., and Mario Garcés (1985). *La explosión de las mayorías, protesta nacional 1983–1984*. Santiago, Chile, Editorial ECO.

Miething, C. (1987). *Saint-Satre oder der autobiographische Gott*. Stuttgart, Metzler.

Monckeberg, M. O., María Eugenia Camus and Pamela Jiles (1986). *Crimen bajo Estado de Sitio*. Santiago, Chile, Editorial Emisión.

Moreiras, A. (1996). The Aura of Testimonio. *The Real Thing: Testimonial Discourse and Latin America*. G. M. Gugelberger. Durham, Duke University Press: 192–224.

Morse, J. (1993). "Words Devoted to the Unspeakable." *American Literary History* 5(4): 715–734.

Nietzsche, F. (1980). *On the Advantage and Disadvantage of History for Life*. Indianapolis, Cambridge, Hackett Publishing Company, Inc.

Oppenheim, L. H. (1993). *Politics in Chile: Democracy, Authoritarianism, and the Search for Development*. Boulder, Westview Press.

Pascal, R. (1965). *Die Autobiographie. Gehalt und Gestalt*. Stuttgart.

Peitsch, H. (1990). *"Deutschlands Gedächtnis an seine dunkelste Zeit"—Zur Funktion der Autobiographik in den Westzonen Deutschlands und den Westsektoren von Berlin 1945 bis 1949*. Berlin, Sigma Bohn Verlag.

Perelli, C. (1990). The Military's Perception of Threat in the Southern Cone of South America. *The Military and Democracy*. L. W. Goodman, Johanna S. R. Mendelson and Juan Rial. Lexington, Mass, Lexington Books: 93–105.

Politzer, P. (1990). *Miedo en Chile*. Chile, Ediciones Chile y America.

Porter, D. H. (1993). "The Gold in Fort Knox: Historical Fiction in the Context of Historiography." *Soundings: An Interdisciplinary Journal* LXXVI(2–3): 315–350.

Prada Oropeza, R. (1986). De lo testimonial al testimonio—notas para un deslinde del discurso-testimonio. *Testimonio y Literatura*. R. a. H. V. Jara. Minneapolis, Society for the Study of Contemporary Hispanic and Lusophone Revolutionary Literatures: 9–21.

Rabinov, P., Ed. (1984). *The Foucault Reader*. New York, Pantheon Books.

Remmer, K. (1991). *Military Rule in Latin America*. Boulder, Westview Press.

Rice-Sayre, L. P. (1986). Witnessing History: Diplomacy Versus Testimony. *Testimonio y Literatura*. R. a. H. V. Jara. Minneapolis, Society for the Study of Contemporary Hispanic and Lusophone Revolutionary Literatures: 48–72.

Roa Bastos, A. (1974). *Yo el Supremo*. Buenos Aires, Siglo Veintiuno Editores.

Rojas, M. A. (1986). *La casa de los espíritus* de Isabel Allende: Un caleidoscopio de espejos desordenados. *Los libros tienen sus propios espíritus: Estudios sobre Isabel Allende*. M. Coddou. Xalapa, Ver., México, Universidad Veracruzana: 83–90.

Rosenberg, D. (1989). *Testimony: Contemporary Writers Make the Holocaust Personal*. New York, Random House.

Scholes, R. (1975). *Structural Fabulation: An Essay on the Fiction of the Future*. Notre Dame, University of Notre Dame Press.

Sepúlveda, E., Ed. (1996). *We, Chile, Personal Testimonies of the Chilean Arpilleristas*. Falls Church, VA, Azul Editions.

Sklodowska, E. (1996). Spanish American Testimonial Novel. Some Afterthoughts. *The Real Thing: Testimonial Discourse and Latin America*. G. M. Gugelberger. Durham, Duke University Press: 84–100.

Sommer, D. (1996). No Secrets. *The Real Thing: Testimonial Discourse and Latin America*. G. M. Gugelberger. Durham, Duke University Press: 130–157.

Suleiman, S. R. (1993). "War Memories: On Autobiographical Reading." *New Literary History* 24(3): 563–575.

Valdés, H. (1974). *Tejas Verdes—Diario de un campo de concentración en Chile*. Barcelona, Editorial Ariel.

Vegh, C. (1984). *I Didn't Say Goodbye*. New York.

Verdugo, P., Ed. (1994). *Chile 1973 "Así lo viví yo"*. Cuadernos Universitarios, Serie Investigaciones No. 4. Santiago, Chile, Universidad Nacional Andres Bello.

Viezzer, M. (1977). *Si me permiten hablar... Testimonio de Domitila una mujer de las minas de Bolivia*. Mexico, Ed. Siglo XXI.

White, H. (1990). *Tropics of Discourse. Essays in Cultural Criticism*. Maryland, The John Hopkins University Press.

Yanes, G., a.o, Ed. (1985). *Mirrors of War—Literature and Revolution in El Salvador*. New York, Monthly Review Press.

Young, J. E. (1987). "Interpreting Literary Testimony: A Preface to Rereading Holocaust Diaries and Memoirs." *New Literary History* 182 (Winter): 403–423.

Yúdice, G. (1996). Testimonio and Postmodernism. *The Real Thing: Testimonial Discourse and Latin America*. G. M. Gugelberger. Durham, Duke University Press: 42–57.

Zimmerman, M. (1996). Testimonio in Guatemala. Payeras, Rigoberta, and Beyond. *The Real Thing: Testimonial Discourse and Latin America*. G. M. Gugelberger. Durham, Duke University Press: 101–129.

LATIN AMERICA
Interdisciplinary Studies

Gladys M. Varona-Lacey
General Editor

Latin America: Interdisciplinary Studies serves as a forum for scholars in the field of Latin American Studies, as well as an educational resource for anyone interested in this region of the world. Themes and topics encompass social, political, historical, and economic issues, in addition to literature, music, art, and architecture.

For additional information about this series or for the submission of manuscripts, please contact:

Dr. Gladys M. Varona-Lacey
Ithaca College
Department of Modern Languages & Literatures
Ithaca, NY 14859

To order other books in this series, please contact our Customer Service Department at:

(800) 770-LANG (within the U.S.)
(212) 647-7706 (outside the U.S.)
(212) 647-7707 FAX

Or browse online by series at:

WWW.PETERLANGUSA.COM

Printed by
CPI books GmbH, Leck

FSC
www.fsc.org
MIX
Papier | Fördert gute Waldnutzung
FSC® C083411

Kolibri 360 GmbH
Ferdinand-Jühlke-Straße 7
99095 Erfurt, Deutschland
produktsicherheit@kolibri360.de